Britain, Japan and Pearl Harbor

Books published under the joint imprint of LSE/Routledge are works of high academic merit approved by the Publications Committee of the London School of Economics and Political Science. These publications are drawn from the wide range of academic studies in the social sciences for which the LSE has an international reputation.

Britain, Japan and Pearl Harbor

Avoiding war in East Asia, 1936–41

Antony Best

London and New York

First published 1995
by Routledge
11 New Fetter Lane, London EC4P 4EE

Simultaneously published in the USA and Canada
by Routledge
29 West 35th Street, New York, NY 10001

© 1995 Antony Best

Typeset in Times by
J&L Composition Ltd, Filey, North Yorkshire.

Printed and bound in Great Britain by
TJ Press (Padstow) Ltd, Padstow, Cornwall.

British Library Cataloguing in Publication Data
A catalogue record for this book is available from the British Library

Library of Congress Cataloging in Publication Data
has been applied for

ISBN 0–415–11171–4

This book is dedicated with love
to the memory of my brother David

Contents

Maps

Usages and abbreviations

In this book I have followed the Japanese style of giving family name first; Chinese names are given in Wade-Giles as this was the contemporary usage and Formosa has been used in preference to Taiwan. The following abbreviations have been used in the text:

ATB	Advisory Committee on Trade Questions in Time of War
BJ	Blue Jacket (The designation given to British decrypts of foreign diplomatic cables)
'C'	Head of SIS
CCP	Chinese Communist Party
CID	Committee on Imperial Defence
CIGS	Chief of the Imperial General Staff
DMI	Director of Military Intelligence
DNI	Director of Naval Intelligence
FEC	Far Eastern Committee
FECB	Far East Combined Bureau
GCCS	Government Code and Cypher School
HSBC	Hongkong and Shanghai Banking Corporation
IJA	Imperial Japanese Army
IJN	Imperial Japanese Navy
IIC	Industrial Intelligence Centre
JIC	Joint Intelligence Sub-Committee
JPC	Joint Planning Sub-Committee
KMT	Kuomintang
MI2c	War Office Military Intelligence section dealing with East Asia
MEW	Ministry of Economic Warfare
NID	Naval Intelligence Division
SIS	Secret Intelligence Service
SOE	Special Operations Executive
USN	United States Navy

Acknowledgements

I started working on the subject of Britain and the origins of the Pacific War in the summer of 1985 as an undergraduate at the University of Leeds. I therefore have nine years' worth of acknowledgements to honour. I would like to thank the staff at the following institutions for their kind assistance in my endeavours: the Public Record Office in Kew; Churchill College, Cambridge; Trinity College, Cambridge; the Bodleian Library, Oxford; Birmingham University Library; the British Library for Political and Economic Science; the School of Oriental and African Studies Library; the National Maritime Museum; the Liddell Hart Centre for Military Archives; the Houghton Library at Harvard. Records from the Public Record Office appear by permission of the Controller of Her Majesty's Stationery Office. I would like to acknowledge Curtis Brown Ltd, London for permission to quote from the Chartwell Papers on behalf of C & T Publications Ltd; the Trustees of the Inverchapel Trust for the Inverchapel Papers; the Trustees of the Liddell Hart Centre for Military Archives; Kings College, London, for the Davidson and Alanbrooke Papers; Sheffield University Library for the Malcolm Kennedy Papers; the Trustees of the National Maritime Museum for the Chatfield Papers; the Avon Trustees for the Avon Papers; Birmingham University Library for the Neville Chamberlain Papers; the Master and Fellows of Trinity College, Cambridge for the Butler Papers.

Among fellow historians I would like to express my deep thanks to Professor Donald Cameron Watt and Professor Hosoya Chihiro for arranging for me to attend the 'Fifty Years After: The Pacific War Reexamined' conference at Lake Yamanaka in November 1991, from which I benefited greatly. I must also mention my debt to others who in conversation have helped to shape my views, in particular Janet Hunter, Iokibe Makoto, Akira Iriye, Kibata Yoichi, and Sakai

Tetsuya. I am, in addition, very grateful to my two doctoral examiners, Peter Lowe and Richard Sims, for their observations and assistance. My greatest thanks go to my doctoral supervisor, Professor Ian Nish, who has helped me enormously over the years, steering me away from generalizations and writing innumerable letters and references on my behalf; he has my deepest respect and gratitude.

For advice and support I would like to thank Orna Almog, Joe Maiolo, Morice Mendoza, Kate Morris, Effie Pedaliu and Jenny Yang and all the other friendly souls I have met along the way at the LSE and the PRO. A special round of applause goes to Andrew Bell, who has put up with me droning on and on about the past for more years than we both care to remember, to 'Arthur' Clarke, a man of taste and discernment, and to Tim Pope, whose opinions are legion. I am also exceedingly grateful to Serena Hirose and her family for their kindness and for introducing me to Japan. I also must give a big thank you to my canine companion, Jasper the Dog, for stopping me from sitting at the word processor too long. Finally my deepest thanks go out to my family, my mother and father not only for being great parents but also for acting as my unofficial cartographer and editor respectively, and to my brother, David, who I wish was here to see this book in print.

1 Introduction

On 8 December 1941 the Japanese Chargé d'Affaires in London, Kamimura Shinichi, was called to the Foreign Office to be presented with a British declaration of war on his country. This document stated, in the lofty tones of diplomatic language

> On the evening of December 7th His Majesty's Government in the United Kingdom learnt that Japanese forces, without previous warning either in the form of a declaration of war or of an ultimatum with a conditional declaration of war, had attempted a landing on the coast of Malaya and bombed Singapore and Hong Kong. In view of these wanton acts of unprovoked aggression committed in flagrant violation of international law and particularly of Article 1 of the Third Hague Convention, relative to the opening of hostilities, to which both Japan and the United Kingdom are parties, I have the honour to inform the Imperial Japanese Government in the name of His Majesty's Government in the United Kingdom that a state of war exists between the two countries.[1]

Later that day in Washington an outraged and embittered United States Congress met and decided in the light of the previous day's attack without warning on the naval base of Pearl Harbor to pass their own official declaration of war against Japan.

The war in the Pacific thus began with both Britain and the United States perceiving themselves as responding to completely unjustified and unprovoked aggression; the Japanese, the Asian allies of Nazi Germany, had not even had the decency to declare war before the first bombs dropped. This conviction that Japan's acts were unwarranted and a violation of international codes of practice has cast a long shadow over the historiography of the origins of the Pacific War. The controversial nature of the opening shots of the conflict has necessarily meant that the study of this period of history has concentrated to a large degree on the question of blame, and the assumption has all too easily been made that because Japan was guilty of delivering the first blows it must be held solely responsible for the outbreak of war. However, to come to any true understanding of the events of 7–8 December 1941 it is important to clear the mind of any preconceived notions of responsibility, with all the moral connotations that word implies. History is fundamentally a process of understanding; it should not be an excuse to indulge in finger-pointing.

The idea of blame is dangerous because it encourages the historian to take short cuts. The desire to attribute blame exaggerates the natural and almost inescapable tendency to study historical events through the prism of hindsight. It is also a process all too easily influenced by the tendency of the victors of wars to describe the origins of the conflict in a manner favourable to themselves. If one is beguiled into such an approach there is the danger that one will be led into manipulating events to fit a pattern, to search for convenient continuities, to discount initiatives that fall outside the expected, and to end up with a very deterministic interpretation of the period. The result can be a history that concentrates far too heavily on the short term and when it does deal with the long term trades in generalizations rather than seeing the rich complexity of the events that led to conflict.

To be more specific, the problem in relation to our understanding of the Pacific War is that the enormity of Japan's attack on Pearl Harbor has done the historian a disservice because it demands explanation and virtually forces one to draw up a narrative in which Pearl Harbor is the only possible destination of events. In particular, it requires us to focus on the major crises of the period to the detriment of any attempt to study the efforts made for reconciliation in a bid to avoid war. In addition, Pearl Harbor is a problem because the very scale of the Japanese attack, and the fact that it took place not on a colony but on a territory of the United States, pushes the historian towards a concentration on Japanese–American antagonism as the key to understanding the origins of the Pacific War to the exclusion of other factors, thus leading to a rather narrow perspective.

The intention of this book is to challenge some of the myths that have grown up about this period and to contribute to our understanding of the origins of the Pacific War by focusing on the evolution of the various strands, both negative and positive, of British policy towards Japan and East Asia from January 1936 to the outbreak of war in December 1941. This is, of course, only one element in the complex mosaic of East Asian history in this period, but the study of British policy is worthwhile because Britain was, at least until 1940, the major extra-Asian player in the region. Indeed, it is possible, as two leading historians of the period, Ian Nish and Hosoya Chihiro, have pointed out, to make a case that the confrontation in 1941 was to a degree an Anglo-Japanese conflict, because Japan's main ambition was to seize control over the mineral-rich territories of South-East Asia and it was Britain which posed the most direct obstacle to this aim, and that the United States became involved because it had tied its own security to that of Britain.[2] The emphasis on Anglo-Japanese competition need not be limited simply to the events of 1941; it can be taken further to demonstrate that throughout the period from 1933 this phenomenon was a major destabilizing element in East Asia. This does not refer just to rivalry over markets in China, or even to strategic concerns, although it is interesting to note that as early as 1933 Japan had clearly replaced the Soviet Union as the chief target of British intelligence-gathering in East Asia; it also points to wider economic factors.[3] In particular, it is important to see how the restrictive trading practices which the British Empire introduced to buttress British industries during the Depression, such as imperial preference and quotas on Japanese exports, pushed Japan towards the desire for autarky and the establishment of a yen bloc, and thus expansionism in East Asia. In addition, a study of British policy is important because it reveals that events in East Asia must be seen as part of the broad struggle in this period between revisionist and *status quo* powers and thus as part of a global conflict. This point is an exceptionally important one, and a difficult one to approach due to the unpleasantness of the revisionist regimes involved, but it is essential to investigate the legitimacy of Japan's cries of discrimination and to see how one leading *status quo* power responded to such claims.

In approaching this subject it would be a mistake to assume that it is merely the sorry story of a slow, inexorable slide towards war. Instead, the period in question represents a series of troughs and peaks as the course of Anglo-Japanese relations shifted one way and then another under the influence of the hectic pace and magnitude of the events that shook the international system during these years. In relating this tale it is necessary to see the relationship between Britain and Japan against the background of a region in turmoil; one cannot hope to comprehend events without studying how Britain viewed the nationalist aspirations of Kuomintang (KMT) China, or how it perceived the machinations of the Soviet

Union in East Asia. In addition, it is vital to see the influence of the confrontation in Europe between the Axis and the Anglo-French blocs, and how this shaped Britain's fears for its security and emboldened Japan into action. Last, and perhaps in the long term most importantly, it is essential to understand the attitude and role of the United States. One must not imagine that American isolationism meant that Washington could be ignored; Britain could never forget that its success in any future war in East Asia or in Europe rested on Roosevelt's benevolent support. In this period American silence spoke as much as its actions.

As well as the external influences on British attitudes towards Japan, policy was also the result of a complex debate between the various government departments in Whitehall about how best to uphold Britain's interests in East Asia and elsewhere. The one constant in this tangle was that the Foreign Office was responsible for the everyday handling of relations, but dissatisfaction with its conduct of policy all too often led to challenges to its authority from the Treasury, the service ministries and, in the wartime period, the Ministry of Economic Warfare; this meant that the formulation of policy was often an acrimonious process. It is also important to realize that there were pressure groups working in this field which at various points and particularly before September 1939 could exert influence on sympathetic government ministries. The China Association, representing the interests of British companies in China, was one such lobby, and there was a more nebulous body of Japanophiles made up of businessmen, journalists, politicians and servicemen seeking to influence policy.

As one of the main themes of this study is to look at what attempts were made to avoid war during the period, the role of those sympathetic to an understanding with Japan is of some concern. It is important to understand that, just as there were those in Britain and Japan, both in and outside government circles, who consistently believed that the depth and range of the clash of interests made conflict inevitable, there was also a competing group who worked for the goal of improving mutual ties. To this latter group the mutual antagonism between Britain and Japan, the erstwhile allies, was not a cause for fatalism; there was a belief that although the problems that had arisen were serious they were not insoluble, and that in the long term the interests of the two empires were not incompatible. To the believers in a *rapprochement* it seemed expedient for Britain and Japan to sit down and negotiate in a spirit of compromise and determination to overcome the obstacle of mutual misunderstanding.

There was, however, a division within these ranks. On one side there were those who were at heart sentimentalists and yearned to return to the Elysian days of the Anglo-Japanese Alliance, while on the other was a group who, for reasons of *Realpolitik*, saw a closer relationship as a vital necessity in the harsh international climate of the 1930s. This difference in motivation was important, for while the sentimentalists in both countries could agree in a rather naive way, the practitioners of *Realpolitik* in Britain and Japan saw reconciliation only in terms of their own countries' self-interest, and were therefore frequently pursuing different and at times directly contradictory ends – this was a significant disadvantage as the members of this group tended to wield the greater influence in their respective countries.

A figure who can be seen as working in the latter manner was Sir Robert Craigie, the British Ambassador to Japan from September 1937 to December 1941, and he plays an important role in this study. An analysis of his attitudes and influence is essential because he was deeply disturbed by the steady deterioration in Anglo-Japanese relations, and sought to alleviate the growing tensions by espousing an alternative to the negative policy pursued by the British government, thus hoping to establish the grounds for a new understanding. The fact that Craigie felt that war could and should be averted and that his opinions on this matter were rejected is an important comment on the origins of the Pacific War. It raises a number of questions, such as why the views of someone so close to the heartbeat of Anglo-Japanese relations were ignored, and whether the alternative path Craigie postulated could have averted war.[4] In addition, it is necessary to study in some detail the proposals put forward in London by the two diplomats who held the post of Japanese Ambassador to the United Kingdom during this period, Yoshida Shigeru and Shigemitsu Mamoru, and to assess the practicability of their efforts to ease tensions.

The fact that programmes for an improvement of relations were ignored also raises the issue of how perceptions of Japan within Whitehall were formulated and what information was fed into this process. In this context it is important to look at the quality and breadth of British intelligence sources in East Asia. This is a difficult area to study, as the government still has strict controls over what records are released into the public domain and therefore the material on this field is far from complete, but it is possible, while acknowledging the crucial gaps in our understanding, to construct an image of what the Foreign Office and the service ministries ought to have known at any one time, and then to point out or postulate how that information influenced policy. This is, of course, an area of some controversy among historians, particularly in relation to foreknowledge of the attack on Pearl Harbor, and an attempt will be made to demonstrate what can reasonably be surmised from the latest records released by the government about Britain's reading of events in late 1941.[5]

The period covered by this survey relates to the years 1936 to 1941. The choice of the former as a starting date was deliberate and reflects a belief that, while the start of the Sino-Japanese war in July 1937 was clearly a vitally important event for Anglo-Japanese relations, to study the development of policy from 1936 leads to a broader and less regionally specific analysis. It allows for a discussion of the tensions that existed between Britain and Japan even before the Lukouchiao incident had taken place, and reveals that in the summer of 1937 a serious attempt was made within Whitehall to construct a new policy towards East Asia.

2 Halting a policy of drift
January 1936 to July 1937

On 17 January 1936 the Secretary of State for War, Alfred Duff Cooper, circulated to his Cabinet colleagues a memorandum entitled 'The Importance of Anglo-Japanese Friendship'.[1] This paper, which reflected the growing concern in the War Office about Britain's position in East Asia, observed that the current state of Anglo-Japanese relations was unsatisfactory and that an amelioration of tensions could only be achieved if the British government displayed a more friendly attitude towards Japan. It warned that this was particularly important in the light of the current state of Europe, where Britain was not only threatened by a resurgent Germany but was also faced with the possibility of conflict with Italy over Abyssinia, and recommended in sombre tones that

> so long as affairs in Europe remain unsettled, our interests in the Far East, at any rate north of Singapore, are at the mercy of the Japanese. It would seem a reasonable precaution, therefore, to try, by every means and even at some cost, to safeguard by amicable agreement with Japan, interests which we are unable to protect by military means.[2]

It also noted that the situation was not entirely black as Japan had recently made a number of overtures to Britain, and that it would be logical considering the strategic position to take advantage of these. This was a powerful argument but in the winter of 1936, while it was relatively easy to suggest that relations should be improved, it was more difficult to see how this could be achieved in practice. This was in part because of the great complexity of events in East Asia but it was also due to grave differences of view in Whitehall about how Britain should treat Japan and maintain, or even expand, its stake in China.

In 1936 British interests in China were fairly substantial. Approximately 6 per cent of Britain's overseas investments were located in

China; it was an important market for imperial exports, and a number of powerful commercial enterprises such as the Hongkong and Shanghai Banking Corporation (HSBC), Butterfield Swire, British-American Tobacco and Jardine, Matheson & Co. relied on China for the majority of their business.[3] China was not, however, a stable trading partner for, although the period of warlord domination had ended in 1928 with the establishment of the KMT government at Nanking led by Chiang Kai-shek, Chinese unity was under threat from outside and within. The external menace came predominantly from Japan which, uneasy at the strident claims of Chinese nationalism and itself weakened by the world Depression, had from 1931 to 1933 turned its economic sphere of influence in Manchuria into the puppet state of Manchukuo, and had then started to exert pressure on China to enter into an ever closer political and economic relationship. Internally Chiang Kai-shek faced the problem that his power-base was more or less confined to the lower Yangtse valley and that his government's authority outside that area relied on a series of fragile alliances with rival KMT leaders and recalcitrant warlords. From 1928 his regime had been faced by a number of rebellions, the most serious of which was that led in the province of Kiangsi by the Chinese Communist Party (CCP), a problem which also complicated China's relationship with the Soviet Union.

The problem for Britain in this situation was to work out how best to protect its stake in China. Should it side with the Nanking regime and renounce its claim to outdated imperial privileges such as extra-territoriality and the Treaty Ports in the hope of a fruitful relationship with the new China? Or should it co-operate with Japan and seek a division of China into spheres of influence, recognizing that otherwise the militarists of Tokyo would simply brush it aside? This conundrum was complicated further by the fact that Britain could not consider its future in East Asia in isolation. Relations with Japan and China covered a plethora of issues which also concerned other powers, and consequently any decisions Britain made would inevitably have repercussions on its ties with countries such as the United States, the Soviet Union and Germany. The overstretched bulk of the British Empire meant that for Whitehall events in East Asia were inextricably linked to those in Europe, and vice versa.

THE ROOTS OF FOREIGN OFFICE POLICY

The controversy within the British government over policy towards East Asia can be dated from February 1934, when the Defence

Requirements Sub-Committee, which had been established to study the state of Britain's military preparedness, produced its first report and suggested that Germany rather than Japan had to be considered the main threat to British interests. That report led the Treasury, and to varying degrees the service ministries, to push for a policy of reconciliation with Japan, only to find that what had seemed to them a logical response to the situation met with substantial opposition from the Foreign Office.

The basis of the Foreign Office's position throughout the period 1934–6 was that any bold initiative to improve relations with Japan was laudable in theory, but that the complexity of local conditions in East Asia meant that such a policy was barely practicable. From their perspective the central element in the politics of the region was the troubled state of Sino-Japanese relations, and there was a belief that any policy which failed to address this problem was doomed to failure. It was believed that progress could only be made with Japan if reconciliation could be brought about between Tokyo and Nanking. However, it was not easy to see how this could be achieved without actually undermining British interests, since Japan's attitude towards China was based upon the premises that tensions were the result of the Nanking government's reliance on Western assistance and that relations could only be improved if the political role of the West was reduced.

The Foreign Office held no delusions about Japan's ambitions, for they perceived that the Gaimushō (Japanese Foreign Ministry) had made its intentions perfectly clear in the Amō Statement of 17 April 1934, in which the head of the Gaimushō's information division, Amō Eiji, had briefed Japanese journalists on the government's position towards China and espoused the idea of a Japanese 'Monroe Doctrine' for East Asia.[4] This declaration was in direct contradiction to the 'open door' policy of equal access to markets and trade which had been espoused in the Nine Power Treaty signed at the Washington Conference in 1922. Although there was a brief flurry of speculation in the press about whether Amō was actually speaking on behalf of the government or simply expounding his own ideas, the Foreign Office had no such doubts because they knew from intelligence sources that Amō's words represented Japanese policy.

The role of intelligence in influencing Foreign Office policy is far from clear due to the British government's strict control over the release of documents, but it does seem to have been important. It is apparent that as early as 1934 the Government Code and Cypher School (GCCS) was forwarding decrypts (known as BJs) of Japanese diplomatic traffic to relevant government departments. The first evidence of this ability can be seen at the time of the Amō Statement, when decrypted telegrams from the Gaimushō revealed that Amō's comments were not his own personal views but rather an expression of the official government line.[5] In particular, a telegram from the Foreign Minister, Hirota Kōki, to the Japanese legation in Peking on 13 April stressed with great clarity that Japan was not prepared to co-operate with the Western Powers and concluded

> Japan does not wish to interfere with the trade of the Powers in China so long as it does not disturb peace and order in Eastern Asia, but Japan will resist any action calculated to disturb that peace and order . . . For these reasons, and because China still hopes to use foreign influence as a curb on Japan, it is important for the time being to proceed on the principle of upsetting the operations of foreign countries in China whether based on common or individual actions.[6]

Clearly this policy represented a threat to Britain's political interests and raised a question mark over the degree of influence Japan was willing to allow Britain in China even if a bilateral *rapprochement* could eventually be agreed. There was therefore a belief that until Japan reversed this policy relations could not be improved.

Another aspect of the Foreign Office's reluctance to make an opening to Japan was their awareness of the divisions within that country, and in particular the belief that the Imperial Japanese Army (IJA) was pushing for a harder line towards China than the Gaimushō and that it was the former which wielded the greater power. Once again intelligence was an important element, as it revealed the Gaimushō's futile attempts to restrain the IJA. For example, in the summer of 1935, just before the signing of the IJA-negotiated Ho-Umezu agreement, which substantially reduced the ability of the Kuomintang government to control events in Hopei province, a telegram from Hirota to the Japanese Embassy in London was intercepted in which the Foreign Minister optimistically observed that tensions in north China were unlikely to lead to any serious developments. It also revealed that the head of the Far Eastern section of the Gaimushō had complained to his opposite number in the IJA General Staff about the army's efforts to destabilize the situation.[7] Here too was evidence that any attempt to negotiate an agreement with Japan was fraught with danger, as there was no guarantee that a policy acceptable to the Gaimushō would win the approval of those seen as the real makers of Japanese policy, the IJA.

There was also the problem, as far as the Foreign Office were concerned, that even if Britain did manage to agree a compromise with Japan it would lead to serious opposition from the other powers with a stake in East Asia. As regards China, there was the danger that a deal bought at Nanking's expense would provoke a Chinese boycott of British goods, making a mockery of any economic concessions Britain had managed to negotiate with Japan. In addition, for Britain to come to terms with Japan would earn the ire of the United States. Washington's policy towards the region rested on the Stimson Doctrine of January 1932, which stipulated that the United States would not recognize any change in sovereignty in the region achieved through infringement of the Nine Power Treaty or of the Kellogg–Briand Pact of 1928, which had banned aggressive war. It was clear that if Britain were to act against the principles underlying this policy it would meet with opposition from the American President, Franklin Roosevelt, and that it could have many unfortunate ramifications in regard to issues such as future Anglo-American defence co-operation in the region, naval limitation and economic relations, and also increase Washington's tendency towards isolationism not only in East Asia but also in Europe.[8]

Another possible unfortunate consequence of renewed Anglo-Japanese friendship was the effect that such a development might have on the tense relations between the Soviet Union and Japan. The antipathy between these two countries had been a central theme in East Asia since 1932, and some elements within the IJA openly talked about the inevitability of war. As far as Britain was concerned tension between the two countries was welcome as their mutual suspicion was so intense that it curtailed their ability to act elsewhere, but there was no desire to see actual conflict. However, there was a danger that an Anglo-Japanese *rapprochement* might tip the balance in Japan's favour and encourage it to go to war with Russia in a conflict that could be detrimental to British interests. There was the possibility first and foremost that such a war might lead Moscow to seek a new understanding with Berlin which would allow Hitler more freedom of movement in Eastern Europe. There was also the threat of the consequences for East Asia should one side emerge as the decisive winner. In February 1934 a Foreign Office memorandum on this subject noted that a victory for Japan would lead to its becoming the predominant power in north-east Asia and allow it to exert further pressure on China, while a Soviet triumph might be even more catastrophic as it would lead to renewed Russian support for the

CCP and possibly the extension of Soviet influence into Sinkiang and Tibet, thus threatening the security of British India.[9]

There was also a realization in the Foreign Office that the Anglo-Japanese clash over China was but one of the areas where the countries differed and that a solution to this problem would not necessarily lead to success elsewhere. One vital issue was that of naval limitation, a process that had begun with the limitations on battleships established in the Five Power Treaty signed in Washington in 1922 and then expanded to cruisers in the Treaty of London in 1930, which had limited Japan to 60 to 70 per cent of the tonnage allocated to Britain and the United States. Here too there were doubts about the Gaimushō's power to direct Japanese policy, this time due to the tough stance taken by the Imperial Japanese Navy (IJN). Throughout the period of negotiations for a new naval limitation agreement from the summer of 1934 to the autumn of 1935 the Gaimushō hinted that a political settlement between Britain, the United States and Japan could lead the IJN to compromise, but each time the Foreign Office attempted to respond to these overtures they were met with an embarrassing silence. Meanwhile the IJN put forward its proposal for a 'common upper limit' which would in essence have allowed Japan parity with the other naval powers and was therefore unacceptable both to London and Washington. Here too was an area of policy in which it was very difficult to see how a mutually acceptable conclusion could be reached.[10]

Another area of concern to the Foreign Office was trade policy, and especially the difficulties raised by what they perceived as Japanese dumping of textiles into the British Empire. This was a problem because these goods were in direct competition with those produced by the Lancashire cotton industry, and were in fact beginning to displace the latter because the textiles from Osaka were cheaper due to Japan's lower labour costs and because Japanese business methods were more efficient. There was little belief that Japan was willing to make concessions in this field, as talks held in 1934 to find common ground had revealed that Japanese companies were not prepared to talk about a global demarcation of markets, with the result that Britain had in retaliation introduced quotas for Japanese cotton textile exports to British colonies. This sense of pessimism was underpinned by the reports received from the Commercial Counsellor at the Tokyo Embassy, Sir George Sansom, who was considered to be one of the world's pre-eminent authorities on all things Japanese. Sansom had from 1934 increasingly felt that Japan's aggressive trade policies and the rise of militarism meant that British and Japanese interests had become dangerously incompatible, and that Japan was not prepared to compromise. These views coming from one so respected had an important effect on the Foreign Office, and Sansom's comments were often used to counter the more optimistic proposals made by the Treasury.[11]

The belief that it would be difficult to come to any satisfactory arrangement with Japan did not, however, mean that the Foreign Office was prepared to swing to the other extreme and espouse an active policy of opposing Japanese expansion. There was an awareness that Britain was simply not powerful enough militarily to justify such a course and there were also doubts about how far America could be relied upon for support. In addition, it needs to be recognized that most of the officials in the Foreign Office, and particularly Sir Robert Vansittart, the Permanent Under-Secretary, were far more concerned with Germany as a threat to British interests and felt that rearmament should be focused initially on Europe.[12]

The conclusion that the Foreign Office drew from the above was that the policy of unilaterally seeking Japanese friendship as a cure to Britain's security problems was self-defeating, as any advantages accruing from such an arrangement would only lead to substantial disadvantages elsewhere, but also that resistance to Japan was too risky an alternative. This led to the belief that East Asian policy had to be based on the premise that nothing positive could be done until Sino-Japanese relations had been improved, and that all Britain could do was to try to provide an atmosphere which would encourage such a development. A summary of this essentially reactive and passive line was produced in a memorandum drafted by Charles Orde, head of the Far Eastern Department, for the Dominion Prime Ministers in March 1935 which noted

> Our interests seem . . . likely to be best served by cultivating friendly relations with both China and Japan, avoiding taking one side against the other, displaying neither undue jealousy towards Japanese aims, so long as they do not directly conflict with our own interests, nor too unsympathetic an attitude towards China's aspirations to be treated as a modern state.[13]

THE TREASURY AND EAST ASIA

The Treasury took a very different view of Britain's relations with East Asia and the initiatives it proposed in 1934–5 led to a battle with the Foreign Office for influence over foreign policy. The crux of the matter as far as the Treasury was concerned was that Britain could not afford the financial cost of rearming against two potential enemies and that therefore it was necessary to achieve a *rapprochement* with Japan while strengthening defences against Germany. However, this attitude was not just a logical consequence of the Treasury's financial rectitude, it was also the result of indications from pro-Japanese individuals in London, such as H.A. Gwynne, the editor of the *Morning Post*, and Arthur Edwardes, the agent for the Manchukuo government, that Japan was keen to draw closer to Britain.[14] The Chancellor of the Exchequer, Neville Chamberlain, made his first major effort to change British policy in autumn 1934 when he argued that a bilateral compromise with Japan over naval limitation could pave the way for a non-aggression pact. Underlying this policy was a rejection of the Foreign Office's assumption that Britain had to maintain good relations with the United States over East Asian issues. As far as Chamberlain and the Permanent Secretary at the Treasury, Sir Warren Fisher, were concerned reliance on Washington restricted Britain's flexibility and led to unnecessary tensions with Japan. In this particular instance the Treasury argued that Britain should ignore Washington's hardline position over refusing Japan naval parity, and instead seek an informal understanding with Japan over building programmes. This policy was completely unacceptable to the Foreign Office as it threatened in one fell swoop to destroy multilateral limitation and ignored the fact that if the United States was not party to such an agreement it would cause the very naval arms race it was supposed to avoid. In the end, however, Japan's own unwillingness to compromise showed that there could be no progress in this field.[15]

Finding its policy over naval limitation rebuffed, the Treasury was forced to realize that an agreement which ignored China and left America to one side could not be successful. The result in early 1935 was a new attempt to seize the initiative in East Asian policy with the focus this time on the financial situation in the region. This was an issue of some importance, since in the autumn of 1934 the Chinese economy had been severely hit by a drain of silver from the country caused by the American Congress's decision to build up the Federal Reserve Bank's silver stocks. This had led to inflation in China and the Nanking government desperately sought a currency stabilization loan from Western governments. The Treasury was opposed to any such loan, but did believe that China could be rescued from economic chaos if Britain, Japan and the United States could collaborate together to reform the Chinese currency and put it under their own control. This proposal was seen as having two advantages: first, it would provide an arena for Anglo-Japanese collaboration and thus pave the way for a more permanent agreement, and second, it would allow Britain a means of reversing the decline of its economic power in China, a phenomenon that was increasingly being brought to the Treasury's notice by the British companies operating there.[16] After six months of discussion, the Treasury's plan, with the support of the Board of Trade, metamorphosed into the idea of sending Sir Frederick Leith-Ross, the Chief Economic Adviser to the British government, to East Asia to investigate the possibility of arranging a joint Anglo-Japanese loan to China in return for Chinese *de jure* recognition of Manchukuo, a proposal which it was hoped would lead to the long-hoped-for breakthrough in relations between London and Tokyo.

The Foreign Office, browbeaten by Chamberlain's dominance over the Cabinet, reluctantly acquiesced to this proposal, but there were some, particularly in the Far Eastern Department, who felt that the Treasury's plan was doomed to disaster. They believed that the Leith-Ross scheme failed to comprehend that Japan's whole approach towards Chinese affairs was antithetical to the concept of international co-operation, and they were soon proved right; Leith-Ross was rather curtly rebuffed when he visited Japan in September 1935. However, even after this reverse Leith-Ross stayed in the region and began work on assisting the Chinese with the launch of a new currency, the *fapi*. This was an act which did not endear him to the Japanese, since one of Leith-Ross's major triumphs was to persuade the Chinese to link the *fapi* to sterling, thus undermining Japan's endeavours to establish a yen bloc in East Asia. In addition, Leith-Ross became convinced that Chinese stability and British business interests would be best served by a British loan to China. This put the Treasury in a very difficult position, first because Leith-Ross made the loan contingent on a Japanese approval which obviously would not be forthcoming, and second because it was also equally apparent that if Britain pressed on with the loan regardless it would antagonize the Japanese, in violation of the Treasury's stated aim of improving relations. The result, to the delight of the Foreign Office, was that the Leith-Ross mission was faced with an impasse, although there was less contentment over the fact that the Treasury's bumbling diplomacy had led to even worse relations with Japan.[17]

THE WAR OFFICE AND EAST ASIA

As the Treasury and Foreign Office squabbled over policy and relations with Japan were left to drift, the service ministries in 1935 concentrated their efforts on trying to persuade the government to agree to address the very grave defence problems in East Asia and in particular to sanction the fortification of Hong Kong and an accelerated completion of the Singapore naval base.[18] Although limited success was achieved in this field, there was still a perception, particularly in the War Office, that tensions were getting worse in East Asia. In particular, there were problems in north China where the IJA was trying to undermine Nanking's authority by pushing for the region to become autonomous; a development which would allow Japan to dominate the economy of the area. This challenge to the KMT was seen as highly dangerous since it could lead to a Sino-Japanese war. In August 1935 Colonel Ismay, the officer in charge of MI2 (the branch of the Directorate of Military Intelligence and Operations which dealt with East Asia), noted with great prescience that as the prospect of a quick Japanese victory over the Soviet Union became ever more unlikely due to Russia's rearmament programme, the chances of a confrontation between Japan and China grew

> Japan's interest is likely to turn more and more to economic – perhaps political – domination of China. This idea, which first arose out of the necessity for securing supplies of raw materials against an *eventual* war with Russia may eventually absorb Japan's attention – and add to her military commitments to such an extent that the Russian objective will fade into the background. . . . [W]hat was intended to be a mere stage in preparation for the long term aim of war with Russia may turn out to be at once a preparation for, and the cause of, a conflict with a naval power – viz. Great Britain. Of this conception, I am convinced no Japanese soldier has more than the first dawning.[19]

The concern within the War Office over events in East Asia continued to mount in the autumn of 1935. The chief cause was the steady escalation of tensions in north China. The IJA's desire for regional autonomy and its fear that the *fapi* would enhance the influence of the KMT government inspired it in December 1935 to establish the East Hopei Anti-Communist Autonomous Council. For a while it appeared that China and Japan were on the brink of war; an impression which was reinforced by intelligence information collected by the Far East Combined Bureau (FECB) at Hong Kong, an inter-Service intelligence gathering organization established in April 1935. One FECB report, based on the interception of a message sent in the IJN's operational code, suggested that IJN ships were heading towards Shanghai and Tsingtao in an effort to bring pressure to bear on the Chinese government. However, in the end Chiang Kai-shek backed away from confrontation and agreed to a joint Sino-Japanese venture which would allow the region greater autonomy: the Hopei-Chahar Political Council, but this was a reprieve from war rather than a solution to Sino-Japanese antipathy.[20]

In addition to the rising tensions in China, there were disturbing developments on a wider scale. Evidence from various intelligence sources suggested that German–Japanese relations were becoming closer. In August 1935 MI2c produced a memorandum which detailed the growth of links between the military and naval commands in both countries, and noted, in particular, that the IJN and the *Kriegsmarine* had agreed to exchange technical information.[21] This was an extremely dangerous prospect as far as the War Office was concerned, for although it was clear that the initial impetus behind these soundings was mutual antipathy towards the Soviet Union, there was a danger that it could become an anti-British grouping which would have the potential to menace British interests at opposite ends of the globe.

In the midst of these troubles there were indications that Japan was interested in improving relations. On 17 December 1935 the British Ambassador in Tokyo, Sir Robert Clive, was approached by Hirota who suggested, in regard to the recent opening of the Second London Naval Conference, that if no agreement on naval limitation could be reached Japan, Britain and the United States should seek to negotiate a Pacific pact. On 27 December this was followed by a report from Clive indicating that the IJA General Staff, who were usually seen as the most radical and uncompromising element in Japanese politics, were sympathetic towards closer ties with Britain.[22] To the War Office these overtures seemed to suggest that, despite all the problems in Anglo-Japanese relations, there was still a possibility that one of Britain's potential enemies could be neutralized; this was an enormously enticing prospect and on 1 January 1936 Ismay noted that this opening should not be wasted. His seniors agreed with this analysis and the result was the War Office's memorandum for the Cabinet.[23]

THE RAW MATERIALS ISSUE

In addition to noting the recent Japanese overtures, the War Office also referred in its memorandum to the potential of a proposal that was currently being discussed in Whitehall as a means of overcoming the disparity between the 'have' and the 'have-not' nations, the idea of a guarantee of equal access to raw materials. This is an area little considered in terms of the origins of the Pacific War, but the debate about this issue and Japan's place within it was considered to be important at the time. It is also important to look at it from a British perspective in the light of the Japanese historian Usui Katsumi's criticism of influential Japanese figures, such as Konoe Fumimaro and Shigemitsu Mamoru, for preferring the unilateralist approach of seeking domination of East Asia to co-operation with Western initiatives for reform of the international system, a judgement which begs the question of how sincere the Western initiatives were.[24]

The Foreign Office's initial debate about this question was precipitated by the rising tensions between Italy and Abyssinia in the summer of 1935. The basis of Italy's claim for 'a place in the sun' was that, as a late arrival to imperialism, it did not have the same access to raw materials and markets as France and Britain and that the post-war *status quo*, underpinned by the League of Nations, denied it the right to expand its territories. Such an argument was, of course, not very different from those used by Germany and Japan. Although there was little sympathy for these regimes in the Foreign Office there did exist a recognition in some quarters that the 'have-nots' case was logical and that to ignore their complaints was a sure way of consigning the world to a new conflagration. It was in this spirit that, on 4 September 1935, Sir George Mounsey, who oversaw the League of Nations Department, noted

> Insecurity as to the availability of necessary supplies of raw materials and inability to find outlets for expanding populations under the restrictive regimes prevailing in most modern states constitute two of the fundamental causes of unrest and friction from which the world is suffering today; and unless and until these problems are frankly tackled in a generous spirit and thrashed out by common agreement there is no hope of any lasting peace in the world.[25]

In seeking to rectify this problem Mounsey and others came upon the idea of incorporating into a speech to be made by the Foreign Secretary, Sir Samuel Hoare, to the League of Nations Assembly at Geneva on 11 September 1935 a passage which referred to Britain's desire out of 'enlightened self-interest' to discuss a guarantee of equal access for all countries to raw materials from colonial territories.[26]

Although too late to distract the Duce from his aggression against

Abyssinia, this was a bold initiative implying that the leading *status quo* power in the world was willing to discuss the need to tackle the wider issues disturbing the equilibrium of international politics. Hoare's speech was met with enthusiasm in many countries including Japan, and this welcome encouraged the War Office to argue in its memorandum that with careful handling the proposal could act as bait to draw Japan into talks.

The War Office's espousal of the raw materials proposal presupposed that Hoare had been sincere when he had made this speech and that the Foreign Office wished to see fruitful international discussion of this issue. In reality there was no consensus and much confusion within the Foreign Office about what Hoare had been trying to achieve. To some, such as Ralph Wigram, the head of the Central Department, and Lawrence Collier, the head of the Northern Department, the idea of a League investigation into raw materials would merely serve the purpose of proving that the British Empire already provided satisfactory access, thus revealing that the revisionist powers' cult of expansionism had no economic justification; to them Hoare's speech was no more than a propaganda exercise.[27] There were others, of whom Mounsey was the most senior, who were sincere about the utility of this initiative, but even among this group there was some division over whether Japan deserved to benefit from such reforms. While Mounsey was willing to see Japanese grievances addressed, others remained profoundly suspicious, largely because of Japanese trading practices, and these doubts manifested themselves in the memorandum that was eventually produced for the Cabinet in January 1936 on the raw materials issue. This document noted that if imperial preference in the colonies was abolished in order to allow foreign countries to build up their sterling reserves and thus have more currency with which to buy raw materials, this

would not necessarily assist the individual European countries such as Germany and Italy, which have been most vocal. Immediately, Japan would probably benefit most by this change, owing to the advantage which she enjoys in her labour costs. Germany and Italy might well not benefit at all.

It has been suggested that some formula might be devised whereby, in effect, existing restrictions were retained on Japanese goods. For example the 'door' might only be 'opened' to the goods of countries who were party to the various International Labour Conventions.[28]

What emerges from this revealing statement is that the Foreign Office and other government departments were agreed that the issue of reform of the international system should not be pursued as a means of establishing greater equality between states in general, but that it was seen as an appeasement measure only to be applied to the revisionist powers in Europe who posed the greatest threat to British interests.

This cynical interpretation is confirmed by a comment written by Vansittart on 31 December, after Hoare's resignation, in which he noted that the raw materials idea had never been a serious suggestion and that

> Sir S. Hoare included it in his speech largely with a view to gaining time for the temperate and dignified consideration of the demand for territorial redistribution, which was then already very obviously coming; for which no preparation had or has been made. We shall get nowhere with any mere discussion of raw materials.[29]

This view also reflected the position of the Foreign Secretary, Anthony Eden, who preferred the idea of an agreement with Germany over the redistribution of colonies. Consequently when the memorandum on this issue was presented to the Cabinet on 29 January 1936 Eden persuaded his colleagues that the issue ought to be dropped until the Abyssinian crisis was over.[30] It was therefore clear that the War Office could expect little progress in this field.

SEARCHING FOR AN OPENING

The War Office's reverse over the raw materials issue was mirrored by the reception given to the wider issues raised by its memorandum. The call for a new policy towards Japan did not find an appreciative audience within the Foreign Office. On 22 January Orde drafted a brief for Eden, which refuted the argument that a *rapprochement* was possible by noting that all the original reasons for not pursuing this policy still existed.[31] Orde could afford to be so dogmatic since he wrote in the knowledge that Hirota's overture the previous month had come to nothing; Clive had later reported that the Foreign Minister was merely thinking out loud and that the IJN remained firmly opposed to Gaimushō interference in naval policy. Hopes for a pact were also dashed by the attitude of the American Under-Secretary of State, William Phillips, who made it abundantly clear in talks with Eden that the United States felt that even a simple consultative pact would not be worth pursuing.[32] In addition, Orde noted that it was a mistake to imagine that an overture to Japan would divert the latter from talks with Germany, since Tokyo and Berlin had a common enemy in the Soviet Union, a view shared by Vansittart.[33]

The War Office memorandum was considered by the Cabinet at its meeting on 29 January 1936. It was given a polite but non-committal reception; Eden's sole comment was to tell his colleagues that he too desired better relations with Japan, but that in the present climate it was difficult to put this into practice, while Chamberlain stressed the need to see what Leith-Ross could achieve.[34] This was hardly a satisfactory outcome for the War Office and the overall impression given was that the Foreign Office and the Treasury would continue to dominate East Asian policy with little regard for the fears of the Services.

With the War Office's challenge dismissed attention could be turned again to the central question in British policy towards East Asia in early 1936, what to do with Leith-Ross. The Foreign Office's attitude was that the Chief Economic Adviser's continued presence in China did not serve any useful purpose since it was clear that any attempt to give a loan to the Nanking government would only lead to a worsening of relations with Japan. The Treasury, however, still believed that their representative could do some good, and were particularly encouraged when in early February hints came from a number of Japanese channels that Leith-Ross would be welcome to make a second trip to Tokyo. The Foreign Office was at first able to resist this idea but by early April Chamberlain's conviction that such a visit would be beneficial persuaded them to give way, although the price for approval was that this should be Leith-Ross's last act and that he should leave East Asia soon after.[35]

Once this visit had been agreed in principle the problem then was to decide what issues Leith-Ross ought to discuss with Japanese officials. It was obvious that China would be at the top of the agenda, but on 9 March Leith-Ross indicated that he was interested to see if the Board of Trade would be willing to put forward a new negotiating line over British colonial quotas on Japanese textiles. This enquiry led to a debate in Whitehall about how far Britain could move in this direction. The Board of Trade's reaction was that these quotas were vital to the Lancashire cotton industry and that they could only be relaxed if Japanese companies were willing to agree to a world-wide demarcation of markets.[36] This was an unfortunate line to take as such a tough stance over the maintenance of protectionism could do little to endear Britain to Japan or divert the latter from its adherence to a policy of autarky, and consequently

Leith-Ross was able to offer very little in this field apart from reiterating that Britain would welcome talks on this issue.

Leith-Ross finally arrived in Tokyo in early June. His reception was considerably warmer than on his previous trip in September 1935, but the talks he held with Japanese officials did little to overcome the problems in Anglo-Japanese relations. Over China there was no meeting of minds and predictably the Japanese Foreign Minister, Arita Hachirō, showed very little interest in the reconvening of talks over cotton, although he did indicate his enthusiasm for Hoare's raw materials initiative.[37] However, despite this lack of substantive progress, Leith-Ross did come away from Japan with the feeling that potential existed for ties to be improved.

In July 1936 Leith-Ross arrived back in London after ten months spent in East Asia. His report on his mission championed the idea that with government assistance it was possible for British enterprise to expand and flourish in China, and that there was no need to acquiesce to Japanese domination of the region. In particular he stressed the potential for Britain to improve its position through its financial strength, and the importance of the supply of British capital to support China's railway projects. As regards Japan, Leith-Ross noted that he had been assured both by the Japanese government and by the military authorities that 'they had no desire to prejudice British interests in China', and that Britain should do its best to wean Japan away from its present policy and back towards the idea of co-operation in exploiting the potential of the China market.[38] This report was received with considerable pleasure within Treasury circles, as it seemed to justify the policy that they had pursued since the start of 1935, and moves were made to implement its recommendations, particularly in the field of railway financing.

The Treasury's optimism was encouraged further by positive signs from Japan, and in particular the arrival in London in June of the new Japanese Ambassador to Britain, Yoshida Shigeru. Yoshida, who had only recently been vetoed by the IJA from taking over as Foreign Minister, was determined to achieve a diplomatic success in London and soon after his arrival he began to develop a plan for a comprehensive settlement between the two countries, the basis of which was co-operation in the economic development of China. These ideas tied in closely with Leith-Ross's conclusions from his mission to China, with the result that Yoshida found the Treasury sympathetic to his views. On 15 October he held a meeting with Chamberlain to discuss his proposals, in which the Chancellor promised that he would approach Eden and prepare the way for the Japanese Ambassador.[39]

On 26 October the Treasury forwarded Yoshida's ten-point plan to the Foreign Office; it began by stating that China was the central problem in Anglo-Japanese relations and that a normalization of Sino-Japanese relations through reaffirmation by Britain and Japan of China's sovereignty south of the Great Wall and of respect for the 'open door' would pave the way for a broader agreement. In addition, it proposed that political and financial aid should be given to Nanking, and that specifically Japan would give the Chinese government long-term credits and military advisers to assist it in its struggle against the CCP. As well as the Chinese issue, Yoshida also proposed an improvement in Anglo-Japanese commercial and financial relations, British benevolent neutrality in any Soviet-Japanese war, a reconvening of the naval limitation conference, and reconstruction of the League of Nations.[40]

This was an ambitious scheme but, despite the Treasury's enthusiasm, it was fatally flawed. The major problem was that it was based on the belief that terms agreeable to Britain and Japan could simply be dictated to China, indeed Yoshida's plan seemed at times to harken back to the infamous ultimatum Japan had presented to China in 1915, the Twenty-One Demands. Difficulties were also raised by the Ambassador's insistence that Chinese sovereignty would only be recognized below the Great Wall, which automatically raised questions about the status not only of Manchukuo but also of Inner Mongolia.[41] Above and beyond these problems was the very practical objection that these proposals emanated not from the Gaimushō but from an Ambassador on his own authority, and there was no guarantee that these terms would be acceptable in Tokyo. Indeed the more Yoshida talked with Eden and Sir Alexander Cadogan, the Deputy Under-Secretary of State at the Foreign Office, the clearer it became that the Ambassador was considerably divorced from his own government. This was also made apparent by Clive's despatches from Tokyo and the conversations held by Sir Eric Drummond, the British Ambassador in Rome, with his Japanese counterpart, Sugimura Yōtarō.[42] In addition, it is likely that seeds of doubt were being sown by GCCS's ability to read the telegrams Yoshida had sent to and received from the Gaimushō, although no such decrypts are currently in the public domain.

Despite their misgivings about Yoshida's credentials, the Foreign Office could not simply dismiss his initiative, as this would be a dangerous signal to give to Japan and could lead to a renewed clash with Chamberlain. Therefore Cadogan was given the task of trying to modify Yoshida's proposals into a shape acceptable to

British interests, and on 7 January 1937 he produced a draft *aide-mémoire* as a reply to the Japanese Ambassador. This toned down many of the more extreme demands in Yoshida's text, removing the reference to the area south of the Great Wall, making Chinese acceptance of aid against communism voluntary, and noting that Britain was keen to improve its commercial and financial links with Japan. Before being forwarded to Yoshida the draft was sent over to the Treasury for comment; Leith-Ross reinstated the Great Wall clause, but a furious Cadogan was soon able to point out to him the ramifications of such a move and have the words removed.[43] On 18 January Eden handed the *aide-mémoire* to Yoshida, who to the consternation of the Foreign Office, returned three days later to report that the document was too detailed and that all he had wanted was a vague assurance that Britain was willing to negotiate a general agreement, which he would then take back to Tokyo.[44] This raised all sorts of problems, as the manner in which Yoshida's original memorandum had been worded demanded a detailed response, and therefore to fit the Ambassador's request it was necessary for Cadogan not only to produce a shorter and vaguer British *aide-mémoire*, but also to rewrite Yoshida's original draft. This farcical episode tried the Foreign Office's patience and in a note of 28 January Vansittart summed up the general feeling by noting 'Mr Yoshida is just plainly no good. We can leave it at that: play him, but don't take him seriously'; from this point on the Ambassador was treated with due suspicion.[45]

RISING TENSIONS IN EAST ASIA

Yoshida's diplomacy, in spite of its bumbling execution, did have some uses in that it helped to stir enthusiasm in Whitehall for an agreement with Japan, and forced departments to consider the means by which a mutually acceptable understanding could be reached. It was, however, not the only stimulus behind a renewed interest in an Anglo-Japanese understanding, for there were other darker forces at play. The year 1936 was one of constant activity in East Asia and the complex interplay of events began to suggest that a cataclysm was impending. The main threat to the region's security was the steady escalation of Sino-Japanese tensions, but in addition there were signs that Japan and the Soviet Union were increasingly involved in a battle for influence over China.

Indications that Chiang Kai-shek's previous policy of non-resistance to Japan might be on the wane came from a number of sources. In the

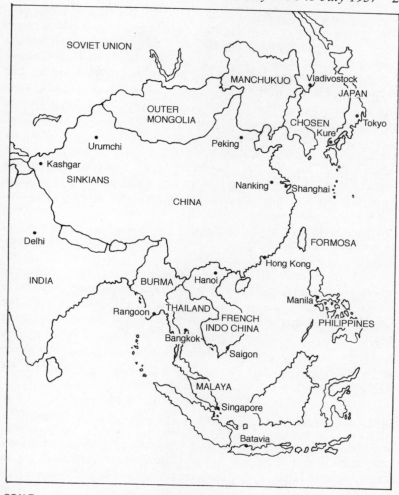

Pre-war East Asia c., 1936

spring of 1936 Sir Maurice Hankey, the Cabinet Secretary, forwarded information to the War Office and the Foreign Office on various military preparations being made in China. These warnings were in turn reinforced by reports from the Army's intelligence centre in

Shanghai which noted that there were signs that China was strengthening its defences along the Yellow and Yangtse rivers.[46] Perhaps even more disturbing was that evidence existed to suggest that the Soviet Union was encouraging this development. In March the intelligence centre in Shanghai reported that it had been reliably informed that the Soviet Embassy had orders to discuss military co-operation in return for a promise of non-interference in Chinese internal affairs, while on 19 June Chiang Kai-shek in his last meeting with Leith-Ross, openly asked what Britain's attitude would be to a Sino-Soviet alliance.[47] Meanwhile the *Manchuria Daily News* and other publications circulated rumours about a secret Sino-Soviet pact and, even though the veracity of this claim was not accepted in London or by the British Embassy in Moscow, they contributed to the general sense of unease.[48]

The rumours sweeping East Asia were disturbing because it was clear that within China there was increasing pressure on Chiang Kai-shek to begin a policy of resistance. The initial feeling within the Foreign Office was that Chiang was too astute to risk resistance against Japan, and it was argued that the defensive moves were to a large extent a propaganda exercise designed to deter Japan and to persuade the West to restrain Tokyo.[49] However, in the autumn of 1936 this complacency was challenged when a series of anti-Japanese incidents, involving the deaths of a number of Japanese nationals, occurred in central and southern China and threatened to escalate out of control. Britain was aware of how dangerous this crisis could be, because the FECB through its reading of IJN messages could follow the orders given to the Japanese naval command in China. This source revealed that, although Japan had no intention of beginning hostilities, its navy was reinforcing its position in China in case a wider conflagration broke out.[50] This made it clear that the avoidance of such a conflict would rest to a large degree on Chiang's handling of events.

It was thus with some trepidation that the Foreign Office learnt on 28 September that Chiang had told the British Army's senior intelligence officer in China, Colonel Burkhardt, that he would 'meet any further aggression by ordering general mobilization'. Faced with the possible escalation of tensions the Foreign Office on 29 September sent the first of a series of warning telegrams to their East Asian ambassadors; informing Clive that he was to advise the Gaimushō that harsh demands on China would only lead to further incidents and harm Anglo-Japanese relations, and telling Knatchbull-Hugessen in Nanking to urge the Chinese to curb anti-Japanese activities.[51]

Even when talks began in October between the Chinese Foreign Minister, Chang Chun, and the Japanese Ambassador to Nanking, Kawagoe Shigeru, British nerves were kept on edge by a series of Secret Intelligence Service (SIS) reports which contained evidence of Chiang's new, tougher approach towards Japan.[52] In November a new threat to peace emerged due to fighting in Inner Mongolia between Chinese and pro-Japanese forces, and the eventual success of the Chinese forces in resisting the Mongolians under Prince Teh acted as a catalyst to a new outpouring of anti-Japanese sentiment, particularly in north China where the CCP were stirring up opinion in favour of a war of resistance. On 12 December events took an even more dramatic turn when the leader of the government forces in Shensi province, Chang Hsueh-liang, kidnapped Chiang Kai-shek while the latter was visiting Chang's headquarters at Sian. At first the paucity of information available to the Foreign Office made it very difficult to assess what was going on and who was behind Chang's venture. The idea that the Soviets were involved was quickly dismissed and intelligence information from the FECB showed that the Japanese were not implicated.[53] All that could be done was to watch and wait, and there was much relief when Chiang Kai-shek was eventually set free on 25 December. Even then, however, there were worries, notably the confusion over what conditions Chiang had agreed to in order to regain his liberty and whether they involved a commitment to pursue an even stiffer line against Japan.[54]

The ever-worsening Sino-Japanese confrontation was not the only problem that Britain faced in the autumn of 1936; in addition there was the fact that Japan's paranoia about communism in East Asia and the threat from the Soviet Union led, on 25 November, to the conclusion of the Anti-Comintern Pact with Germany. Although Britain, through the BJ source, had been aware for some time that such an agreement was likely, it was still met with some misgivings in London. This was not because the pact was seen as the basis for an eventual alliance against British interests but because of the fear that this was a major step towards the establishment of ideological blocs which would polarize international relations as did events preceding the First World War. Such anxiety was not without substance, as the first reaction of the Soviet Ambassador in Japan, Konstantin Yurenev, was to suggest to Clive the formation of an Anglo-Soviet-American-Chinese bloc.[55] In addition, the Foreign Office was disturbed because, despite protestations from Arita to Clive that the pact was merely intended as a curb on Comintern activities, it was known that a secret protocol had been signed relating to the conduct of the signatories in case of war between one of them and the Soviet Union.[56] Although the commitment for both powers in such a scenario was strictly limited to refraining from providing any assistance to Moscow, the precedent of common action against a mutual enemy had been set.

The potential military threat to Britain from this development was worrying not only in abstract terms but also because of evidence of Japan's growing interest in expansion of its influence in both south China and South-East Asia. Even before the Anti-Comintern Pact had been signed, the Joint Planning Sub-Committee (JPC) which reported to the Chiefs of Staff had recommended that a Far Eastern Appreciation be prepared which would consider the possibility of war with Japan. In particular the JPC was interested to learn whether Japan could launch an assault on Singapore without Britain being forewarned. This prediction was investigated by the newly constituted Joint Intelligence Sub-Committee (JIC), which reported in October that Japan's proven ability to keep radio-silence during a large expedition, the ease with which Formosa could be used as a base for concentrating air and land forces, and the inadequacy of information received from the SIS organization in Japan meant that there could be no absolute guarantee that warning would be received of a Japanese expedition towards Singapore or Hong Kong.[57] This, in addition to continued budgetary restraints on British defences in the East, emphasized that Britain could not contemplate with any comfort the idea of a simultaneous conflict in Europe and Asia.

The linking of the European and East Asian theatres through the Anti-Comintern Pact, the possibility of Sino-Japanese conflict, the potential Japanese threat to British possessions in the East, and the subsequent overstretching of Britain's defensive resources meant that in late 1936 there was increasing disquiet about the state of Anglo-Japanese relations and a desire to improve ties. In December Vansittart produced a long memorandum entitled 'The World Situation and British Rearmament', which among many other matters considered the state of relations with Japan. He argued in regard to the Anti-Comintern Pact that

> What this agreement clearly does . . . is to introduce Japan into the orbit of European affairs at a particularly delicate and dangerous phase, and to increase the probability that, in given circumstances, Germany and Japan will now act together.[58]

He therefore proposed that Britain should initiate a new policy towards Japan designed to counter any further development of

Japanese–German ties by improving Britain's naval defences in the East and taking advantage of the obvious disapproval in many circles in Tokyo of the activities of the pro-German faction. This view won the approval of the First Sea Lord, Admiral Chatfield, who on 5 January 1937 noted in response to Vansittart's memorandum

> An understanding with Japan . . . is . . . the first essential and, difficult as it admittedly is, should not be unobtainable if we make it not a weak aim but a decided policy. Having thus secured our Eastern Empire against our *first* commitment, we should be in a stronger position to sit on the fence in Europe.[59]

This opinion was shared by the other Chiefs of Staff and by the members of the Committee of Imperial Defence (CID), and as a result the Review of Imperial Defence drawn up in February 1937 for the forthcoming Imperial Conference stressed that an agreement with Japan would 'enormously strengthen the Empire'.[60]

AN END TO DRIFT?

Opinion in Whitehall was therefore by the winter of 1937 far more united than before in believing that an understanding with Japan was necessary. The problem remained, however, of trying to find mutually acceptable terms while at the same time not provoking American and Chinese animosity. An opportunity emerged in March 1937 when Satō Naotake was made the new Japanese Foreign Minister. Satō had previously been the Ambassador in Paris and had gained a reputation for being a moderate and pro-Western diplomat, in contrast to China-orientated figures such as Hirota and Arita. From the time he took office Satō lived up to this reputation, declaring that relations with China ought to be based on equality and making clear his desire to see an improvement in Anglo-Japanese relations.[61] At the same time it became apparent that Roosevelt was having a change of heart about American policy towards the Pacific, and was prepared to see negotiations to formalize a new *status quo*.[62] Meanwhile, as regards China, there was also cause for hope in that official sources and SIS reports indicated that Chiang had emerged from the Sian Incident with heightened authority and that, using this influence, he had in February 1937 managed to convince the KMT's Central Executive Committee to approve a policy of negotiating to improve relations with Japan on the basis of equality and reciprocity.[63] At long last it appeared that there was a genuine chance for a lasting settlement.

The wave of optimism among British officials in spring 1937 led to a number of actions and proposals designed to improve relations with Japan. One positive step was that on 13 March it was announced that Sir Robert Craigie was to be the new British Ambassador to Tokyo.[64] This was an interesting choice, as Craigie had never previously served as a diplomat in East Asia and his only experience of negotiating with the Japanese had been in the naval limitation talks. However, in these talks Craigie, as well as showing his considerable skills as a negotiator, had come to know a number of influential figures, such as Matsudaira Tsuneo, Yoshida's predecessor, who now held the key post of Minister of the Imperial Household, and Admiral Yamamoto Isoroku, the Navy Vice-Minister. He had also consistently shown an interest in better relations with Japan as a means of improving Britain's global position and preventing any further development of German–Japanese ties. In addition to these qualifications, Craigie's appointment was noteworthy in that he was one of the most willing of the senior figures within the Foreign Office to see Britain tackle the problems in the international system by far-reaching reforms. In summer 1936 he had written a memorandum recommending the negotiation of a new Locarno Treaty to guarantee security in Western Europe and of a Mediterranean pact based on the same principles as Locarno, and argued that many in Britain underestimated Germany's fear of Bolshevism.[65] In December 1936 he had noted in response to Vansittart's memorandum 'The World Situation and British Rearmament' that he agreed with the idea of a colonial settlement with Germany and put forward the opinion that '[w]hat puts us in the wrong not only with Germany but with the whole world is the slogan, when applied to mandates, of what we have we hold'.[66] His appointment to Tokyo therefore suggested a greater British willingness to negotiate on equal terms.

The new mood also encouraged the emergence from outside Whitehall of three policy initiatives for improved relations with Japan. The first came from Knatchbull-Hugessen, who on 2 March proposed that Britain should take advantage of the decline of Japanese pressure on China to push for a regional *détente*, which would also meet the security needs of the Soviet Union by arranging for a reduction of Japanese forces in Manchuria and Japanese recognition of Outer Mongolia.[67] This was a bold plan but it was met with little enthusiasm within the Foreign Office, where it was felt that Soviet–Japanese antagonism remained a useful way of diverting Japan from southwards expansion. The second proposal emanated from the United States, and consisted of a plan for the neutralization of the Pacific as a means of replacing article XIX of the Five Power Treaty of 1922, which had prohibited the fortification of islands north of Singapore or west of Hawaii. This idea was, however, also rejected by the Foreign Office because, although the general idea of neutralization was welcome, there was no guarantee of security in the American proposal.[68]

The third idea came from the Australian Prime Minister, Joseph Lyons, who proposed at the Imperial Conference in London in May 1937 that a new, enlarged version of the Four Power Pact of 1922 should be negotiated which would uphold the *status quo* in the Pacific and provide an apparatus for economic and cultural collaboration. Once again the Foreign Office approved of the general aim of the proposal but saw it as being difficult to negotiate.[69] In part the reluctance of the Foreign Office to back any of these proposals unreservedly was based on doubts about the practicality of their multilateral approach. The desire in London was for a more incremental policy, a view espoused, in response to the Lyons Plan, by Craigie who noted in June

> I would . . . suggest that a wiser procedure would be to confine our efforts at first to the settlement of some of the outstanding problems in Anglo-Japanese and Sino-Japanese relations. If success can be achieved in these two fields, the way would then be open for an advance to a wider international settlement.[70]

There was then within the Foreign Office a cautious attitude to the opportunity provided by Japan's apparent reversal of policy and a recognition that only a careful and balanced policy would harvest results. This concern was reflected in the decision by the Far Eastern Department in the winter of 1937 to initiate their own thorough investigation of British policy towards East Asia. A first draft of a memorandum was sent by Frank Ashton-Gwatkin of the Economic Section of the Foreign Office to Leith-Ross for comment in February. The document began by contending that British policy had until that time been nothing more than a set of delaying tactics and that it was necessary for a more active policy to be pursued. It proceeded to argue that Britain's position in East Asia could only be improved if there was a substantial effort to improve defences in the region, and that with such an improvement it would be easier to persuade Japan to agree to engage in serious negotiations about its grievances. The memorandum was also heavily influenced by Leith-Ross's report, and recommended a number of initiatives to revitalize Britain's position in China, including an end to extraterritoriality and renunciation of Britain's right under the terms of the Boxer Protocol to station troops in north China.[71]

Leith-Ross's response to this paper was to welcome its general outlook while criticizing its tendency to treat Japan as an inveterate enemy. In replying to Ashton-Gwatkin, Leith-Ross sent his own memorandum which took a much more liberal stance, arguing that Britain should make an effort to improve its commercial relations with Japan, and that the Foreign Office should stress that if Japan desired to see the economic development of China then London and Hong Kong were the only capital markets with the money and experience to support such ventures. On the issue of the need for more British armed forces in East Asia, Leith-Ross, in a manner suited to a Treasury official, skirted round the issue by proposing greater multilateral co-operation in the Pacific as a means of supplementing Britain's defences.[72]

The Foreign Office, while willing to tone down some of the passages on Japan, remained convinced that *rapprochement* could only be achieved if Japan was convinced that Britain had the forces and will necessary to defend its interests. Consequently Eden at a meeting of the Cabinet Defence Plans (Policy) Committee in May argued strongly in favour of a plan presented by the Admiralty in April 1937 for a 'New Standard of Naval Strength', while at the same time stressing his hope for an improvement in Anglo-Japanese relations which 'rested on a community of interests as regards the joint policy of England and Japan towards China'.[73] Eden's apparent optimism was bolstered further by evidence that the Japanese themselves were also seeking better relations, despite Satō's replacement by Hirota as Foreign Minister in early June. Open confirmation on the diplomatic front came when Yoshida informed Craigie on 2 June that he was awaiting new instructions from Tokyo, while Britain was also able to follow this trend through the BJ source.[74] In June the Far Eastern Department's memorandum on policy towards East Asia was completed, and it was decided that the document should be circulated to the Cabinet and then discussed in detail by an interdepartmental committee.[75]

The Far Eastern Department's memorandum was, however, not the only initiative discussed within Whitehall that dealt with the state of Anglo-Japanese relations, for there was also debate at an interdepartmental level about trade with Japan. The initial impetus behind this development was the revival by the Cabinet Committee on Foreign Policy in July 1936 of the raw materials proposal. The aim was to use this as a means of side-stepping German demands for colonies, and it led on 25 September 1936 to Eden making a speech to the League of Nations General Assembly reiterating Hoare's call for an investigation into the question of access to colonial raw materials. Both the League Assembly and Council voted over the next few months to back this initiative and finally in March 1937 a Raw Materials Committee began its proceedings in Geneva.[76] Germany did not attend these deliberations, but Japan, although no longer a member of the League, was enthusiastic about this investigation and sent its Commercial Counsellor in Berlin, Shudō Yasuto, as its representative.

While the preparations were being made in Geneva, Whitehall considered what line Britain should take in the forthcoming discussions. The consensus reached at an interdepartmental meeting in February was that Leith-Ross, who was to act as the British representative, should support a guarantee of equal access, except in the case of League of Nations sanctions or Britain being at war; that the Committee should not be allowed to consider India, which was deemed not to be a colony; and that an initiative to expand the 'open door' in tropical Africa might be made as long as its benefits did not apply to Japan – conditions which reflected the innate conservatism of the British attitude, and in particular the dead hand of the Board of Trade. It was thus with some embarrassment that Leith-Ross reported on 9 March that Shudō, in his opening statement to the Committee, had made clear that Japan desired freedom of distribution for raw materials, free access to the development of backward areas, an end to restrictions on access to markets, and free movement of people.[77]

This positive statement contrasted sharply with the British position, particularly considering that the proposal had originally been Hoare's initiative and on 18 March the Cabinet Committee on Foreign Policy discussed, as part of a general discussion of the colonial issue, what could be done to make the 'open door' proposal more attractive. Both Chamberlain and Lord Runciman, the President of the Board of Trade, argued that to make the scheme work it was essential to reach some sort of agreement with Japan under which the latter would agree to limit its exports to the region.[78] Support for this policy came from Eden, who six days later proposed to Chamberlain that an Interdepartmental Committee on Trade Policy should be established and that, in particular, it should study trade relations with Japan. In this context the Foreign Secretary noted

At present we are engaged in damming back Japanese goods from our colonial empire (and elsewhere if we can) by that policy of quotas, which we are the first to condemn in other countries; while the Japanese cut off from normal economic expansion and nervous about their supply of raw materials are busy establishing by force of arms a preferential area in Manchukuo and North China. This cannot be regarded as an ideal state of affairs. Yet a settlement with Japan is, I believe, not unobtainable.[79]

Chamberlain accepted this argument, and in May an interdepartmental committee met to consider the 'open door' in Africa and trade relations with Japan. Its report was produced on 7 June; it warned that it was vitally necessary to address the legitimate economic complaints of the 'have-not' powers and concluded in regard to Japan that, although it would be necessary to continue to restrict Japanese exports to Africa after the 'opening of the door', it would also be wise to try to reach a broad agreement. In forceful language it argued that Britain should agree to the abolition of colonial quotas on imports from Japan in return for Japan's voluntary agreement to restrict its exports, and supported this case by observing that

> On general political and strategic grounds it is hardly necessary to emphasise the importance of concluding even a limited agreement with Japan. The Far East constitutes the exposed flank of our strategic position. A friendly Japan is the best remedy for this weakness, and reacts at once on the strength of our position in Europe. After years of mistrust there are definite signs of Japan adopting more moderate policies in China and showing a desire for good relations with the United Kingdom. . . . For this reason alone we feel that any sacrifice which Lancashire might be called upon to make in the interests of an agreement . . . would be more than compensated by the larger advantages which we contemplate. . . . We should regard it as a serious blunder if we were to miss an opportunity of clearing away one of the points of constant friction between us and Japan by refusing a concession which for trade reasons we may ultimately be compelled to grant.[80]

This showed a far-sighted vision and demonstrated the extent to which views within Whitehall had evolved over the previous months, but when the report was considered at two meetings of the Cabinet Committee on Foreign Policy on 11 and 16 June the momentum behind these suggestions was dissipated. Both Ormsby-Gore, the Secretary of State for the Colonies, and Hoare, the Home Secretary, criticized the idea of making trade concessions to Japan, and, in addition, there were demands that the 'open door' proposal should only be made if other colonial powers reciprocated.[81]

This conservative backlash could only have a detrimental effect on the talks in Geneva. By this point Shudō was anxious about the lack of progress and on 22 June emphasized to Leith-Ross that it was urgently necessary for positive measures to be suggested by the Raw Materials Committee if Hirota was to stand up to pressure from the IJA for a more radical policy to solve Japan's problems.[82] Despite this plea no move was made by the British government to assist the Gaimushō, since the general consensus was that the best thing was to allow the Committee to wind down its activities and to conclude that there was no problem of access to raw materials. Indeed, the final report of the Committee, published on 7 September 1937, noted that the real difficulty was fundamentally one of payment rather than restricted access and that the 'have-not' powers were weakening their purchasing power by concentrating on rearmament.[83]

While Whitehall debated how best to approach the Japanese and the finishing touches were put to the Foreign Office's paper on policy towards East Asia, tensions in the region began to escalate once again. On 7 July, two days after the Far Eastern Department wrote the covering note to their memorandum, fighting broke out between Japanese and Chinese troops at Lukouchiao, west of Peking, and began to spread as both sides, for reasons of prestige, refused to compromise. Portents of such an outcome had been evident over the last few months. The Chinese had not responded to Satō's overtures with much enthusiasm, noting that there was no incentive to do so until evidence was received that the Japanese Army was willing to follow the Gaimushō's lead. In fact evidence from an SIS source in Nanking that talks were taking place between the KMT and CCP to forge a united front suggested that Nanking was preparing for resistance.[84] The caution of the Chinese was apparently justified when, in June, the Hayashi government was replaced by one led by Konoe Fumimaro and Hirota returned to the Gaimushō. By 7 June Knatchbull-Hugessen was reporting that the trend in Sino-Japanese relations should be considered negative rather than positive and that there was little hope of any early settlement.[85]

With the start of the Sino-Japanese war the first part of Ismay's prophecy of August 1935 on how Japan and Britain would eventually come to blows had come true, and the chance for improved Anglo-Japanese relations and co-operation in the development of China passed. Britain in the summer of 1937 had seen a greater consensus over the need to negotiate with Japan than at any time since 1933. There was a genuine hope in a number of quarters, including the Foreign Office, that a revival of British naval strength and concessions in trade policy, combined with a more enlightened Japanese policy towards China, could lead to mutually beneficial agreement. As far as Britain was concerned such a deal would ease the severity of the 'strategic nightmare' of Britain being threatened by three powers, Germany, Italy and Japan simultaneously, thus allowing Britain to focus on the containment or appeasement of the European dictators and allow for the expansion of its economic stake in China. Indeed, events in the first six months of 1937 hinted that Britain was on the verge of a new dawn in China as talks for HSBC financing of a series of railway projects progressed and the Chinese Finance Minister, H.H. Kung, on a visit to London in May reiterated China's desire for a government loan from Britain. There was even in Cabinet a discussion of the possibility of reopening negotiations with China about an end to extraterritoriality if Nanking should raise the issue.[86] The events of 7 July 1937 revealed all this to be a chimera, for war meant that all talk about the future of China had to be postponed indefinitely and that no one was willing to invest in the country. The greatest tragedy was, however, reserved for Craigie, the man who was to have negotiated a new understanding with Japan, for even before he had left Britain his task had changed, he was now to be the diplomat with the responsibility to make sure that tensions in China did not lead to an Anglo-Japanese war.

3 New circumstances, new problems
July 1937 to September 1938

From its very outset the Sino-Japanese war had a profoundly detrimental effect on Anglo-Japanese relations. To some extent this was only natural, as any fighting close to important centres of commercial and financial activity such as Shanghai and Hong Kong was bound to lead to British concern about the future of its interests. However, the mutual antipathy that developed during the conflict had broader roots than this alone; it was also the consequence of a British perception that Japan was responsible for the war, and of a Japanese perception that Britain, while posing as a neutral, was aiding Chinese resistance. Such hostility made obsolete any call for *rapprochement* on the lines being considered in London and Tokyo in June 1937, but this did not mean that the two countries were necessarily set on a path to war. Japan had its hands full trying to win the war in China while still keeping up its guard in Manchukuo against the Soviet Union; Britain had the European situation to consider and felt that its only feasible ally against Japan, the United States, was unreliable. The period from July 1937 to September 1938 could thus be categorized as a time of caution; neither side was willing to push matters to a point of no return, and there was even some desire amongst elements on both sides to reach some kind of *modus vivendi*.

To the British government, the start of the war in East Asia meant a breakdown in the loose consensus that had so recently been formed over policy towards the region. Increasingly there was to be acrimonious debate, with arguments taking place not only between the various departments within Whitehall, but also between London and its diplomatic representatives in the region, particularly the new Ambassador to Japan, Sir Robert Craigie. The crux of the matter was to work out how to perpetuate British interests in East Asia in a way that would not have dangerous repercussions elsewhere, either at home, in terms of public opinion, or in capitals such as Washington,

Berlin, Rome and Moscow. The next few years were to show that all these disparate interests could not be reconciled.

THE OUTBREAK OF WAR

On 12 July 1937 MI2c produced a memorandum on the possible consequences of the fighting that had broken out five days earlier at Lukouchiao. It noted that, while the government in Tokyo would try to settle the incident, there was a danger that local Japanese commanders might be difficult to restrain, in particular because of the recent bellicosity of the Chinese.[1] This was an astute judgement of the situation for, although neither Tokyo nor Nanking desired war, events on the ground soon began to spiral out of control as local commanders on both sides sought to reinforce their positions. The reaction within the Foreign Office to this haphazard drift towards war was to try to provide a brake and contain the incident in the realization that a full-scale Sino-Japanese war could only harm British interests. On 12 July Eden met Yoshida and warned him that any escalation of the fighting would affect the chances of an Anglo-Japanese settlement, and on 13 July he asked Sir Ronald Lindsay, the Ambassador to Washington, to enquire whether the State Department was willing to join Britain in a joint representation to Tokyo advising against the movement of Japanese troops into north China.[2]

These efforts did not, however, prove successful; the United States was determined to avoid joint action, while Chiang Kai-shek contributed to the growth of tensions by his Lushan Declaration of 17 July which stated that he was not prepared to sign any agreement which infringed the territorial integrity or sovereignty of China.[3] Eden was thus forced to watch impotently from the sidelines as the fighting began to spread. By 9 August the conflagration had reached Shanghai, threatening a repeat of the fighting between Japan and China that had taken place in the city in 1932. This necessitated a renewed attempt to separate the two sides, and on 16 August Knatchbull-Hugessen proposed that Japanese forces should be withdrawn from Shanghai and that the other powers in the International Settlement should take on the responsibility of protecting Japan's civilians and interests.[4]

Five days later Japan dismissed this idea out of hand on the grounds that the forces of the other powers were too small to perform such a task, although it was prestige as much as practicability that influenced this response. This was, however, to be a fateful decision, for on 23 August the Chinese Foreign Minister, Wang Chung-hui, told

Knatchbull-Hugessen that China was prepared to agree to this solution.[5] An impression was thus established that China was more sincere in its desire for peace than Japan, which began a process whereby the original muddled origins of the war were forgotten and instead the myth developed that the escalation of the fighting was completely Japan's responsibility. This was important because it had been difficult to state categorically who was at fault in the first month of the war, and indeed some had argued that China had been the more provocative in July; certainly in August it had not only begun the fighting in Shanghai but had also bombed the International Settlement, albeit accidentally.

The perception that Japan was to blame for the war in East Asia was reinforced by other Japanese acts, notably the news on 16 August that the IJN was preparing to initiate a partial blockade of the Chinese coast, and the attack on 24 August by Japanese naval aviators on a car containing Knatchbull-Hugessen.[6] This incident, which occurred while the Ambassador was travelling between Nanking and Shanghai, not surprisingly caused consternation in Whitehall and led to outraged demands for an apology. However, not everyone in London agreed with this response. On 30 August Captain Malcolm Kennedy, who worked on decrypts of Japanese material at GCCS and had been formerly the Reuters correspondent in Japan, observed in his diary, in response to Eden's formal protest to Tokyo, that

> not content with demanding redress, the Note proceeds to deliver a lecture on ethics – a sort of schoolmasterly admonition such as might be delivered to a naughty school-boy or to a small unimportant state which cd be over-awed by such means. But to deliver admonitions of this kind to country like Japan . . . seems to me to be the height of folly.[7]

Kennedy supported this rather surprising outburst by noting that one had to remember when judging Japanese actions that Knatchbull-Hugessen had undertaken a journey through a war zone without having had the sense to inform the Japanese authorities. Kennedy also noted in his diary his disapproval of what he considered to be the hysterically anti-Japanese tone of the editorials in *The Times*. Clearly, as far as one Japanophile was concerned, a dangerous emotionalism was beginning to pervade the Establishment in its attitude towards Japan.[8]

THE ARRIVAL OF SIR ROBERT CRAIGIE

Alarm over the British reaction to the attack on Knatchbull-Hugessen was also voiced by Sir Robert Craigie, who arrived in Tokyo to take up his post as Ambassador to Japan on 3 September 1937. Craigie, like Kennedy, was appalled at the rapid deterioration of relations with Japan, and he worked hard in his first fortnight to negotiate a mutually acceptable settlement to the Knatchbull-Hugessen incident. In so doing he revealed his determination to avoid the deepening of the gulf between Britain and Japan. It would, however, be a mistake to suggest that this was due to any Japanophile tendency on Craigie's part; it was rather a reflection of his belief that Britain had to neutralize its East Asian difficulties in order to allow for greater flexibility in its dealings with the dictators in Europe. Craigie also shared Kennedy's distress at the tone of the British newspapers, particularly as there was a perception in Japan that editorials in *The Times* represented the views of the British government, and on a number of occasions in the autumn of 1937 he advised the Foreign Office to try to curb the press's enthusiasm.[9]

Craigie's concern about the growth of Anglo-Japanese antagonism was also demonstrated in early October when he learned that the Archbishop of Canterbury had agreed to speak at an anti-Japanese meeting at the Royal Albert Hall. After a stormy interview with Vice-Minister for Foreign Affairs, Horinouchi Kensuke, in which the latter complained vehemently about the proposed gathering, Craigie urged the Foreign Office to persuade the Archbishop to cancel his appearance, stating that

> what now appears to be happening in England is . . . the reverse of salutary and may in the long run have serious consequences for ourselves. Judging from what one sees here in the Japanese press, opinion in France is passive, the Soviet press appears to be exercising a remarkable moderation, while United States opinion, though critical of Japan, appears from here to be far less vocal than in Great Britain and less inclined to advocate strong measures. Germany while fearful for her trade with China and Japan, is careful not to antagonize opinion here, while Italy loses no opportunity of encouraging Japan. Thus we bear the brunt of growing resentment untempered by any apprehension that words will be followed by deeds. There can I fear be little doubt that a continuance of this state will discourage moderate elements here, pushing this country further into German–Italian camp and tend to prolong hostilities in China.[10]

In other words the reaction in Britain to the Sino-Japanese cc
appeared to be encouraging the very situation which Craigie had
appointed to prevent.

However, the outpourings of the British press were not the only
factor poisoning Anglo-Japanese relations; developments on the diplomatic front, in particular the Chinese desire to involve the League of
Nations in the dispute by invoking article XVII of the Covenant, also
contributed to widening the gulf between London and Tokyo. From
the first the Foreign Office had realized that the League's involvement
would serve only to make peace even more remote, pushing Japan
closer to the Axis Powers and encouraging the possibility of an Anglo-
Japanese confrontation. At the same time, however, there was still a
belief in Britain that adherence to the League's principles strengthened them in the battle for world opinion. With this in mind, Eden,
with the support of the French Foreign Minister, Yvon Delbos, and the
League's Secretary-General, Joseph Avenol, was prepared to agree to
go as far as reviving the Advisory Committee which had been first set
up during the previous Shanghai crisis in 1932; one advantage was that
the United States was a member of the Committee and thus the burden
of any action against Japan would be shared. However, the Chinese
were determined to see more than talk, and on 17 September insisted
that the Committee agree to drastic measures against the Japanese
such as denying them access to credit and munitions and even
initiating economic sanctions.[11]

Craigie, who was all too aware of Japan's antipathy towards the
League, argued strongly that Britain should ignore Geneva and
instead make a unilateral offer of good offices to Japan. He was
encouraged in this by an interview with Hirota on 15 September,
when the latter assured him that Japan's peace terms would be very
reasonable. Two days later Craigie learnt from a reliable source that
these terms consisted of a neutral zone to the south of Peking and
Tientsin, an assurance of a friendly regime in north China, economic
concessions, and co-operation against communism, which was a
fairly moderate package. Even when further demands – the right to
station five thousand troops in north China, an autonomous Inner
Mongolia, the *de facto* recognition of Manchukuo, and the lowering
of Chinese import duties – were communicated through the same
channel a few days later, the terms still appeared reasonable considering the scale of the Japanese victory in north China. On 25
September Craigie therefore pressed the Foreign Office to act on
these proposals, noting that this was a real chance for peace.[12]
Chamberlain, now Prime Minister, was impressed with this analysis

of the situation, and on 27 September persuaded a reluctant Eden to forward the Japanese proposals to the Chinese. The result was that, on 29 September, Eden instructed the British Counsellor in Nanking, Robert Howe, to inform the Chinese authorities of the Japanese terms, which were promptly dismissed by Chiang Kai-shek as unacceptable. Craigie's policy thus met with a serious setback.[13]

EDEN AND ANGLO-AMERICAN CO-OPERATION

In arguing in favour of achieving peace through the Japanese formula Craigie was running in the face of opinion in the Foreign Office. The latter was increasingly inclined to see the conflict in China as a direct result of Japanese machinations, and consequently had little faith in the Gaimushō's initiative. In addition, there was a realization within the Foreign Office that for Britain to pursue a line in any way favourable to Japan would harm relations with the United States, not only in East Asia but also in Europe. A particular concern was that as recently as 1936 Henry Stimson, the former American Secretary of State, had published an account of his policy during the Manchurian Crisis of 1931–3, in which he had given the impression that he had been restrained from initiating economic sanctions by the timidity of the then British Foreign Secretary, Sir John Simon.[14] This raised the fear that a compromising line towards Japan in the present crisis could lead to a further outbreak of mudslinging. In contrast, a strong line towards Japan promised the possibility of improving relations with Washington; this prospect appealed to Eden, who hankered after close ties with America as a means of strengthening Britain in its struggle with the revisionists.[15] Eden was also encouraged by the strong sense of outrage at Japanese actions, and several Cabinet colleagues wrote to him urging the need for tough action; the most significant came from Lord Halifax, the Lord Privy Seal and Eden's successor as Foreign Secretary, who noted on 27 September

> I am terribly shocked with the Japanese indiscriminate bombing –
> Can we – with the USA – do anything more effective than protests
>   ? Trade
>   ? Withdrawal of Craigie
> It does seem to me to be the worst thing – for morality and
> civilization – that we have yet seen![16]

Eden's enthusiasm for Anglo-American co-operation was given a further boost on 5 October, when Roosevelt made a speech in which he proposed the need to 'quarantine' aggressor nations. The next day in Geneva the Advisory Committee published a report in which it argued that a conference of the signatories of the Nine Power Treaty should be convened in Brussels to hear the Chinese and Japanese cases, and recommended that in the interim League members do nothing to hinder the Chinese war effort. These events encouraged Eden to believe that a situation was being created in which there was a possibility that the United States and the League might be prepared to do more than just criticize Japanese policy, and consequently he ordered the Foreign Office to investigate the possibility of economic sanctions against Japan.[17]

In addition to pursuing what would prove to be the mirage of Anglo-American co-operation, Eden was also keen to support the Chinese because he believed that China was fighting Britain's war. The minutes he added to incoming telegrams during this period reveal an absolute conviction that aid must be found for the nationalist regime. For example, on hearing that there was a delay in the assembly in Hong Kong of Gloster Gladiators which Nanking had already paid for, Eden noted in desperation 'we handicap our friends too much'.[18] On another occasion he observed that there were many who believed 'that Japan was going to her "1812" in China' and that Britain's role was to 'do what we cautiously can to make it possible'.[19]

Eden's policy did not, however, have the complete backing of Chamberlain, who had grave doubts about the wisdom of the anti-Japanese line being pursued by the Foreign Office. As early as a Cabinet meeting on 6 October he had made clear his opposition to any policy of sanctions by stating

> He could not imagine anything more suicidal than to pick a quarrel with Japan at the present moment when the European situation had become so serious. If this country were to become involved in the Far East the temptation to the Dictator States to take action in Eastern Europe or Spain, might be irresistible.[20]

In this assessment Chamberlain had the support of the Chiefs of Staff, who also feared the implications of a war in the East. In a memorandum of 23 September Admiral Chatfield poured cold water on a proposal from the Cabinet Committee on British Shipping in the Far East that two battleships should be sent to Singapore, observing that to divide the Royal Navy between the Eastern and Western hemispheres was more likely to encourage the revisionist powers than to deter them.[21] This was followed on 4 October by a letter from the

Admiralty to the Foreign Office in response to Chinese calls for economic sanctions against Japan, which pointed out that, even if the League as a whole were to take action against Japan, this in essence meant Britain would be acting unilaterally as it was the League's only significant naval power.[22] The strength of opinion outside the Foreign Office to the idea of sanctions was further demonstrated on 13 October, when an interdepartmental meeting was convened to discuss how such a policy could be implemented and how Washington should be approached. Orde, who was chairing the meeting, soon found himself faced by a virtually solid wall of disapproval with the Treasury, Admiralty and War Office representatives all criticizing Foreign Office policy and demanding that the issue be taken before the Committee of Imperial Defence's Advisory Committee on Trade Questions in Time of War (the ATB Committee) where such proposals were supposed to be discussed.[23]

Despite this negative reaction Eden continued along the same lines; he was not willing to let the caution of others undermine his policy, and although he held out little hope for the Brussels Conference itself he still hoped that it would lead to closer relations with the United States. The conference finally began on 3 November with Eden leading the British delegation. At first it appeared that his optimism was going to pay off, as the chief American delegate, Norman Davis, hinted that a failure by Japan to accept the conference's recommendations could lead the United States to opt for sanctions. Eden, tantalized by this prospect, tried to draw Davis out by intimating that Britain would be agreeable to sanctions if Washington concurred. In doing so Eden was going beyond the policy that had been agreed in Cabinet, but in the end little harm was done as Davis too was considerably overstepping his brief and was ordered by Washington to retract his vague promises.[24] Eden, however, still hoped that some good could come of the conference, and was keen to obtain Cabinet approval for upholding the policy of non-recognition and banning credits to Japan.[25]

Unfortunately for Eden his espousal of an active policy had already been undermined in his absence. The initial reverse came in the ATB Committee's report of 5 November 1937, which concluded that sanctions against Japanese exports would take between one or two years to have any serious effect on Japan's war effort.[26] This setback was followed by a meeting of the Committee on British Shipping in the Far East on 9 November at which it was decided to reject Eden's scheme for the assembly in Hong Kong of military aircraft for China.[27] Therefore Eden was in a weak position when the Cabinet met on 17 November and he was unable to persuade his colleagues to agree to his policy.

The Cabinet's reluctance to support Eden was due not only to suspicions about the United States' reliability, but also to concern about the possible effect on Japan of British coercion. In particular, there was a fear that British involvement in the international pillory-ing of Japan might encourage the latter to reduce its diplomatic isolation by increasing its ties with the Axis Powers. That Japan was prepared to move in this direction was demonstrated on 6 November when Italy joined the Anti-Comintern Pact; a fact not made any the more pleasant by the knowledge, through the BJ source, that in so doing Japan had ignored Yoshida's warning that London would interpret this as an anti-British move.[28] The drift of Japan towards the Axis was worrying not only because of its contribution to global polarization, but also because it raised the possibility that Germany would offer to help mediate the Sino-Japanese war and thus increase its influence in East Asia. Aware of this threat, Craigie on 13 November urged Britain to offer its good offices, noting

> What I fear principally is the loss of our prestige throughout the Far East if conclusion of Pact with Italy were to be followed by a successful German mediation. Moreover some concrete action on our part is necessary if we are to stop the present drift here towards Germany and Italy. Even to China we shall be of little use as a friend if our influence here sinks to zero.[29]

Craigie's telegram found a receptive audience in Chamberlain, and influenced the latter's suggestion at the Cabinet meeting of 17 November that Britain and the United States should jointly try to mediate.[30]

Although this proposal, due to both American and Japanese reluc-tance failed to lead to progress, Chamberlain still remained optimistic that relations could eventually be improved with Japan. In a letter to his sister Hilda on 21 November he made clear his determination to curb the Foreign Office's desire for 'fist shaking at Japan' and noted that he was hopeful that peace talks would begin soon. Then at a meeting of the CID on 2 December he noted his approval of the policy of trying through Craigie 'to keep the door open for the future'; a view he repeated at a full meeting of the Cabinet on 8 December.[31]

THE *LADYBIRD* CRISIS

Any optimistic hopes that Chamberlain may have had were soon dashed by a new crisis in East Asia. On 12 December news arrived in London that two British gunboats, HMS *Ladybird* and HMS *Bee*, had been bombarded by Japanese artillery, and that an American gunboat, USS *Panay*, had been sunk by Japanese dive-bombers. Even though it seemed clear that the attacks were not sanctioned at a high level, these events had all the makings of a very serious crisis. In Tokyo Craigie promptly made an official protest to the Gaimushō, while similar action was taken by his American counterpart, Joseph Grew.[32] In London the Cabinet met on 15 December to discuss what further action should be taken, and agreed that Whitehall should investigate the practicality of sending part of the fleet to Singapore. A move in this direction was greatly encouraged on 16 December when Roosevelt, in a talk with Ronald Lindsay, the British Ambassador in Washington, responded to Eden's suggestion for a joint naval demonstration by suggesting that secret naval staff talks be held between an American naval officer and the Admiralty in London, and that the ground should be prepared for an Anglo-American naval blockade of Japan.[33] The Foreign Office recognized the latter to be a 'fantastic chimaera', as it involved a logistical nightmare, but believed that the President's attitude meant that he was at least ready for some form of joint action and that therefore he could be directed towards a more practical expression of opposition to Japan's policies.[34]

Suddenly it appeared that Eden's hopes that the East Asian crisis could lead to closer ties with America had become a reality, and the result was a flurry of activity in Whitehall to investigate how Britain could take advantage of this situation. One development was that the issue of sanctions against Japan was reopened, and on 28 December the head of the Industrial Intelligence Centre (IIC), Colonel Desmond Morton, received orders to put aside a memorandum he was preparing on the use of economic pressure against Germany and to concentrate instead on Japan.[35] Meanwhile the Foreign Office dwelt on what it hoped to achieve by sending a fleet to the East. A memorandum produced in the Far Eastern Department made it clear that there was no desire for war with Japan but rather the hope that a show of force would be useful in persuading the Japanese to agree to a reasonable settlement of the conflict in China. This paper then sketched an outline of what Britain should aim for in any such settlement, placing great emphasis on the re-establishment of the

'open door' and the upholding of the Nine Power Treaty, but reject-
ing the idea of a complete return to the *status quo ante bellum*.[36] This
was a fairly moderate line to take and it met with approval from
Cadogan who noted on 28 December

> we must recognise that her [Japan's] ambitions arise from her
> grievances and difficulties. That she has sought to remedy these
> in the wrong way should not blind us to their existence, and we
> should be wrong in thinking that a mere return to the status quo
> (if that were possible) would be a solution of the Far Eastern
> problem.[37]

He then observed that if Britain could devise a reasonable settlement
it might act as a useful example to the rest of the world and
particularly to the revisionist states in Europe. This was an interesting attitude to take, as it appears to suggest that, just as in the case of
the raw materials issue, there was an awareness in the Foreign Office
that blind adherence to the *status quo* would not solve any fundamental problems and that a fair peace was necessary to secure
harmony in the future. The idea was not to punish Japan, which
would require war, but to persuade it to make peace on reasonable
terms.

The desire to broker a settlement was not, however, just the result
of broad thinking about reform of the international system; it was also
a response to more specific pressures. First, Germany had now begun
efforts to mediate a peace settlement; second, and linked to this, after
the fall of Nanking on 12 December the Japanese had made their
terms much harsher. Third, as a result of naval signals picked up by
the FECB, there was reason to believe that Japan was preparing to
launch amphibious operations in south China, a move which would
threaten the security of Hong Kong and and allow Japanese encroachment into a region which, like Shanghai, was vital for British financial and trading interests.[38] Here were clear motives for acting in
unison with the United States.

However, the optimism engendered in London by the prospect of
Anglo-Saxon solidarity soon proved to be groundless. On 7 January
Cadogan, in response to reports from Shanghai that Japanese troops
had assaulted British policemen, sent a telegram to Lindsay asking
him to enquire whether the United States would now be prepared to
order naval preparations just short of mobilization. The lacklustre
American response was received on 10 January 1938, when Lindsay
was told by Sumner Welles, the Under-Secretary of State, that
Roosevelt would be prepared to dry-dock the Pacific Fleet to ready

it for action and bring its already scheduled manoeuvres at Hawaii forward to the second week in February, but only if Britain announced that it was making preparations for the Royal Navy to be sent to Singapore.[39] This came as something of a disappointment to the Foreign Office, as it showed that the United States was already lagging behind the British and thus underlined the need for caution. In this mood fears that the movement of the fleet would only lead to problems in Europe gained the upper hand, particularly as the absence of the navy might undermine Chamberlain's plan to achieve an understanding with Italy.[40] The British response was therefore to state that before proceeding with a naval demonstration the Foreign Office would attempt to gain an apology from the Gaimushō. With this the brief possibility of joint action began to slip away, a process not helped by the simultaneous rejection by Chamberlain of Roosevelt's plan for a 'world conference'.[41] A postscript to this sorry episode came in April when the State Department, in response to a Foreign Office enquiry about what would constitute acceptable peace terms, indicated that it did not feel that a Western naval presence in the region would convince the Japanese to make peace and that the best thing was to wait until the combatants had exhausted themselves.[42]

A RETURN TO DRIFT

The collapse of Anglo-American co-operation meant that the line Eden had pursued since September 1937 had come to nought, and that the Foreign Office now had to construct a new policy towards East Asia making a choice between rebuilding bridges to Japan or coming out in open support for China. This was not an easy decision to make, for as always adherence to either policy threatened unacceptable ramifications elsewhere; the basic problem was that Britain could not afford to arouse either Japanese or American antagonism, but that any decision relating to China was bound to upset one of the two. Policy formulation was not made any easier by the fact that the Foreign Office was still only one of a number of government ministries concerned with Japan, and that no consensus existed between these departments since they each interpreted events in East Asia through the prism of their own bureaucratic interests. In addition, the Foreign Office was faced with pressure from its own representatives in East Asia with the newly arrived Ambassador to China, Sir Archibald Clark Kerr, arguing for pro-Chinese measures while Craigie pushed for a moderate policy towards Japan.

The position taken by the Far Eastern Department was to favour Clark Kerr and the idea of providing China with greater assistance. The logic behind this was the belief that a Japanese victory in the war would mark the death-knell of British commercial interests in China and that, since Britain was not in a position to obstruct such a development by coercing Japan, the next best thing was to ensure that Chinese resistance to Japan continued. The idea of a return to the policy of improving relations with Japan was summarily dismissed, for as Sir John Pratt of the Far Eastern Department noted in a memorandum on 24 January

> There are many who still regret the passing of the Anglo-Japanese alliance: there are many more who, realising that it cannot be restored, yet desire that His Majesty's Government should cultivate close relations with Japan because she is the strongest power in the East. There is however only one ground on which alliances, ententes or a common policy can be based and that is community of interest. . . . Great Britain desires to see a prosperous and united China. To Japan this is as great a nightmare as a Europe united under one sovereignty would be to British statesmen.[43]

The desire for more open support of China was also driven by events in East Asia; in mid-January the Konoe government had withdrawn recognition of Chiang Kai-shek's government and ceased all peace efforts, and in February the League passed a resolution calling for members to assist China.[44]

This policy ran into vociferous opposition from Craigie. As far as Craigie was concerned the events of January 1938 had confirmed two crucial beliefs; first that Britain could not rely on American support in East Asia, and second that the likely outcome of the war was a Japanese victory. The corollary of this was that Britain should remain strictly neutral in the Sino-Japanese war, since a policy of backing China would only lead to tensions which Britain could ill afford in the light of the European situation and which would encourage Japan to move closer to the Axis Powers. Even in the smaller-scale context of defending Britain's interests in East Asia Craigie believed that his policy was correct, since he held that if Britain backed China, then Japan, on achieving its victory, would inevitably seek to eliminate them. Craigie's views were neatly summarized in a telegram of 9 February to the Foreign Office in which he wrote

> As I have more than once ventured to urge, British interests (strategic as well as economic) stand to suffer most from a

prolongation of this struggle. . . . My conclusions are that it would
be most unwise from our own point of view to take any step
calculated to encourage Chiang Kai-shek to prolong resistance
. . . and that we should watch carefully for any sign that nationalist Government might be prepared to make peace on terms which
leave China temporarily weakened, it is true, but capable of
ultimate resuscitation.[45]

However, the logic of Craigie's case was not accepted by the
Foreign Office. In seeking to understand why it is important to look
at the prejudices of the 'experts' within the Foreign Office. The
majority of the senior figures within the Far Eastern Department
were diplomats who had served in China and naturally had a greater
sympathy for that country than Japan, a bias underlined by the fact
that most had at various times been witness to Japanese high-
handedness. Of those with experience in Japan the doyen was
Sansom, who was now more convinced than ever that a collision
between British and Japanese interests was more or less inevitable,
and that *rapprochement* was impossible because there were too many
issues over which diametrically opposed opinions were held. Sansom
had a wide circle of admirers both in London and in the Tokyo
Embassy and his opinions were treated with the greatest respect.
The result therefore was that he and the 'China hands' were able to
form a consensus that Britain's East Asian policy should consist of
support for China and resistance to Japan.

Craigie's ability to alter this consensus within the Foreign Office
was minimal, his main drawback being that, never having been posted
to China or Japan, he had very limited experience in East Asian
diplomacy. In addition, however, he made a grave tactical error; on
finding Sansom unsympathetic to his idea of placating Japan, Craigie
increasingly relied for advice on the Military Attaché, Major-General
F.S.G. Piggott. Piggott had originally been assigned to Japan in 1904
as one of the first of the British Army's Language Officers, and had
already served one term of office as Military Attaché between 1922
and 1926 before being asked by the War Office in 1935 to return to
Tokyo.[46] He was renowned as a Japanophile of the most extreme
tendency who, unlike Sansom, refused to accept that Japan had
changed from the days of his youth. He was convinced that his
principal mission was to lay the basis for a *rapprochement* and
believed that many within the Japanese élite shared this aim. It was
therefore quite understandable that Craigie should have seen Piggott

as a very useful vehicle for bringing him into contact with Japanese 'moderates', and particularly those within the army.

There were, however, grave dangers in the Ambassador's reliance upon Piggott's advice. Piggott's crucial fault was that he was out of touch with current trends in the Japanese Army. This was ably demonstrated by a minute he wrote in 1938, in which he commented

> At present the only safe guide to the future development of the pro- and anti-British factions in the Army, is the undoubted fact, I repeat fact, that the heads of the army (Generals Sugiyama, Tada, Umezu, Homma . . . Hata, Ikeda etc.) wish to restore and strengthen friendship with Great Britain.[47]

The error in this judgement was to presume that the senior officers named above, who were all old acquaintances of Piggott from the period of the alliance, were representative of Army opinion. The reality was that power rested with younger men, such as Generals Tōjō, Itagaki, Ōshima, Ishiwara and Mutō, who had risen to prominence in the 1930s and demonstrated very little concern for Britain's welfare; these were men whom Piggott barely knew.[48] His second weakness was that he was all too desperate to be conciliatory towards the Japanese, thus giving a false impression to his contacts of Britain's desire for an understanding.

These faults were serious and were obvious to many of those who came into contact with Piggott; for example, Edmund Hall-Patch, the Financial Adviser to the Tokyo and Shanghai embassies, noted to Clark Kerr in 1938

> he [Piggott] is . . . looming too large as an interpreter of Japanese motives to the Ambassador, and as an exponent of our point of view to many Japanese who think his influence is greater than it really is. . . . I do not place great faith in him in either capacity. Not that he is actuated by base motives: far from it, but he genuinely believes that the Japanese are people of much the same stamp as ourselves. . . . In other times: in other circumstances his: 'get together boys' and his heartiness with the Japanese might be valuable. But not now.[49]

The Far Eastern Department also held the opinion that Craigie's judgements of Japan were heavily influenced by Piggott, with the result that the former's missives on the need for caution when dealing with Japan were not taken as seriously as they should have been because they were in the Foreign Office's eyes tainted with what was referred to as 'Piggottry'.

Outside the Foreign Office, however, Craigie's opinions were treated with greater sympathy. In particular, his warning that Britain should not risk tensions in East Asia at the same time as war threatened in Europe was well received in the Treasury. An example of the esteem in which he was held was demonstrated by Sir Warren Fisher, who noted in July 1938 that 'the official F.O. has always crabbed Craigie who is one of the very few in that branch of the Service who can think . . . detachedly'.[50] Craigie was also fortunate in that Chamberlain was by no means convinced that Britain could afford to base its East Asian policy on backing China; indeed in a meeting of Ministers on 14 February the Prime Minister had informed his colleagues that 'he would not like it to be thought for a moment that all chances of appeasement with Japan had slipped away'.[51]

THE CHINA LOAN ISSUE

In an effort to overcome the divisions in Whitehall, Eden decided in February 1938 to call an interdepartmental meeting to discuss how Britain should react to the League of Nation's call for assistance to China. The meeting on 11 February discussed a number of options, but the only firm decision made was that Britain ought to finance the building of a road linking China and Burma. On the issue of whether army surplus *matériel* should be sent to China it was decided that it was safest to continue to adhere to the policy approved by the Cabinet in November 1937 of providing neither side with arms.[52] Another scheme discussed at the meeting was the idea of a loan to China. This was by no means an original proposal, for as early as November 1937 Dr Quo, the Chinese Ambassador, had told Eden that China required a loan of £100 million to purchase munitions, and in January 1938 he had made a fresh foray requesting a £30 million loan for currency stabilization.[53] It was not, however, an issue that lent itself to easy decisions. On one hand Eden and Leith-Ross were keen to see a loan to China, not only because of the desire to support China but also to ensure that it could still service the interest on its foreign loans; on the other there was opposition within the Treasury from the likes of Sir Warren Fisher and the Second Secretary, Sir Frederick Phillips, and from the Governor of the Bank of England, Sir Montagu Norman, who were convinced that a loan would be inadvisable on both political and economic grounds.[54] By the time of the interdepartmental meeting it was clear that a government loan would not win approval, but there was still the possibility of encouraging a loan from a private source and it was therefore decided on 11

February to press the HSBC to provide China with money for currency stabilization.[55]

Although the HSBC was eventually persuaded to provide a £2 million silver loan in March it was soon clear that the desperate financial straits of the Chinese government necessitated aid on a far greater scale. On 11 March Dr Quo told Leith-Ross that China required a British government loan of £15 million and that this could be secured by linking it to Chinese exports of wolfram and antimony, two metals which were crucial to the manufacture of munitions. The initial reaction to this plan was favourable, many Ministers, including Chamberlain, Halifax, who had in February succeeded Eden as Foreign Secretary, and Sir John Simon, the Chancellor of the Exchequer, expressing an interest in a scheme that would, while supporting China, also deny Germany access to these vital commodities.[56] Events began to move in earnest in late April, when Chiang Kai-shek pressed the new British Ambassador to China, Sir Archibald Clark Kerr, to appeal for greater aid from Britain, and on 9 May Halifax wrote to Simon that

> We are embarking on an expenditure of two milliards of pounds in preparations for war. Here, for an infinitesimal fraction of that sum, we may be able, at no risk to ourselves, to preserve our vital interests in the Far East.[57]

However, the view that no risk was involved was not accepted by all parties, and was resisted most notably by Craigie and the Treasury. The former's response to the proposal of a loan was to deprecate its potential for escalating Anglo-Japanese tensions, as any such move would be of a blatantly political nature and would compromise Britain's neutrality in the China war. In addition, he felt that the loan would, in any case, be a waste of useful assets because China was doomed to defeat. On 10 May he noted that there could be an 'overwhelming outburst of fury against Great Britain' if the loan were made, and argued that the decision to agree to it had to be seen on more than an East Asian scale in that

> whereas in a World War the attitude of China would not be a determining factor, the reverse is true of Japan. Any breach in our relationship with Japan which is of such a character as to bring her irrevocably under German domination is bound sooner or later to act upon our defensive position in Europe.[58]

Craigie's fears had little impact on the Foreign Office or on Leith-Ross, the latter casually dismissing Craigie's arguments in a letter of

12 May by noting that as the Japanese themselves were desperate for credits from the London market they would not wish to establish a precedent by blocking the Chinese.[59] The Treasury, however, were deeply impressed by Craigie's warnings, and began to move away from their earlier enthusiasm for the loan project. In particular, there was agreement with Craigie that to induce Japanese anger could have very dangerous consequences, particularly in the light of tensions in Europe over the Sudeten issue. Therefore at a meeting of the Cabinet Foreign Policy Committee on 1 June, Craigie's 10 May telegram became the centrepiece of an argument between the Foreign Secretary and the Chancellor of the Exchequer; Halifax, on the advice of the Far Eastern Department, dismissed the Ambassador's contentions that China would lose the war and that Japan would be provoked to military action by the loan, while Simon reported that he and his advisers were in full agreement with Craigie. The meeting ended without any definite conclusion, although it appeared that the policy of caution was in the ascendant.[60]

Just as it appeared that the Foreign Office was on a losing wicket a new proposal arrived from Cyril Rogers, a Treasury official on loan to the Chinese Government, who suggested a reversion to Kung's idea of a £20 million currency loan. This idea, unsurprisingly, met with support from the Foreign Office and from Leith-Ross, who was still concerned at the possible ramifications for British banks should China default on its interest payments.[61] Within the Treasury opposition remained high, and on 18 June Fisher noted in typically hysterical tones to Chamberlain and Simon that

> As I see it the issue is a perfectly clear one – are we prepared to support China financially in her resistance to Japanese aggression? If so we must face the consequences & recognise that we shall earn the undying hostility of Japan who sooner or later – perhaps at a time when we are at death-grips with Germany – will take her revenge. Thus to risk our country's security, indeed survival, wd [sic] be nothing short of a crime, equalled only by the folly of it, as nothing that has been suggested in the way of financial assistance can be effective. . . . I sincerely trust that the govt [sic] will have nothing to do with this dangerous – & in the long run possibly suicidal – nonsense.[62]

The Treasury's distaste for the proposal was shared by the very financial institutions the Foreign Office hoped would lend the money. On 6 July Sir Charles Addis, the British representative to the China Consortium, noted his disapproval, and on 8 July his doubts were echoed by J. Fisher of the Bank of England who observed, in a letter to Sigismund Waley of the Treasury, that he did not believe that £20 million would be enough to shore up the *fapi* and that in any case a Japanese victory in East Asia might not be so catastrophic since while

> it would certainly mean that Chinese trade would be exploited so far as possible primarily for Japanese benefit . . . I don't think that that necessarily connotes complete ousting of British trade, unless – as may be necessary – it was found impossible . . . to recognise the new state of affairs. For it seems to me that Japan cannot hope adequately to finance the trade and development of China unaided.[63]

In addition, opposition continued to come from Craigie, for although his position this time was less rigid than before he still affirmed that a currency loan would be seen by Japan as an 'unfriendly act' unless it could be assured that the money given to China would not be used for military funding.[64]

The divide between the Treasury and the Foreign Office was therefore still considerable, and at an informal meeting on 28 June between Chamberlain, Halifax and Simon it was decided to put the issue before a full Cabinet meeting on 1 July.[65] The Treasury memorandum for this next meeting continued to reflect Craigie's arguments and again quoted heavily from his 10 May telegram. In contrast the Foreign Office, in an effort to refute the Ambassador's case, argued that Britain's global strategic position would in fact be weakened if a loan were not given, on the grounds that it was only China's resistance that kept Japan from pursuing 'her expansionist ambitions in the South Seas and throughout Asia'.[66] At the Cabinet meeting a final decision was postponed until the American Ambassador and Craigie were consulted. It was clear, however, that the Foreign Office was losing ground largely due to the growing international tensions, for as Chamberlain commented 'if we were to become embroiled in the Far East, Germany might seize the opportunity to do something in Czechoslovakia or Italy in Libya'.[67] The issue was next discussed at the Cabinet meeting on 13 July, by which time it had been established that no parallel American action could be expected and that Craigie still felt that caution was the best option; as a result Halifax acquiesced in a decision not to go forward with any loan.[68]

THE CRAIGIE–UGAKI TALKS

While the debate over the loan issue raged in London the situation in East Asia was becoming increasingly complex. One of the major problems that the Foreign Office faced was that the dislocation of British trade in the Yangtse valley and elsewhere caused by the initial outbreak of war had turned into a Japanese policy of persistent discrimination against British companies. This in turn led to the presentation of a series of protests to the Japanese government, but these had on the whole been ignored. The result was that by the summer of 1938 there was a feeling within the Far Eastern Department that the time had come to coerce the Japanese into respecting British interests through the use of economic countermeasures. This view was shared by Britain's Ambassadors in East Asia; on 23 June Clark Kerr insisted that the time for sanctions had come and on 29 June Craigie added his voice to the chorus.[69] There was, however, an important condition to Craigie's support for a tough line, and that was that such a policy should only be pursued after a period of six weeks had elapsed in which he would attempt to persuade the Japanese government to reconsider.

Craigie's cautious posture was due to his hope that Japan might be on the verge of a serious change in its attitude towards Britain and the war with China. Elements within the Japanese government had been hinting that they were favourable to an improvement of relations with Britain ever since February 1938, but it was only in late May, when Konoe changed his Cabinet to include Ikeda Seihin as Finance Minister and General Ugaki Kazushige as Foreign Minister, that this desire gained momentum. Ugaki, a former Army Minister, had in January 1938 opposed the decision to refuse to negotiate with Chiang Kai-shek, and had consistently argued for closer ties with Britain. Craigie, with prompting from Piggott, saw Ugaki's appointment as an asset and felt that it would make the Gaimushō more receptive to British claims for compensation arising from the war. In addition, he felt that it might even be possible to achieve a broader *modus operandi*, which he saw as increasingly necessary in the light of the Japanese decision to launch a local currency in north China.[70] There was also lurking beneath Craigie's proposal for talks about trade frictions in China the idea that there was still a 'moderate' element within the Japanese élite who desired closer relations with Britain.

The Foreign Office's attitude towards Craigie's suggestion of talks in Tokyo was positive in terms of its provision of a forum for discussion of the problems arising from Japan's discriminatory practices. It needs to be recognized in this context that the Foreign Office had since the start of the Sino-Japanese war not taken an entirely negative view towards co-operation with Japan, and that it was willing to make compromises over specific issues affecting British interests even in the face of American and Chinese objections. The most obvious example was the Customs Agreement signed with Japan in May 1938, under which it was agreed that the revenue raised under the auspices of the Chinese Maritime Customs in occupied China would be deposited in the Yokohama Specie Bank and be used to service China's foreign debts.[71] As far as talks over trade friction were concerned it would obviously be beneficial if they were successful, but there was also the realization that if the negotiations failed this could be used to support the introduction of a more coercive policy.

However, in terms of Craigie's broader motives for conversations, there was much greater doubt about their utility. On 13 July Lord Halifax made clear to the Cabinet his pessimism about the Ambassador's hopes, stating that he felt there was not likely to be any change in 'the long-range policy of Japan'.[72] On the same day the Foreign Office noted to Tokyo that in their view recent Japanese overtures did not display any noticeable change of heart. To Craigie such an opinion was typical of the unimaginative and conservative thinking prevalent in the Foreign Office, and he responded by expanding on his proposal for talks, observing

the prospect of a re-established friendship . . . would afford the best hope visible today of weaning Japan from her foolish policy of armed imperialism. Of the cynic who denies that any such hope exists, I would enquire whether the alternative of constant bickering and impotent condemnation is not likely to leave China for years in a state of unrest and economic distress. I maintain that such a hope in fact exists; that a test of its strength involves no risks; and that, given encouragement from our side, Japan's recent experiences in China may tend to hasten rather than to retard its fruition.[73]

Underlying this tirade was his frustration at the role he had hitherto been forced to pursue as Ambassador, which was little more than to act as a post office for complaints to the Japanese Government from British firms in China.

To the Foreign Office such views only heightened their suspicions of negotiation with Japan, but their ability to resist talks was undermined by the lack of support within Whitehall for their favoured policy of sanctions against Japan. An interdepartmental meeting on 12 July discussed the options open to Britain in the economic field, and not surprisingly the Foreign Office's proposals met with opposition from the Board of Trade and the Treasury. The argument used was that economic retaliation could not be introduced until the Anglo-Japanese Commercial Treaty of 1911 had been abrogated, and that a far wiser course of action was to warn Japan that abrogation could take place, rather than simply to go ahead and make a precipitous move which might only provoke Japanese retaliation.[74] In the face of this opposition the Foreign Office somewhat reluctantly agreed to the start of conversations in Tokyo.

The first official meeting in the Craigie–Ugaki talks took place on 26 July. It dealt with two main issues; the first was the need for Japan to deal more promptly with British grievances. In this context Craigie presented five specific demands for Ugaki to consider all relating to cases of trade discrimination in occupied China, the most important being the reopening of the Yangtse river for trade. Ugaki's reaction was to state that the reopening was not possible until Hankow had been captured, but that he would get the Gaimushō to investigate all five points.[75] The second major issue which Craigie raised was that of the future of the Sino-Japanese conflict, and in particular whether mediation was possible. Ugaki's response was singularly unpromising on the surface, in that he went into a lengthy criticism of Chiang Kai-shek's insincerity, but he did not totally rule out such an option.[76]

While Craigie and the Foreign Office were mulling over Ugaki's words and waiting for his response to the five demands, the situation was once again thrown into the air, this time by a Chinese suggestion on 4 August for Anglo-American mediation of the war.[77] Clearly this was a double-edged sword, for though it intimated that China was reaching the limits of its endurance there was also the possibility that the proposal had been made in the sure knowledge that such talks would fail and that the West would blame Japan for their collapse and thus be forced to side more openly with China. The perception that success was unlikely was very probably influenced by British awareness, through SIS sources in Shanghai and Hong Kong, that informal Sino-Japanese talks had been going on since the spring but had failed to make any significant process.[78] Craigie was also deeply uncertain about the Chinese initiative, and observed on 12 August that Japan would not want talks until after the fall of Hankow and that in any case the prospect of joint Anglo-American mediation would only bring to mind the analogy of the Triple Intervention of 1895, which had reversed the successes of Japan in the first Sino-Japanese war.[79]

The idea of mediation was therefore pushed aside, which meant that the success of the Craigie–Ugaki talks relied on the progress made over Britain's five demands. However, the meetings between

Craigie and Ugaki in August and September failed to achieve any real advance over the issue of discrimination. The failure was not just a result of the two parties having very different agendas, it was also a reflection of the domestic pressure on Ugaki to take a tough line and of the growing possibility of war in Europe. As the Sudeten problem escalated to the brink of war Japan stood transfixed, not wishing to make any commitment for the future until the course of events in Europe had become clearer. The last unsuccessful meeting between Craigie and Ugaki took place on 22 September; a week later Ugaki, in protest against the plan to establish a China Board which would take responsibility for China away from the Gaimushō, tendered his resignation.[80] Craigie saw the passing of Ugaki from the scene as a great tragedy, and wrote later in his memoirs that although he had found Ugaki a 'hard bargainer' he also felt that some progress was being made. In relating the story of the General's resignation he noted 'so ended the last determined attempt to curb the activities and policies of the Japanese military in China'.[81]

This portentous judgement certainly had some truth in it. On both sides there was in September 1938 a palpable lack of enthusiasm for negotiation. In the main this was due to the shadow of the Sudeten crisis but at least in Britain it also reflected observations drawn from a separate confrontation. In July and August a dispute between the Soviet Union and Japan over territorial control of the hill of Changkufeng on the Korean–Russian border had led to a brief clash of arms. Although this struggle took place in an obscure location there was a great interest in Whitehall in its outcome as this might say a lot about the relative worth of the Soviet and Japanese armed forces. The final assessment in military terms was that the conflict revealed that the IJA was superior to the Soviet Far Eastern Army, since a smaller IJA force was able to hold off a superior Russian one. However, in diplomatic terms it was clear that the crisis was a victory for Moscow because by making use of the fear in Japan that the incident might lead to a wider war it was able to achieve an armistice on favourable terms.[82] To the Foreign Office this was a very interesting development. On 23 August Nigel Ronald of the Far Eastern Department noted, after reading a decrypt of a telegram about Changkufeng by the French ambassador to Tokyo, that the lesson to be drawn was that the Japanese government was able to restrain the IJA and that it was afraid of being dragged into a war with a major power. This led Ronald to conclude that Britain had perhaps been too wary of Japan and if the Foreign Office took 'that "stronger line" so ardently advocated by British business men in China we should not in effect be running more than a very small risk indeed'.[83] Such an interpretation of events, added to the many other difficulties in Anglo-Japanese relations, meant that British policy was on the verge of becoming much more forthright in defence of its interests.

4 Growing tensions
October 1938 to August 1939

October 1938 witnessed the start of a substantial deterioration in Anglo-Japanese relations that was to continue until the outbreak of the European war in September 1939. In part this had its basis in Japan's attempt to widen the Sino-Japanese war both geographically through the extension of fighting to south China, and politically through the promulgation of the 'New Order in East Asia'. The escalation of the war raised concerns in Britain about the future of commerce in China, but in addition, due to the Japanese seizure of Canton and Hainan, there was for the first time a real threat to the security of British territories in South-East Asia. There were also other pressures working on Britain during this period; first, there were signs that the United States was beginning to stir itself and to realize that China needed its support, and second it was increasingly apparent that Western failure to provide assistance to Chiang Kai-shek could mean that China would be forced to rely exclusively on the Soviet Union.

These months also coincided with the immediate origins of the war in Europe, and this too had a corrosive effect on the Anglo-Japanese relationship. The burgeoning crisis between on the one side, Britain and France, and on the other, Italy and Germany meant that the polarization the Foreign Office had so long feared was coming to pass. This had implications for East Asia in that the Axis Powers were attempting to inveigle Japan into a defensive alliance, thus threatening Britain and France with a three-front war. This complicated British diplomacy inordinately, for it meant that there was marked disagreement in Whitehall about whether Japan could best be deterred from entering such an alliance by coercion or by appeasement. The situation was made more complex still by the uncertainty over the Soviet attitude towards the European crisis and whether Anglo-French association with Moscow in Europe would require similar co-operation in East Asia. Such a fluid and dangerous situation called for skilful and cautious diplomacy at both the macro and micro levels, for there was a grave danger that any clash with Japan over British interests in China would have dangerous repercussions both within the region and elsewhere; unfortunately the Foreign Office was to prove itself inadequate to this task.

BRITAIN AND THE 'NEW ORDER IN EAST ASIA'

In the wake of Munich, Robert Howe, as head of the Far Eastern Department, produced a review of East Asian policy in which he noted that British policy was producing the worst of all possible worlds; Britain was losing its influence over China due to its lack of positive assistance and was being alienated from Japan because of its continuing adherence to the Nine Power Treaty. He concluded that for the past year Britain had merely 'been sitting on the fence' and recommended that the government should take a firm decision over whether it was to support China or not. Howe's superiors agreed with his conclusions and on 14 October Halifax minuted that more must be done to aid China.[1] The urgent need for such help was made apparent that month with the news that both Hankow and Canton had fallen to the Japanese. As far as British interests were concerned the capture of Canton was a serious blow; it meant that Hong Kong now shared a common border with Japanese-occupied territory, that a threat existed to the continuation of British trade in south China, and that Japan had gained a jumping-off point for further expansion to the south. In addition, the loss of this area constituted a severe setback for Chinese morale and called into question how long the country could continue to resist.

The Foreign Office's concern over China's future was also fed by a new round of pleas for assistance from the Nationalist government. On 24 October Clark Kerr reported that T.V. Soong had proposed the establishment of a stabilization fund to prop up the *fapi* and that the Chinese were willing to put up £3 million if British banks would do the same.[2] On 6 November Chiang Kai-shek held a long talk with Clark Kerr and gave notice that Britain's stock in China was falling dangerously low; he was alarmed that even after the fall of Canton the British were not prepared to come out in open support of China. Chiang warned that without greater Western assistance only two paths remained open to him; to seek peace with the Japanese or to rely completely on the Soviet Union for support.[3]

The option of turning to Moscow was not a idle threat, for ever since the start of the Sino-Japanese war the Soviet Union had provided the Chinese with material assistance in terms of both munitions and advisers and in May 1938, with the withdrawal of the German military mission to China, had become the sole provider of such help. From the first the Foreign Office had been deeply wary of Soviet intervention, and in August 1937 had tried unsuccessfully to prevent the Chinese from signing a non-aggression pact with Russia due to the fear that Moscow would use the conflict for its own ends.[4] British suspicions grew as the scale of Soviet assistance became apparent and there was particular concern about the presence in China of Russian 'volunteer' pilots and aircraft; by April 1938, according to Air Ministry information, there were 300 such personnel.[5] In September the monthly Shanghai intelligence report gave voice to British fears noting

> It may be assumed that any Russian Military Mission, unlike the German, will have no altruistic motives in helping China. While Russia is willing enough to see China inflict damage on Japan and willing to give China limited help in doing so, her main object is to create a pro-Soviet bloc in KANSU and SHENSI whereby support can be given to the 8th Route Army.[6]

However, the Soviet threat went beyond the danger that north-west China would come under its control; there was also the prospect that if China achieved a victory based on Moscow's support it might lead the Nationalists to pursue an anti-Western line. This had the potential for undermining the West's commercial position in China for, as Nigel Ronald of the Far Eastern Department observed in September 1938, such a policy would result in a Chinese move to 'abolish extraterritorial and other privileges of every kind and impose numberless tiresome restrictions on legitimate international trade'.[7]

Chiang's plea for assistance and his playing of the 'Soviet card' was a powerful weapon, but it was not the only issue that pushed the Foreign Office towards a more openly pro-Chinese policy in the autumn of 1938. As important was that on 3 November the Japanese Prime Minister, Konoe Fumimaro, announced the establishment of a 'New Order in East Asia', a grouping of Japan, China and Manchukuo into one political, economic and cultural bloc, and this was followed on 18 November by a formal repudiation of the Nine Power Treaty. Konoe's statement also made it clear that the Chinese conflict could come to an end if Chiang were willing to accept co-operation with Japan and pursue an anti-Soviet and anti-Western regional policy.[8]

This move by Japan substantially raised the ante in East Asia as it constituted an open challenge to the Western position in China and to the practice of basing complaints to Japan on the premise that discrimination infringed the Nine Power Treaty. It demonstrated that a Japanese victory over China would not merely lead to a change in the bilateral relationship between Tokyo and the Nationalist government, but also that it would have dire implications for the preservation of the whole Western stake in China. This was not a matter that the Foreign Office took lightly and there was a decided move towards a toughening of policy which manifested itself not only in London but also in the British Embassy in Tokyo.

During October Craigie had held to his position of resisting aid to China or coercion of Japan, but in the wake of the 'New Order' statement his advice began to change in the realization that the new radical policy being pursued by Japan made his moderate line obsolete. Craigie's views were influenced by a number of talks he held with the new Japanese Foreign Minister, Arita Hachirō, in November and December on the meaning of and justification for the 'New Order'. On 16 November Arita told Craigie that the Japanese action was simply a response to the formation of other closed economic blocs, which included the British Empire.[9] Craigie refused to accept this argument and on 24 November presented Arita with a memorandum drawn up by Sansom which demonstrated that during the 1930s Japanese exports to the British Empire had actually increased. The document observed authoritatively

> This remarkable expansion could not have been achieved if the British Empire was a closed economic group. It was, on the contrary, achieved precisely because the economic policy of the British Empire as a whole was liberal and based upon the autonomy of its separate parts. Japan enjoyed and continues to enjoy the same free access to raw materials in the British Empire as is enjoyed by members of the Empire.[10]

Such an argument failed to impress Arita, who on 12 December responded by observing that quotas and preferences did exist within the British Empire, and that therefore it was ridiculous and hypocritical to pretend that it that it did not constitute an economic bloc. Moreover, he noted that in times of crisis the Empire had the capability of tightening its ranks and excluding foreign trade; a portent of things to come.[11] The talks thus came to an impasse and Japan ignored Britain's protests.

Further evidence of Japan's new assertiveness came through

GCCS's decryption of telegrams from Japanese ambassadors in Europe, which showed that talks had begun to turn the Anti-Comintern Pact into a military alliance. As long ago as March 1938 hints had been received from the BJ source that Ōshima and Ribbentrop had been discussing the extension of Axis-Japanese ties, but on 14 September GCCS decrypted a document showing that Germany had put formal proposals to Italy and Japan.[12] Through the autumn of 1938 Whitehall was able to follow the talks in Berlin, which revealed that Germany's aim was not just a pact aimed against the Soviet Union but one with a wider geographical scale; a move that clearly had the potential to restrict Britain's freedom of action by threatening her with a war in East Asia if conflict arose in Europe and vice versa.[13]

The bellicose nature of Japanese policy persuaded the Foreign Office that it was essential to provide financial assistance to China. The rationale behind this was summed up by Leith-Ross, who noted on 11 November that in the light of the alliance talks in Berlin it made sense on purely strategical grounds to give aid to China and 'thus keep the Japanese resources fully occupied'.[14] On 25 November a Foreign Office memorandum was produced for the Cabinet stressing that the currency stabilization plan was less likely to lead to a clash with Japan than the proposal put forward in July. However, this contention was challenged by the Treasury who once again produced their own memorandum refuting the Foreign Office's arguments. On 30 November the Cabinet met to discuss these two views and after an inconclusive discussion decided that nothing could be done until Craigie and the United States had been consulted.[15]

If the Treasury supported such action in the belief that these consultations would uphold their position they were soon proved to be wrong, for the sea change in attitudes in the British Embassy in Tokyo was matched by new thinking in Washington. This had first manifested itself in October when Grew had put pressure on the Gaimushō to reopen the Yangtse to commercial shipping and had gained momentum when in November the Japanese repudiated the Nine Power Treaty. The result was that on 1 December Sumner Welles asked Lindsay what Britain thought of economic reprisals against Japan. This was followed on 11 December by news that Roosevelt was considering a $20 million credit to China, a move that was formally announced on 21 December.[16] These actions confirmed not only that Britain should investigate the idea of a loan more fully but also that the question of sanctions had to be reconsidered. The latter was also an initiative which appealed to Craigie who on 4

December informed the Foreign Office that he had proposed to his American counterpart in Tokyo, Joseph Grew, that the three Western Powers should co-operate in giving a joint currency loan to China and announce the abrogation of their commercial treaties with Japan.[17] On 1 January 1939 the newly bellicose Craigie went as far as to propose that the Western Powers should unite in refusing to purchase any further gold from Japan and warned that

> it is no longer a question merely of protecting this or that vested or trade interest in China but of preventing, while there is yet time, the formation in East Asia of a valid and economic entity which may have serious repercussions on credit of every category of power.[18]

Within the corridors of Whitehall the idea of sanctions was even more controversial than the proposal for a loan, as both the Treasury and the Board of Trade strenuously objected to anything that threatened a repeat of the Abyssinian fiasco. However, the fact that the question was raised by an American initiative meant that it could not be dismissed for an entirely negative British response to Washington might be construed as a repeat of the Simon–Stimson incident. In addition, the position of the Foreign Office was bolstered by reports from Craigie and Sansom that the Japanese economy was in dire straits due to its negative balance of payments and the outflow of gold from the country to pay for vital raw materials.[19] The result of the debate within Whitehall over sanctions was that on 23 January, in an effort to put the onus of responsibility on the United States, a telegram was sent to Washington asking if Roosevelt would support a British move to denounce its Commercial Treaty with Japan.[20] The American reply came on 3 February when Welles told the British Counsellor in Washington, Victor Mallet, that the United States preferred to offer aid to China rather than to take direct action against Japan.[21] This did not come as a surprise to Whitehall, which had suspected that American hints of a desire to coerce Japan were largely bluster, but it did act as a further stimulus for increased assistance to China. Already at a Cabinet meeting on 18 January it had been agreed to give positive consideration to the loan proposal and after the arrival of the American advice it was finally agreed at a meeting between Chamberlain and Simon on 23 February that Britain would give £5 million to the stabilization fund, a decision made public on 8 March.[22]

JAPAN AND THE CRISIS IN EUROPE

While the decision to give assistance to China demonstrated a shift to a more active East Asian policy, there still remained the question of how Japan could be deterred from entering into an alliance with the Axis Powers. Evidence from the BJ source in January 1939 suggested that the talk of sanctions in the United States and Britain had had a salutary effect. In late December Ribbentrop had put forward a plan for a three-power military alliance to be directed against any fourth power; the previous draft having specified action against the Soviet Union. This met with Italian approval, but Japan was more cautious. On 26 January GCCS decrypted a telegram from Arita to Ōshima, who was now Ambassador to Germany, in which the former noted that Japan was concerned about the effect of such a pact on its relations with Britain and the United States and that

> It was essential that imports required in connexion with the Sino-Japanese War from these two countries must continue to be available, and it must be realized that the immediate conclusion of the Suggested Pact might conceivably lead to the loss by Japan of these highly important sources of supplies. In this respect, Japan's relations with England and America are necessarily different to those of Germany and Italy at the present time.[23]

On 29 January and 1 February two more decrypted telegrams, to Berlin and Rome respectively, revealed that Ministers in Tokyo had decided that Japan should put forward its own draft treaty and that this would be delivered by a special envoy who would arrive in Europe in the latter half of February.[24] This was naturally a welcome delay as far as the Foreign Office was concerned but there was no room for complacency; evidence from BJs demonstrated that Britain could not afford to take a collapse of the alliance talks for granted. The chief problem was that Ōshima and the Ambassador to Italy, Shiratori Toshio, were determined to pursue an alliance in line with Ribbentrop's draft, and that Ōshima in particular was using his pro-Axis contacts in the IJA to outflank Arita.[25]

The strength of feeling in favour of an alliance was also suspected to be a motive behind the moves that Japan made early in 1939 to establish itself in the South China Sea. On 10 February Japanese forces occupied Hainan Island and this was followed on 31 March by the announcement that the Spratly Islands were to be brought under the jurisdiction of Formosa. The fear in Whitehall was that Japan was being encouraged to expand in this area by Germany and

Italy with the aim of forcing Britain and France to divert scarce resources to East Asia. The obvious answer to this challenge was Anglo-French co-operation to force Japan to back down, but there were grave problems in trying to put such a policy into operation in that both powers lacked the means and the resolution to coerce Japan.[26]

The most significant difficulty for both countries in deterring Japan from adherence to the Axis Powers and from expansion in the South China Sea was their lack of military power in the region. This was a matter that the British diplomatic representatives in East Asia had attempted to address in late 1938 by proposing that naval reinforcements should be sent to Singapore to stem the advance of Japanese influence, a move which they saw as far more convincing than any number of British protests to Tokyo.[27] This proposal met with complete approval in the Foreign Office, who proceeded to put pressure on the Admiralty to commit a squadron to Singapore. However, this suggestion had the misfortune to coincide with a major change of strategy by Admiralty planners. The increasing threat of war in Europe had led to a reassessment of the assumption that, in the case of a crisis in East Asia, the main fleet would automatically be sent to Singapore without reference to the situation in Europe. Instead the Admiralty was developing the idea that if a conflict with the Axis Powers were already in progress in Europe it would be better to delay the sending of the fleet at least until Italy had been defeated and the Mediterranean secured. The Admiralty therefore had little time for Foreign Office plans for a squadron to be permanently stationed in the East, and the reply to the Foreign Office of 29 March recorded that the Royal Navy's commitments in the Mediterranean and the restricted number of capital ships available in 1939 made it impossible to station any battleships in the East until 1942.[28] The idea that one ship might be available in three years' time was hardly an adequate assurance of security and the Foreign Office therefore had to abandon this particular approach.

The other possible method of coercing Japan was to return once again to the idea of economic sanctions. Within the Foreign Office this was still the favoured policy, in part because recent BJs had revealed Japanese fears over such action. On 28 February Nigel Ronald observed that in the light of Japan's economic weakness a decision to cut off supplies of oil, iron, nickel and other vital raw materials could have the effect of bringing the Japanese war effort to a standstill and thus not only prevent any potential expedition against Singapore but also possibly end the war in China.[29] In addition he contended that the belief that such action would lead to an immediate Japanese outburst was mistaken as Japan was restricted by its inability to predict the reaction of the United States and the Soviet Union. This proposal led Halifax on 30 March to circulate a memorandum on this subject to his Cabinet colleagues. The document noted that sanctions would be useful as a warning to Japan of what could be expected if a European war should break out, and observed that

> Germany and Italy could by no stretch of the imagination supply Japan with raw materials . . . even if they did declare war and strike in the West. Indeed the Japanese must recognise that, as things are at present, it would not be an altogether mixed blessing for them if Great Britain became involved in a war with a Third Power for, if she did, many of Japan's vital sources of supply would be automatically imperilled.[30]

This argument did not persuade the Treasury or the Board of Trade, who remained convinced that nothing Britain did alone could ever persuade the Japanese to take a more conciliatory attitude. In the face of their opposition Halifax decided to withdraw the memorandum as it stood and to try to reach a consensus with the Board of Trade. However, their positions proved to be incompatible, and the Foreign Office was forced once again to retreat.[31] The difficulty in building a consensus behind sanctions directly hindered the development of co-operation with France. The French reaction to the Japanese seizure of the Spratly Islands was to introduce a ban on the export of mineral ores from Indo-China to Japan, and on 17 April the Counsellor at the French Embassy in London, Roger Cambon, suggested to Ronald that Britain should do the same for zinc and iron ore from Malaya. The Foreign Office responded to this overture by consulting other government departments and the State Department in Washington only to find that there was no support for introducing restrictions of any type against Japan, so on 2 June a negative reply was given to the French Ambassador.[32] However, there was progress in the field of defence co-operation. In March the Governor of Indo-China had proposed an exchange of information to Sir Shenton Thomas, the Governor of the Straits Settlements, and this led in late June to the holding of an Anglo-French defence conference in Singapore.[33]

British willingness to see greater co-operation with the French as a means of strengthening the Western position in East Asia was, however, limited, and Whitehall was prepared to go no further than preparatory talks in building up an anti-Japanese bloc in East Asia. There was a recognition that a more drastic change of policy could push Japan inexorably into the Axis camp, which also influenced the response in March 1939 to an initiative from Chiang Kai-shek suggesting Anglo-Chinese co-operation in case of a European war. The reaction of Sir George Mounsey, who was now overseeing the Far Eastern Department, was to warn that a pro-Chinese move of this nature would be disastrous as Japanese abstention from a general war was worth far more than Chinese assistance.[34]

This opinion was also a factor in the question of whether East Asia ought to be included in the agenda of the Anglo-French-Soviet talks in Moscow which had been inspired by the German seizure of the rump of Czechoslovakia and the threat to Poland. There were some in the Foreign Office, notably the head of the Northern Department, Lawrence Collier, who held that it would be to Britain's advantage to co-operate with the Soviets in East Asia on the grounds that no matter what Britain did Japan would join with the Axis Powers.[35] A more cautious faction believed that Japan's mind was not decided, that any hint of alignment with Moscow against Japan would have the effect of pushing Tokyo into the German camp, and that in any case the Soviets would be worthless allies as Changkufeng had shown that the Red Army could not be relied upon to defeat the Japanese.[36]

These doubts were encouraged by reports from Craigie, who was witnessing in Tokyo a titanic struggle within the Japanese government over the alliance issue. In May, with talks already under way in Moscow, Craigie reported that the moderates were holding their ground and that the only thing that could now undermine their position was Anglo-Soviet co-operation in the East.[37] In London there was broad agreement with Craigie's view, and this was further encouraged by talks held between R.A. Butler, the Parliamentary Under-Secretary at the Foreign Office, and Shigemitsu Mamoru, who had replaced Yoshida as Ambassador in late October 1938. Shigemitsu had previously been Ambassador in Moscow and had come away with a deep mistrust of the Soviets; he was also, as the Foreign Office had discovered from BJs, an opponent of closer relations between Japan and Germany, and in his conversations with Butler he made it abundantly clear that Anglo-Soviet co-operation in East Asia would force Tokyo into Berlin's arms.[38] The result of this pressure was that the talks in Moscow remained focused on Europe. This circumspection may also be linked to another important consideration that arose in spring 1939 and that was the gradual loss of the ability to read the Japanese diplomatic code. In late February the new 97-Shiki O-bun Injiki cypher machine was introduced on the Berlin-, Rome- and London-to-Tokyo circuits, and while some messages were still sent in the old code the overall effect was to render Britain, for the first time in five years, blind to Japan's diplomatic manoeuvrings.[39]

TENSIONS AT TIENTSIN

In the background, as these momentous issues were grappled with, what started as a routine dispute in north China began slowly to impinge upon the already stony path of Anglo-Japanese relations. The crisis concerned the position of the British and French Concessions at Tientsin, which stood as two small enclaves of Western rule in north China. Their existence posed two problems for the Japanese, who otherwise had almost complete political and military control of the region: first, the Concessions were used by Chinese nationalists as a safe haven from which to launch terrorist attacks against the Japanese; second, and perhaps more important, they acted as an economic challenge to the Chinese puppet government at Peking due to their continued use of the official Chinese currency, the *fapi*, which weakened the Peking government's attempt to dominate the economy of north China. Added to this was the presence in the British Concession of a substantial amount of silver belonging to the Kuomintang government, which the Japanese wished to see transferred to the reserves of the puppet government to strengthen its financial position.

Tensions in Tientsin first manifested themselves in October 1938 when the Japanese government protested to Craigie about the refusal of the British authorities at Tientsin to hand to them Ssu Ching-wu, a man who they alleged was the head of a 25,000-strong band of Nationalist guerrillas. This complaint sparked off a debate in British circles, for it raised a difficult legal argument. Craigie and Edgar Jamieson, the British Consul-General at Tientsin, held that if Ssu was guilty he should be handed over and that the best policy for Britain was to remain strictly neutral. Clark Kerr and the Far Eastern Department saw matters differently; they believed that Japanese pressure on Tientsin was part of a broader policy in line with the 'New Order' statement and designed to push British interests out of China altogether, and that therefore Britain ought to stand firm.[40] This impasse meant that no decision was taken over Ssu and policy was left to drift, with the result that on 14 December the Japanese, in an attempt to capture Chinese illegally entering and leaving, barricaded every road leading into the British and French Concessions and turned away residents who failed to produce identity cards or passports. In addition, an export ban introduced in the summer for animal skins was extended to include wool, a vital commodity for British business.[41] This state of affairs continued until 8 February when the newly arrived commander of the IJA forces at Tientsin, the Anglophile General Homma, ordered the barriers to be raised and the searching of Concession residents stopped.

This proved to be only a lull in the storm. On 10 March the Chinese puppet government at Peking declared the *fapi* to be an illegal currency and once again extended export restrictions so that they now covered 70 per cent of Britain's trade.[42] A week later tensions were raised even further when the Chairman of the British Chamber of Commerce at Tientsin, a Mr H. Dyott, was kidnapped by Chinese bandits in the pay of the Japanese. At this stage Jamieson lost all patience and noted in a letter to Homma on 25 March that the IJA had attempted to obstruct efforts to mount search parties and warned that if Dyott was not recovered 'the effect on reputation not only of yourself but of the Japanese army as a whole will be most deplorable'.[43] Whether Jamieson realized how insulting this phrasing was to a Japanese officer, let alone to the Japanese nation, is not made clear from the documents, but the note certainly caused a volcanic uproar in both Tientsin and Tokyo. Craigie, in particular, took fright at the possible implications of the confrontation and with the Foreign Office's reluctant approval sent Piggott to the city to calm the situation, a repeat of a mission that the Military Attaché had undertaken to Shanghai in June 1938. Piggott, who was close to Homma, was able in his short stay in April 1939 to persuade both sides to have greater respect for the other's point of view.[44]

On 9 April, the day that Piggott left Tientsin, the new atmosphere of co-operation received its first challenge, for the newly appointed pro-Japanese Inspector of Customs in Tientsin, Dr. Cheng Hsi-keng, was murdered while watching the film *Gunga Din* at the Grand Theatre in the British Concession. Within a few days four Chinese suspects were captured in a joint Anglo-Japanese raid in the British Concession; they were then handed over to the Japanese for interrogation and confessed to the crime. However, once back in the Concession the men retracted their statements, which they claimed had been extracted under torture. This left Jamieson in a dilemma, for while the Japanese demanded that the men be tried by the local Chinese court and punished the only evidence against them was deeply suspect. In his search for advice Jamieson turned to Clark Kerr and the Foreign Office and thus began an acrimonious debate that was to last for almost two months.[45]

Jamieson's opinion, influenced by Piggott's visit, was that the men should be handed over whether guilty of this specific crime or not as they were members of a terrorist gang and their presence therefore prejudiced the neutrality of the concession. His opinion was also influenced by his recognition that Japanese patience with the British over Tientsin had worn thin and that to take too legalistic a stance might lead to a dangerous escalation of tensions.[46] In this he was opposed by both Clark Kerr and the Foreign Office, who were determined to act strictly within the bounds of legal propriety; for as long as there was no irrefutable evidence linking the men to the crime there was no reason to hand them over. For Clark Kerr the need to adhere to principles was underlined by his faith in Chiang Kai-shek's cause. In the Foreign Office's motivation there was as well as sympathy for China a view that Britain would win no concessions from the Japanese by compromising.[47]

The result of the prolonged and inconclusive debate about how to proceed over the four men was that British policy continued to drift, with Homma being neither appeased nor convinced that Britain was in a position to resist. The situation was not helped by the fact that Jamieson's and Clark Kerr's individual handling of the crisis left much to be desired. Jamieson was a weak character who overreacted at times of crisis and seemed incapable of negotiating his way out of a corner. He was also guilty of failing to provide Clark Kerr and the Foreign Office with detailed, accurate information, including the fact that the men had confessed their crime to Jamieson's deputy, Major Guy Herbert, news that when eventually released led one official in London to note that had they been in possession of such material they might well have acted differently.[48] In addition, Jamieson delayed the implementation of instructions which did not accord with his own views; a fault that could also be applied to Clark Kerr, who prevaricated throughout the crisis.

The behaviour of the diplomats in China was matched in incompetence by the Far Eastern Department, who displayed the most blatant complacency in the face of numerous reports of Japanese bellicosity, not only from Jamieson but also from Craigie and Lieutenant-General Grasett, the General Officer Commanding at Hong Kong.[49] This failure to register the seriousness of the crisis was a result of their long-ingrained belief that Japan was not as formidable as it appeared and that Britain merely had to make clear its willingness to resist in order to force the Japanese to back down. This was a dangerous presumption on which to base a policy when the Admiralty had made clear in the winter their opposition to a 'main fleet to

Singapore' policy and when the Treasury and Board of Trade had still not agreed to economic retaliation against Japan. Another problem was that the Department dealt with the developing crisis without drawing the situation to the attention of the higher echelons of the Foreign Office. During most of May and June the senior official involved was Mounsey; it was only on 7 June that the issue was brought before the Cabinet and even then Halifax, on the advice of the Department, tended to play down the dangers.[50] On 20 June Cadogan, now Permanent Under-Secretary, noted in his diary

> As regards Tientsin, we have bungled the thing sadly. F.E. Department and Mounsey have been working their little groove and *never* referred a paper to me. That puts me in the awkward position that I can't explain or shift the blame. I saw copies of the telegrams . . . and did not ask what it was about. I ought to have.[51]

The failure to consult also applied to relations with other Ministries and was particularly important in relation to the War Office, which was directly responsible for the defence of the Concession. At no point did the Foreign Office ask the Army how they planned to respond to military action by Japan at Tientsin.[52]

The result of the Foreign Office's laxity was that on 14 June Homma, faced with a lack of compromise over any of the issues raised, reintroduced the barrier system, stopped food passing into the Concessions and ordered his troops to search all Concession residents, both men and women, who passed through the barriers.[53] This great insult to British prestige, allied to the ever tighter commercial blockade of the Concession, forced the British government to consider how to react to the high-handed policy of the Japanese Army; whether to retaliate through economic or military measures or to seek conciliation.

TO THE BRINK OF WAR

The Foreign Office's mishandling of relations with Japan could hardly have come at a worse moment, as by June 1939 Europe was growing increasingly tense. Britain not only faced a possible conflict over Danzig but also had to contend with Germany and Italy coming together in the Pact of Steel and a renewed Italian threat to Mediterranean security.[54] The reprehensibly casual attitude of the Far Eastern Department had thus brought Britain to the brink of a catastrophe. The questions facing Whitehall once the Japanese blockade had been established were first how to persuade Japan to back down, and second how to deal with the specific issues arising from the Concession's existence. Once more Britain's paltry armoury had to be inspected to ascertain whether coercion was possible either by sea-power or by economic means, and furious activity began in London to prepare memoranda for the Cabinet.

Meanwhile from Tokyo a voice of seething righteousness rang out. On 18 June Craigie sent a long and damning critique of Foreign Office policy directed not merely at events in Tientsin but also at the line taken by London since the very start of the Sino-Japanese war; he noted caustically

> Relations with this country have now become so strained and the feeling against us has been aroused to such a pitch that unless some fundamental change in policy – or at least in tactics – can be envisaged there is a serious danger of two countries drifting into a long conflict.
>
> Tientsin is but symptomatic. The major cause of our trouble is of course a vast clash of interests in China, especially acute during the present hostilities, but bound to continue with varying intensity for many years, but such clashes of interest between powerful states in relation to the fate of a weaker state are nothing new in history and have by no means always led to war: nor need the present clash lead to war if the Japanese policy can be rendered less intransigent and British policy be pursued with more regard for realities.
>
> There has been an open partisanship about our policy which in the circumstances of today does more credit to our heart than to our head. No doubt if we were in Sir A. Clark Kerr's place I should be tempted to adopt the same vigorous championship of a valiant cause. But from this post I feel bound to emphasise deadly dangers to which we are heading if we cannot get back to a position of stricter neutrality such as the Americans have been clever enough to maintain.[55]

He concluded that, as a means of settling the present crisis, talks should be opened in Tokyo to examine the whole range of problems thrown up by the Tientsin crisis.

This was, of course, in marked contrast to the views Craigie had expressed in the winter of 1938/9. The change was influenced by his beliefs that once again the Americans had retreated into their shell, that Britain lacked the means by itself to coerce the Japanese, and that the failure of Japan to tie itself to what became the Pact of Steel demonstrated that the 'moderates' were still a powerful element in

Japanese politics.[56] He therefore felt it foolish for Britain to pick a quarrel with Japan as this would play straight into the hands of the hardliners. However, Craigie did not turn his back completely on coercion – he saw that the threat of reprisals could be useful in making the Japanese see sense – but made it clear that talks should be the first priority.[57]

In the bellicose atmosphere within the Far Eastern Department it was the call for retaliation that appealed rather than the proposal for negotiations, but due to the gravity of the crisis the Foreign Office was no longer responsible for policy-making, which was now in the hands of the Cabinet. The crucial meeting in deciding a response to the crisis was a gathering of the Cabinet Foreign Policy Committee on 19 June. Memoranda produced for the meeting differed in their approach. A paper from the Foreign Office argued strongly for economic sanctions, preferably in parallel with the United States, on the grounds that to compromise would undermine China, antagonize the United States and encourage Japan to undermine the British Empire in the East. Another memorandum, jointly presented by the Foreign Office and the Board of Trade, considered the prospects of economic retaliation in more detail and, showing the influence of the latter ministry, argued that the most effective measure Britain could take was to restrict Japanese exports, thus striking not only at Japanese industry but also at Japan's poor foreign exchange reserves. It concluded, however, on the cautious note that Britain could not rely on American support, which might not be forthcoming. The report from the Chiefs of Staff on the strategic situation went a stage further, stating that to initiate the 'main fleet to Singapore' policy at this juncture would endanger Britain's position in Europe 'to an extent which, from a military point of view, would be quite unjustifiable'. In view of the British guarantees to Romania and Greece and the pact with Turkey, the Royal Navy was in a position where very few capital ships could be spared, and it was calculated that only two could be sent to Singapore. This reiterated the conclusion that action could only be taken if Britain had the active support of the United States.[58]

The decision facing the Committee was therefore a complicated one, made more complex by a lack of information about the American attitude towards the crisis. From the start it was apparent that Chamberlain was not impressed with the Foreign Office's policy of introducing sanctions and preferred the proposal for talks from Craigie, which at least appeared to offer a way out of the crisis.[59] Halifax and Cadogan were, however, able to restrain the Prime

Minister from ordering talks to begin immediately by stating that it was necessary first to hear from the United States and to consult more with Craigie, but this only put matters in abeyance as pressure from other members of the Cabinet for a diplomatic solution continued to grow. On 19 June Chamberlain received a letter from Lord Runciman, the Lord President of the Council, which urged him to take the line recommended by Craigie and warned that

> If ultimately we are to be effective in our use of the Fleet it will be wiser of us to look after the European position first of all, and when we are secure in this theatre we can later on deal with the Japanese Navy. That I submit is the correct order . . . to go to war with our present divided forces without the active cooperation of the U.S.A. would in my judgement be disastrous, and I could not accept any responsibility for this course.[60]

The need for caution was further confirmed by a meeting the following day between Chamberlain and Admiral Chatfield, the Minister for the Co-ordination of Defence, in which the latter made clear his agreement with the Chiefs of Staff that Britain could not afford to contemplate a war in the East which might lead Hitler and Mussolini to take advantage of British preoccupation with Japan.[61]

On 20 June a second meeting of the Foreign Policy Committee was convened at which Chatfield expanded on Britain's naval dilemma and stated that the Chiefs of Staff had indicated that, if necessary, the Royal Navy could send seven battleships to Singapore by late August, but that they could not recommend this course of action due to the dangers elsewhere. The Prime Minister's response was to conclude that the unfavourable naval position made it imperative to try to reach an early settlement of the dispute at Tientsin by diplomatic means, a conclusion that was reinforced by the lack of any sign of support for Britain from the United States.[62] The Foreign Office line was thus defeated by the practical objection that Britain simply could not afford to run the risk of war through a policy of economic retaliation. This was not a policy of any real choice, but one of necessity. The stage was set for Craigie to try to achieve some kind of settlement in Tokyo.

Even before approval was received from London, Craigie had on 18 June sounded out Arita, stressing how important it was for talks to be held in Tokyo rather than in the heated atmosphere of Tientsin, and had met with a favourable response.[63] Over the next week the situation remained fluid due to the Japanese Army's dislike of negotiations and its insistence that all problems should be settled in

Tientsin. However, through the use of an intermediary between Craigie and Prime Minister Hiranuma the army was circumvented, and on 28 June a communiqué appeared stating that talks were to be held about Tientsin; with that there was a slight easing of tensions in the city and a drop in the number of body-searches of British subjects.[64] To some in London the mere fact that Craigie had managed to get this far was success enough, and Chamberlain noted hopefully in a letter of 2 July to his sister Hilda that the crisis showed 'some prospects of relief now that Craigie has very skilfully managed to get the venue removed to Tokyo'.[65]

Despite Craigie's success in relaxing tensions and arranging for talks to begin, this approach found little favour in the Foreign Office, who continued to push for retaliatory measures against Japan and raged against the timidity of the Services and the Board of Trade. On 22 June a meeting of the ATB's Economic Pressure Sub-Committee was held at which it was decided that a new report on the options open to Britain should be produced, and that each department would send its thoughts on the subject to the secretariat of the CID.[66] The ATB report was completed on 20 July and much to the chagrin of the Foreign Office still reflected the innate caution of the Board of Trade, in particular in its emphasis on the inadvisability of unilateral action.[67] However, the report did indicate that there were a few areas where real economic damage could be inflicted; of these the most interesting and relevant for the future was the harm that the British Empire could do to Japan if sales of raw materials were restricted. Information from the IIC showed that 50 per cent of Japan's iron ore came from Malaya, that the jute necessary for producing rice-bags came almost solely from India, and that Japan also relied on Malaya and India for manganese. In addition, Colonel Morton of IIC noted that he had received a report from Professor Hall of the National Institute of Economic Research which demonstrated that Japan would find it very difficult to find alternative sources of supply for these raw materials.[68]

While the ATB report was being put together the Foreign Office also attempted to escalate the momentum towards sanctions by pressing the Board of Trade to draw up draft legislation that would legitimize restrictive measures by Britain against a country that broke a treaty to which it and the British government were party. Once again this was a proposal that led to conflict between the Foreign Office and the Board of Trade, but on this occasion Halifax was able to defeat the ever-cautious bureaucrats in the latter by appealing directly to the President of the Board of Trade, Oliver Stanley.[69]

By late July the legislation was ready to be set in motion if the talks in Tokyo collapsed before Parliament went into recess on 2 August.

To a large degree the Foreign Office's enthusiasm for sanctions was predicated on the belief that Japan still had no intention of going to war with Britain and that it was bluffing in an attempt to force a compromise, a view that was strongly influenced by the presence in London of Sir George Sansom, who had just returned from Tokyo. This was not an opinion shared by Craigie, who continued to warn that the situation still had the potential to spiral out of control and that it would take little for Britain and Japan to 'drift into a state of things scarcely distinguishable from open hostilities'.[70] The Far Eastern Department felt this view to be needlessly alarmist and blamed Craigie's apparent hysteria on the malign influence of Piggott. However, to many in the Cabinet it was Craigie's attitude that appeared to be more judicious and this acted as an obstacle to the Foreign Office's efforts to construct a tougher line. Chamberlain, in particular, backed Craigie and noted to his sister Hilda on 15 July

> Thanks to the ineptitude of our Foreign Office we have been manoeuvred into a false position where we are single-handed and yet are being attacked over a policy as essential for America, France and Germany as ourselves. . . . The only thing that gives me any confidence is Craigie's attitude. He always seems to preserve his calm and never seems to get rattled. . . . But the anti-Japanese bias of the FO in the past has never given him a chance. If he gets us through this mess I shall insist on his having an honour to mark our gratitude.[71]

THE TIENTSIN NEGOTIATIONS

On 15 July the talks between Craigie and Arita finally opened in Tokyo. The latter began by presenting the Japanese agenda for the negotiations, which consisted of a general settlement of Anglo-Japanese relations in China, the legal problems arising from Tientsin, and the economic problems. In furtherance of the first item Arita presented Craigie with a formula for Britain to accept, which read

> The British Government fully recognise the actual situation in China, where hostilities on a large scale are in progress and note that, as long as that state of affairs continues to exist, the Japanese forces in China have special requirements for the purpose of safeguarding their own security and maintaining public order in

the regions under their control, and they have to take the necessary steps in order to suppress or remove any such acts or causes as will obstruct them or benefit their enemy. The British Government, therefore, will refrain from all acts and measures which will interfere with the Japanese forces in attaining their above mentioned objects.[72]

This wording was quite unacceptable to Craigie because it would have forced Britain to become in effect a benevolent neutral and because it did not just apply to the Tientsin area but to the whole of occupied China. However, he realized that for Britain simply to reject the idea of a formula would be extremely dangerous as it would very likely precipitate the end of the talks, and therefore proposed to London that the best policy was to dilute the Japanese wording to make it innocuous.[73]

Clark Kerr objected strongly to this line, but in spite of the Foreign Office antipathy towards any such agreement it was recognized that the talks could not be allowed to collapse; work was therefore started on an alternative formula which accepted the Japanese line as far as possible while at the same time reserving Britain's legitimate rights in the region.[74] On 19 July Craigie duly presented this document to Arita, and after two further days of discussion a mutually acceptable document emerged. The final text, which was officially signed on 24 July and became known as the Arita–Craigie Agreement, was a subtly worded and vague work which was, in the tradition of agreements with Japan, open to various interpretations. It differed from the original Japanese formula only in the last sentence where it stated

His Majesty's Government have no intention of countenancing any act or measures prejudicial to attainment of the above mentioned objects by Japanese forces and that they will take this opportunity to confirm their policy in this respect by making it plain to British authorities and British nationals in China that they should refrain from acts and measures.[75]

The crucial change of emphasis was that the onus of the agreement now rested on the British Concessions in China and committed them to uphold a policy of neutrality without restricting the British Government itself from assisting the Chinese.

The reaction in China and the United States to the publication of the Agreement suggested that these subtleties were lost on the wider audience; the general opinion was that this was an example of 'perfidious Albion' at its worst. In the British press too there was displeasure at the apparent appeasement of Japan. In Whitehall, however, news of the Agreement was generally met with great relief and with admiration for Craigie's negotiating skills; Chamberlain, for example, noted to his sister Ida his admiration of Craigie's 'great skill' and observed that 'if only a little restraint can be exercised on our side the inflammation should gradually subside'.[76] In a Cabinet meeting of 26 July Halifax defended the formula by noting that its most important achievement had been to lessen tensions and to gain time; he described the British policy as being one of holding on and doing anything necessary 'to extricate ourselves from a difficult position'.[77]

Craigie too was pleased with his achievement, which served to convince him that the talks could lead to a real improvement of relations with Japan. With such hopes he reversed the support he had previously shown for the introduction of legislation to legitimize economic restrictions and reacted angrily to news from London that the Export Credit Guarantees Department was on the point of giving a £3 million loan to China. In both cases his objections had the necessary effect as, with the European situation still so uncertain, there was no wish to risk antagonizing the Japanese at such a critical juncture. At a meeting of Ministers on 31 July it was decided to postpone the announcement of the export credits for a fortnight and to allow Craigie to assure Arita that the credits would not cover arms or munitions.[78]

With the Arita–Craigie Agreement signed it was possible for the talks on Tientsin proper to open. These began on 24 July with the Japanese setting an agenda of issues that they wished to discuss which consisted of twelve points taking in the position of the four suspects, general problems of public order and the economic problems. By 31 July a provisional agreement had been thrashed out over the first two areas, namely that the four men should be handed over to the Japanese for interrogation and that the Japanese should be allowed to observe the work of the police in the Concession.[79] Over the economic issues, however, no such easy progress was made and as early as 27 July Craigie reported that deadlock had been reached over both the currency and the silver questions.[80] The result was that on 1 August Craigie asked the Foreign Office to moderate its position over the silver, which he saw as the more important of the economic problems. His proposal was to meet the Japanese demand that the silver be handed over to the Federal Reserve Bank or the Yokohama Specie Bank, but to demand that it remain sealed.[81] In London it was realized that the deadlock over the economic issues was very threatening but that any compromise would affect the rights of other powers such as France, the United States and, obviously, China. In a Cabinet meeting of 2 August Halifax summed up his fears by confessing that 'the position in the Far East was now causing him more anxiety than the position in any other part of the world'.[82]

The position of the British Government was further complicated by the American announcement on 26 July that they would abrogate their 1911 Commercial Treaty with Japan in six months' time. This momentous decision was made without any prior consultation with London and came as a complete shock.[83] To those in the Foreign Office who deprecated Craigie's efforts the American action came as a demonstration that Britain no longer had to appease Japan but could begin to stand its ground and even move to abrogate its own commercial treaty. The resurgent opposition within the Foreign Office to a policy of compromise influenced Halifax, who on 2 August proposed to the Cabinet that Britain should use the continued anti-British demonstrations in both Japan and occupied China as an excuse to break off the talks, and that if it was decided that retaliation was necessary then Britain should denounce its commercial treaty with Japan. This view did not find much support with Chamberlain, who told the Cabinet that in his opinion due weight ought to be given to Craigie's opinions. Chamberlain's recommendation received general support and it was decided that, before a position over the economic issues was settled, it was necessary to consult Craigie further and also to sound out France and the United States.[84]

While these problems were mulled over, the talks in Tokyo were suspended. Craigie was far from happy with this enforced lull and he supported his case for a compromise with a number of arguments that illustrate his hopes and concerns at the time. As early as 1 August he had noted that the Foreign Office should not make too much of the apparent toughening of American policy as his experience was that

> the present United States Administration run away so often from their own initiatives that I hesitate to regard the action very seriously and believe the new American treaty will be negotiated well before expiration of six months limit. We must be sure it is not just another flash in the American pan before putting any reliance on this new development.[85]

Having dismissed the possibility of co-operation with the United States, Craigie saw the position as little different from that in June, apart from the fact that he was now even more convinced that

China c., 1939
Note: shading indicates areas under Japanese occupation

British concessions could strengthen the position of the Japanese 'moderates'.

Craigie's arguments were not, however, accepted within the Far Easten Department. The most influential criticism came from Sansom who produced a memorandum on 3 August attacking Craigie's assessment of the Japanese 'moderates'.[86] Sansom held that the 'moderates', if they existed at all, differed from the 'radicals' in methods and not in aims and were small in number and not very influential. Bearing this in mind, he also addressed the issue of what it would actually take to come to an understanding with Japan, a topic which Craigie had largely skirted over, and came to the conclusion that it would involve at the least giving up British privileges in China and might also require a compromise over colonial quotas. Such opinions tallied with that of the Department, but carried considerably more weight from the pen of the man who was deemed the doyen of Japanese experts.

In addition to the opposition within the Far Eastern Department, Craigie's hopes were also undermined by the views received from France and the United States about the economic issues. The French reported on 11 August that, as the silver deposited in their Concession was in the hands of a private bank, they would find it very difficult to order it to be handed over to the Japanese. The United States meanwhile indicated their opposition to any agreement that would restrict the use of the *fapi* in north China.[87] To the Foreign Office this proved that Britain could not comply with the Japanese terms and, as neutralization of the silver was not likely to find favour with Tokyo, it was argued that no British counterproposal should be made; a suggestion that was reinforced by the improbability that Japan would risk war over this issue. On 16 August Halifax wrote to Chamberlain to explain the Foreign Office's rejection of Craigie's call for a compromise. In his letter he noted

> I feel pretty clear . . . that we cannot do what Craigie wants by way of compromise over silver, and I feel that if we did we should be very likely to get very little positive result in exchange for the great worsening of our present position vis-à-vis the United States and China.[88]

In reply Chamberlain gave his assent with a heavy heart to Halifax's proposals and agreed that there seemed to be little prospect that a compromise on silver would lead to any substantial improvement in Japan's treatment of British interests.[89]

On 17 August the Foreign Office's terms were communicated to a disgruntled Craigie who passed them on to the Japanese the next day. As a result the Gaimushō announced on 20 August that the talks had broken down. Craigie was naturally resentful that his advice had been rejected and his telegrams over the next few days clearly reveal his bitterness.[90] This was not simply because he believed that the talks could have succeeded but also due to his belief that tensions at Tientsin could once again bring Britain and Japan to a crisis point. These fears proved in the end to be unsubstantiated owing to two events of the last days of August.

On 20 August severe flooding at Tientsin left most of the British Concession under water in conditions so atrocious that it would have been impossible for the local Japanese forces to increase their pressure.[91] The other, and much more important, event was that on 23 August the Nazi–Soviet Pact was signed in Moscow. In Tokyo there was bewilderment and anger at the German betrayal. Japanese policy, which had since 1936 been based on alignment with Germany, was thrown into turmoil with the IJA, which had renewed pressure for an alliance earlier in the month, unsure how to react and the moderates convinced that the time had come to return to the fray by pushing for closer relations with Britain and America. The Hiranuma government was caught in the middle of this furore, and on 28 August announced its resignation and was replaced by a new Cabinet led by General Abe Nobuyuki.[92] In such an uncertain atmosphere there was little likelihood the Japanese would risk the alienation of Britain by raising the stakes at Tientsin, and therefore the end of the talks passed without any serious recriminations. Whether this would have happened had the above events not occurred is a moot point, and the question of how justified Craigie's fears were must remain unanswered.

Craigie quickly recognized that the signing of the Nazi–Soviet Pact raised the possibility of a backlash in Japan against Germany which Britain would be wise to exploit, and on 24 August he recommended to Halifax the renewing of the Tientsin talks and, on a broader scale, an attempt to push for a Sino-Japanese peace settlement. He justified these proposals by arguing that this was a rare window of opportunity which if acted upon quickly could rebound to Britain's advantage.[93] These suggestions met with some approval in the Foreign Office and Craigie was told that he could make soundings about Tientsin but that peace talks were still too controversial. Interest in reopening the Tientsin talks was also displayed by the Japanese Embassy in London. In late August Shigemitsu, realizing that the signing of the Nazi–Soviet pact could have a salutary effect on Anglo-Japanese relations, began to make diplomatic manoeuvres of his own, and on 26 August sent Arthur Edwardes, who was now working as an adviser to the Japanese Embassy, to ask Butler if it would be worth starting new talks based around the sealing of the silver. This was followed by a talk between Shigemitsu and Halifax on 28 August in which the former hinted that, as Japan had been double-crossed by Germany and Britain by Russia, London and Tokyo ought to improve their mutual relations.[94] However, before anything could come of Shigemitsu's soundings they were overtaken by events. On 1 September Germany invaded Poland and two days later Britain was at war.

5 A false dawn

September 1939 to June 1940

The diplomatic revolution that took place in the late summer of 1939 with the signing of the Nazi–Soviet Pact and the outbreak of the European conflict had grave repercussions in East Asia and raised a number of questions about future alignments in the region. Would Japan now lean towards the democracies in the hope of using their influence to solve the China Incident or favour Germany and its new-found Soviet partner in order to force a full retreat of the West from the region? Would the Soviet Union, as a benevolent neutral towards Germany, now seek to threaten British interests in Asia, and if so what would be the Japanese attitude to an Anglo-Soviet war? The inherent unpredictibility of the situation led within Whitehall to a heightened desire to work for stability in East Asia. The question was, as so often previously, how to achieve this: one possibility was that, in the interests of power politics, China might be sacrificed to the higher strategic goal of appeasing Japan. However, a policy of complete appeasement carried with it many problems, the most important of which was that any such move would irrevocably alienate Washington, and that this would have a detrimental effect not only in East Asia but also on the level of American assistance to the Allied war effort in Europe.

The logical alternative was to pursue a policy of limited appeasement in relation to a number of specific issues affecting Anglo-Japanese relations, for example, by the settlement of the Tientsin problem and by granting various concessions in the economic field, in the hope that this would create an atmosphere in which relations could improve. This was the option that Britain chose to follow from September 1939 to the summer of 1940, but even efforts in this field were hindered by wider factors. In particular, Britain was presented with the problem that the conflict against Germany required both the marshalling of its imperial resources for the war effort and economic warfare to limit Germany's imports, both policies which had the potential to heighten tensions with Japan, who wanted guaranteed access to raw materials from the British Empire and the continuation of its trade with Germany. Britain was thus faced with a conundrum; was it worth diluting measures designed to cripple Germany for the sake of gaining Japan's benevolent neutrality?

EAST ASIA AND THE EUROPEAN WAR

From the very first Whitehall recognized that the conflict with Germany radically changed the nature of Britain's position in East Asia. The struggle to retain British interests and investment in China now had to be subsumed within the wider task of ensuring that events in the region did not detract from the task of winning the war in Europe. This naturally led to some debate in British circles about how to proceed and specifically what conditions would best assist the British cause. In theory a number of options were available, but in practice Britain's room for manouevre was severely limited.

One possible avenue to pursue was to work for a speedy conclusion of the Sino-Japanese war, thus removing the major source of tension in Anglo-Japanese relations. This was, of course, not an easy task to accomplish, and events in September and October underlined the difficulties. On 22 September Craigie was approached by General Koiso Kuniaki, a senior Japanese Army figure, with a proposal that Abe should meet Chiang Kai-shek in Hong Kong to discuss peace. Koiso claimed that this plan had the support of Abe and of the new Army Minister, General Hata Shunroku.[1] The Foreign Office and the War Cabinet saw this as an interesting proposition, but it soon turned out that Koiso had not consulted the Gaimushō before making his proposal, and on 11 October the new Foreign Minister, Admiral Nomura Kichisaburō, told Craigie that he was firmly opposed to any talks with Chiang Kai-shek.[2] There was, in any case, opposition in Whitehall to such a solution, particularly from the Chiefs of Staff who noted in an influential memorandum for the War Cabinet on 28 September that, with Italy's ambitions still unclear, there was a great necessity to prevent any extension of the war to East Asia and that the best way of achieving this was to ensure that the war in China continued to act as a drain on Japan's resources.[3]

The value of Chinese resistance meant that in theory Britain might have benefited from increasing its assistance to the Nationalist cause, but in reality this was not a practical option as aid could not be given without diverting resources from the British war effort, and anyway such a policy might lead to Japanese retaliation. Consequently, the only line that could be followed in regard to Chungking was to encourage resistance verbally and not to undermine Chiang Kai-shek's position by showing any willingness to deal with the rival Chinese regime that the Japanese were establishing at Nanking under Wang Ching-wei.

This still left the question of how to mollify Japan, as clearly Britain could not afford to leave relations at the low point they had reached in the summer and there was obviously a danger in allowing Japan to remain a loose cannon in the East which could at any time threaten British interests. On 22 September Butler, who now held the ministerial brief for overseeing British policy towards East Asia, produced a memorandum in which he argued that the international situation, and particularly the confusion about Soviet motives, made it essential to rebuild bridges with Japan. He argued, in the light of the Soviet decision to attack Poland five days earlier, that

> Much depends on which way Russia goes. If she is to become the inveterate enemy of the British Empire, it is essential that we should harness Japan to ourselves. It is therefore wise to take precautionary steps now. Russia and Japan are bound to remain enemies, and with our position in India and the East it would pay us to make a return to the Anglo-Japanese alliance possible. It does not appear that there are the makings of a war between America and Japan: the American interests in the Far East are insufficient to justify a major war. I do not believe that it will in the end pay us to keep Japan at arm's length and distrust everything she does for the sake of American opinion. I believe it is still possible to obtain American interest on our side in fighting dictators in the West, while improving our relations with Japan.[4]

This was a controversial view, particularly in its assessment of American sensibilities, but Butler realized this and made it clear that his eventual aim could only be achieved through a programme of incremental progress, and specifically an effort to improve trade relations and new talks over Tientsin. While there were doubts in the Far Eastern Department about Butler's overall vision, there was agreement that the initial focus should be to remove the more overt sources of tension.

The logical starting point was to settle the differences over Tientsin. Craigie had suggested on 18 September that this might be possible and had noted that a proposal from Jamieson that the problem over the silver could be overcome by selling some of the deposits to raise money for flood-relief at Tientsin might be feasible. This proposal was considered by the War Cabinet on 23 September and a new attempt to start talks was approved, although there was a preference for the Foreign Office line of first trying to get the silver sealed in a neutral bank and only if this proved impossible allowing it to be used for flood-relief.[5]

Despite some optimism progress was initially slow. Craigie found Nomura unresponsive and the Foreign Office became loath to press the issue after a speech by the American Ambassador in Tokyo, Joseph Grew, which strongly criticized recent trends in Japanese foreign policy, which would have rendered any British concession to Japan impolitic. It was only in late October and November that talks began to make headway with the suggestion of a mutually acceptable compromise under which the silver would be deposited in the Yokohama Specie Bank and some of it used for flood-relief.[6] Craigie in particular became optimistic about the chances of success and on 16 November informed London that a settlement would be of great symbolic importance and pave the way to better relations. At the end of November Halifax asked the War Cabinet to agree formally to reopen the talks, but his decision to make this request was not just the result of Craigie's optimism, but also because the need to conciliate Japan was becoming ever more imperative.[7]

The main reason for this urgency was the growing fear in Whitehall about Soviet ambitions in Asia and the nature of Soviet–Japanese relations; a concern which arose from a number of disturbing developments. One element was that it appeared that the Chinese government was coming under ever greater influence from Moscow. There had, of course, been worries about this for some time, but in October these mounted when it was reported that a Soviet military mission had arrived in Chungking to negotiate a Sino-Soviet military pact. Suspicion was heightened further when Chiang Kai-shek responded to Clark Kerr's queries about this rumour in a most evasive manner, noting only that, though he would prefer to rely on the democracies for support, the lack of Western assistance forced him to turn instead to Moscow.[8] This situation was disquieting, as now that Russia was openly hostile to Britain, the Soviets posed an even greater threat than before; on 17 November Clark Kerr warned that a variety of sources indicated that Moscow was clearly working for the complete eviction of British interests from China.[9]

In addition to disturbing developments in Chungking, Britain was also concerned in October 1939 about evidence that Soviet troops were beginning to mass in Sinkiang. This province had been under strong Soviet influence since 1934, but with the Sino-Japanese war Russian control had markedly increased as the major supply route for Soviet war material to China passed through the province's two largest cities, Urumchi and Hami. One of the results of Soviet domination had been pressure on Indian traders in southern Sinkiang to leave the province and measures had also been taken to isolate the British Consulate at Kashgar. However, the arrival of large numbers of Soviet troops in the autumn of 1939 posed a new and somewhat elliptical threat. It was accepted that the impenetrable barrier of the Himalayas meant there was no immediate danger to India, but this still left the question of why this reinforcement had taken place. A number of theories were postulated; that Soviet troops were there to prevent a possible Japanese offensive against Kansu, or to forestall a Japanese-sponsored rebellion by the Tungans around Kashgar and Aksu, or that the Soviets believed that the Chinese were going to make peace with Japan and therefore wished to consolidate their hold over the province.[10]

It was the last of these suppositions that most worried the Foreign Office because, if true, it might suggest that the Soviets and the Japanese had reached an agreement on the partition of China into spheres of influence. Concern about the possibility of a Soviet–Japanese understanding and of a division of China had emerged in Britain and France almost as soon as the Nazi–Soviet Pact had been signed, and had gained momentum with the news on 15 September that an armistice had been signed to end the fighting between the Soviet Union and Japan at Nomonhan on the Mongolia–Manchukuo border during the summer of 1939.[11] In November these fears were revived due to reports that elements within the IJA were leaning towards the Soviets as a means of facilitating an end to the war with China. On 22 November Craigie informed the Foreign Office about this tendency and warned that there was a real danger 'that Japanese foreign policy may fall into the hands of inexperienced extremists'.[12] This news was reinforced by reports from Sir William Seeds, the British Ambassador in Moscow, and by French information which suggested that a partition of China was under active consideration in the Kremlin.[13]

These disturbing rumours led to a debate within the Foreign Office about their significance. The view held by the Far Eastern Department and Collier of the Northern Department was that these reports were part of a deliberate Japanese campaign to use the Soviets as a bogey to frighten Britain into becoming more amenable, and that in fact there was little hard evidence to show that Japan and the Soviet Union would be able to overcome their antipathy. This was also the view expressed by Sumner Welles to the new British Ambassador to the United States, Lord Lothian.[14] Others, however, including Butler and Colliers' deputies, Fitzroy Maclean and Daniel Lascelles, were not so convinced that Britain could afford to be complacent. For example, Lascelles noted that Britain had previously assumed that no deal was possible between Germany and the Soviet Union and warned that

> a serious Soviet–Japanese rapprochement would be little short of disastrous, however little scope it might give *Japan* for harrying us. It would redouble the danger of Soviet encroachment in Central Asia – our weakest spot – and might well enable the very large Soviet submarine fleet to cripple our shipping in Far Eastern waters.[15]

The situation was such that the Foreign Office had to err on the side of caution, and on 27 November Halifax told the War Cabinet that Japan was split over this issue and that Britain could influence its decision by agreeing to reopen formal talks over Tientsin.

ANGLO-JAPANESE TRADE RELATIONS

In addition to the complications caused by the Soviet role in East Asia, the drive towards a settlement over Tientsin was also influenced by the state of economic relations between Britain and Japan. As early as 19 September the FECB (now relocated to Singapore) had decrypted a consular telegram revealing Japan's concern over possible restrictions on its supply of raw materials from the British Empire now that war had started.[16] It was therefore not surprising when, on 23 September, a proposal was received from the Japanese Commercial Counsellor in London, Shudō Yasuto, for Britain and Japan to negotiate a *modus operandi* over trade which would allow Britain to buy Japanese foodstuffs and silk in return for continued Japanese access to British machinery and imperial raw materials. In the Foreign Office this idea fell on fertile ground, as only the day before Butler had asked Sansom to enquire into the possibility of making a friendly gesture to Japan in the economic field.[17]

However, this was not solely a Foreign Office matter, as the Treasury, the Board of Trade and other ministries also had a say in commercial policy, and therefore on 26 September the matter was discussed at an interdepartmental meeting. This gathering agreed that no binding trade agreement should be signed and that the aim should be to gain concessions over commodity exports to, rather than to agree to increase imports from, Japan. Shortly afterwards a detailed outline of the Japanese position was forwarded by Shudō and at a second meeting on 5 October it was decided that these proposals could act as a basis for negotiation, but with the proviso that any concessions should be linked to a relaxation of restrictions on British trade in China.[18] This decision was communicated to Shigemitsu by Sansom on 6 October and met with some optimism, although the former rejected the attempted linkage between trade with Britain and trade in China.[19]

At this stage the prospective agreement, though potentially useful, was still of relatively minor importance, and it is noticeable that initially the Ministry of Economic Warfare (MEW) showed little interest in the talks on the grounds that it was difficult to see how a deal with Japan could affect its campaign against Germany.[20] The MEW's complacency was, however, rudely shattered on 20 October by the arrival of a telegram from Craigie which changed the whole basis of Britain's economic relations with Japan. Craigie began by noting that he supported the idea of improving trade relations with Japan on the grounds of the general good it would do for Anglo-Japanese relations, but then proceeded to observe, somewhat prosaically, that it would also be useful because of 'the danger of supplies reaching Germany via Japan and Siberia'. He then went on to report that he had heard from 'good sources' in Tokyo that the Germans were trying to arrange with Japan for the delivery of Manchurian soya beans via the Trans-Siberian Railway. Craigie concluded that this demonstrated the need for a trade agreement with Japan, and that in negotiations Britain should

> indicate to the Japanese that they can hardly expect us to facilitate supplies unless they on their side undertake not to export Japanese, Manchurian or Chinese produce to our enemies by any route and unless they undertake also to prevent the transit to our enemies of goods from third countries either through their territories or by their vessels.[21]

He did not, however, go as far as proposing a formal link between the Siberian issue and Anglo-Japanese trade, realizing that any attempt to do so would only increase the agitation of the radicals against the weak Abe government. At first the MEW appeared too shocked to take in the gravity of this bombshell, but within days further reports from Japan made it clear that a major circumvention of the British blockade on Germany had emerged which constituted a major threat to the Allied war effort as it allowed Germany continued supplies of rubber, nickel and tin from the Dutch East Indies, wolfram and antimony from China, copper from the United States and Japan, and vegetable oils from Manchukuo. The MEW was therefore galvanized into co-operating with the Foreign Office to push for some kind of trade agreement along the lines suggested by Craigie which would indirectly link favourable terms for Anglo-Japanese trade to a commitment by Japan not to supply Germany with raw materials, and in November both ministries began to prepare memoranda for the War Cabinet arguing in favour of such an agreement.[22]

However, the plan for a trade agreement soon ran into strong opposition from the Treasury and the Board of Trade. The Treasury's objections rested on their concern that too generous an agreement with Japan would allow the latter to accrue large stocks of sterling which, if sold for dollars on the open market at Shanghai, would have the effect of lowering sterling's value and thus affecting Britain's ability to buy war materials from markets such as the United States. The Board of Trade's position was that no trade agreement was possible until enough time had passed to see what Britain's wartime needs would be, and that to enter precipitously into an agreement with Japan and commit Britain to the purchase of goods it may not need would be very unwise.[23] The result was that it was decided at an interdepartmental meeting on 24 November that it was impossible to continue along these lines, and the idea of a trade agreement was dropped.[24] This was highly ironic, for the two ministries which had obstructed all of the Foreign Office's previous attempts at sanctions against Japan, on the grounds that Britain could not afford to antagonize Japan, had now defeated a policy whose object was to appease the Japanese.

The blocking of this avenue was not the only obstacle to an improvement in commercial relations. It had long been hoped by Chamberlain and others that effective economic warfare could bring the German economy close to collapse in a relatively short space of time, and in an attempt to increase the pressure on Berlin it was decided in November to introduce Orders in Council to allow for the seizure of German exports. The idea was that this would drastically reduce Germany's acquisition of foreign exchange and thus curtail its ability to purchase imports, although the official justification was that it constituted retaliation for Germany's indiscriminate use of mines off Britain.[25] The initiation of such a policy may have been necessary for the pursuit of the war but it portended a series of clashes with Germany's trading partners, including Japan. The seriousness with which Japan viewed this British move was made evident when on 27 November, the day that the Orders in Council came into operation, Shigemitsu handed a vigorous note of protest to Lord Halifax which declared that there was no justification for Britain's act under international law. He also protested over a number of other issues, such as the British requisitioning of machinery Japan had ordered from British factories before the war and the future of £1,200,000 worth of goods from Japan for Germany which had been seized at British ports.[26]

The need to make a decision over Tientsin therefore came at a point when Anglo-Japanese economic relations were increasingly strained and when a real fear existed of a Soviet-Japanese understanding. However, despite all of these reasons for using the Tientsin talks as a means of conciliating Japan there was still opposition within the War Cabinet to renewing the negotiations, notably from Winston Churchill, the First Lord of the Admiralty, who was already showing signs of a dangerous underestimation of Japan's martial capabilities and the importance of East Asia.[27] Halifax was able to fight off this challenge, in part because of news that the United States was undertaking talks with Japan designed to reopen the Yangtse to commercial shipping, which blunted fears of American criticism, but also because Japan continued to be conciliatory over Tientsin. On 4 December, after a week of discussion in the War Cabinet, it was finally decided that a settlement ought to be pursued.[28]

OBSTACLES AND DELAYS

On the day his instructions arrived from London Craigie forwarded the first draft of a formula under which the disputed silver was to be deposited in a neutral bank under the joint seal of the HSBC and the Yokohama Specie Bank, £100,000 being earmarked for flood-relief, and followed this the next day with a draft to cover the currency issue.[29] The Foreign Office took fright at this rapid diplomacy and urged Craigie to be more cautious, but the real obstacle to the talks proved to be neither the timidity of the Foreign Office nor the excessive demands of the Japanese, important though these were, but the opposition of the Chinese Government. On 13 December Clark Kerr reported that the Chinese were against any sale of silver to raise funds for flood-relief, an announcement that threw the Foreign Office into a state of utter dismay.[30] In response a telegram was sent to Clark Kerr for him to forward directly to Chiang Kai-shek which vociferously defended the silver formula negotiated by Craigie and noted

96 A false dawn

His Majesty's Government are not prepared to allow this situation to continue indefinitely and they, especially in view of the moral and material support which they have given to the Chinese Government, feel that they are entitled to expect the latter to afford such help as may be possible or at any rate not to adopt too rigid an attitude. ... It is in the interests of the Chinese Government not to place obstacles in the way of our relations with Japan which hamper our war effort, since the victory of the Allies in Europe is in the best interests of an independent China.[31]

However, this pompous and self-serving note could not be delivered immediately as Chiang Kai-shek had gone to the front. This caused a considerable delay, but it was in some respects fortunate as the negotiations in Tokyo had moved into a new minefield; on 20 December the Japanese indicated that the figure of £100,000 was too low for flood-relief, and the Foreign Office opposed Craigie's subsequent proposal to raise the sum to £300,000.[32]

As the Tientsin talks stagnated, Japan kept up its pressure on Britain to relax restrictions on trade with Germany. On 5 December Shigemitsu handed Howe an *aide-mémoire* asking for special treatment over machinery that had already been ordered from Germany, for Japan to be allowed to order further vital goods in the future, and for the Orders in Council not to be applied before 1 January 1940. Then on 10 December Shigemitsu requested that the *Sanyo Maru*, a Japanese ship which was just about to leave Rotterdam, be exempted from British contraband control. This posed a difficult problem because the MEW had received information that the vessel was carrying a cargo of 'secret naval goods' from Germany for the IJN.[33] Any decision over the searching of the ship therefore had to be made at the highest level as it raised important policy questions. In the War Cabinet Churchill argued, with his usual bellicosity, for a strict search of the ship, but this was countered by Halifax who argued that any search would cause political difficulties with Japan. The eventual decision made on 14 December was that the ship would only be given a cursory search if there was an assurance that the whole cargo was for the Japanese government and that none of it would pass into German hands in East Asia. Subsequently on 15 December Shigemitsu agreed to these terms in exchange for British agreement that the introduction of the Orders in Council would be postponed until 1 January 1940, and the issue was settled.[34]

These minor concessions raised the question of whether Britain was willing to go any further to appease the Japanese in the economic field. Sansom felt that it was worth indicating to the Japanese that a beneficial economic deal may be possible in six months, a policy which found support from Butler and Halifax. However, before anything could be done a new obstacle emerged in the increasingly rigid attitude of the United States towards Japan. Lothian had in late November and early December tried to gauge the Roosevelt administration's attitude towards East Asia, even to the point of asking Welles what sort of Sino-Japanese settlement the Americans would be willing to support. The official American response was delivered to Lothian on 9 December by the State Department's political adviser for Far Eastern Affairs, Stanley Hornbeck, who made it clear that he foresaw no acceptable peace in the near future. He also took the opportunity to decry the idea of making concessions to Japan to encourage the 'moderates' and warned that the latter were too insubstantial ever to be in a position to take power, a view similar to that espoused by Sansom during the latter stages of the Tientsin crisis.[35]

On top of this cautionary advice, it was also clear that the Roosevelt administration believed that the talks Grew had been holding with Nomura over the Yangtse had failed to make satisfactory progress and that it therefore planned to proceed with the abrogation of its Commercial Treaty. Moreover, Morgenthau indicated on 12 December in a conversation with Arthur Purvis, the Chairman of the Anglo-French Purchasing Commission in the United States, that Roosevelt wished in collaboration with Britain and France to introduce an embargo on the export of strategic ferro-alloys, such as molybdenum and nickel, to Germany, the Soviet Union and Japan.[36] These intentions made it abundantly clear that Britain could not afford to make the slightest move towards conciliating Japan without becoming seriously out of step with the Americans; more seriously the American wish for co-operation over ferro-alloys put Britain in a position in which it had to contemplate taking restrictive measures against Japan. Such a decision could only be taken by the War Cabinet, which met to consider the issue on 23 January 1940. A joint Foreign Office-MEW memorandum made clear that this was a serious step, noting that it might very well halt the recent conciliatory mood in Tokyo and that there was no guarantee of American support should Japan retaliate, but it also observed authoritatively

When the course of war cannot be foreseen, and when all that is certain is that we are fighting for our lives, it is clear that the Allies cannot afford to reject any friendly approach by the President of the United States nor fail to examine to the full the potentialities of the joint control of raw materials which Mr Roosevelt has tentatively outlined.[37]

This was enough to persuade the War Cabinet, although even Eden, hardly a Japanophile, observed sadly that it was 'unfortunate that the United States should wish to take a firm line with Japan, just when we were trying to improve our relations with that country'.[38]

The result of the War Cabinet's discussion was that it was agreed to propose to the French that a joint delegation be sent to Washington to discuss the American plan with Morgenthau and, in the interim, to restrict the sale of strategic ferro-alloys, of which the most important was Canadian nickel, to Japan. However, this was not the first formal restriction on exports to Japan, for, unknown to Whitehall, Sir Shenton Thomas had already in December refused the export of rubber and tin from Malaya unless guarantees were given that they would not be re-exported to Germany.[39] Thus, despite all efforts to the contrary, Anglo-Japanese trade relations by January 1940 were on a collision course and a breakthrough had still not been achieved in the Tientsin negotiations. But worse was yet to come.

THE *ASAMA MARU* CRISIS

On 30 December 1939 the Admiralty received information that a number of German sailors stranded in the United States were planning to return to Germany via Japan and the Trans-Siberian Railway. The first part of this journey entailed travelling from San Francisco to Yokohama on a Japanese merchant ship, the *Asama Maru*. The Admiralty therefore decided to intercept the ship and detain the sailors. This plan was discussed with the Foreign Office and the MEW, who raised no objections, and on 9 January the relevant orders were sent to the Commander-in-Chief China Station with the explicit instruction that the vessel was not to be stopped within sight of the Japanese coast.[40] On 21 January the *Asama Maru* was intercepted by HMS *Liverpool*, and twenty-one Germans, thirteen officers and eight technical ratings, were taken into British custody. However, there was a problem; the ship had been intercepted at a distance of thirty-five miles from Japan or what the Japanese termed as 'within sight of Mount Fuji'. The high-handed nature of the British action allied to its proximity to the Japanese coast led to outrage within Japan and on 22 January Vice-Minister of Foreign Affairs, Tani Masayuki, protested strongly to Craigie and demanded the return of the detained Germans.[41]

Craigie was aghast at this turn of events and his mood was little improved the next day when he learnt that the Admiralty were now planning to intercept another ship, the *La Plata Maru*, which led him to send a telegram warning in no uncertain terms that another incident could lead to war.[42] In the Foreign Office too there was a sense of bewilderment at the sudden appearance of this crisis and a desire to try to placate the Japanese, and thus the Admiralty was restrained from further actions. Luckily for the British the Japanese Government was also at this stage anxious to avoid a break in relations as a change of government had taken place on 14 January installing Admiral Yonai Mitsumasa as Prime Minister and Arita Hachirō, who was keen to see better relations with Britain, as Foreign Minister once again.[43] The first promising sign came on 24 January when Shigemitsu informed Halifax that his government was keen to ease the situation in whatever way it could. The next day Arita did just that by ordering the two main Japanese shipping companies, NYK and OSK, not to take any more German passengers of military age.[44]

On 27 January Craigie met Arita to present the British plan for a solution of the crisis. In keeping with the concern in the Foreign Office he offered a very moderate proposal; a Japanese promise not to carry anyone valuable to the German war effort in exchange for a British commitment not to stop and search Japanese ships for German passengers and, if necessary the return of those removed from the *Asama Maru* who would not be of use to the German Navy. After some discussion Craigie and Arita finally arrived at a solution based on the British formula on 5 February, with the proviso that nine of the Germans should be returned to Japan.[45]

The settlement of this potentially explosive incident was a matter of satisfaction for both sides and in London Craigie was roundly praised for his astute diplomacy. The question that now faced Whitehall was whether this success could be built upon as the basis for a more permanent easing of Anglo-Japanese tensions. In Craigie's opinion this was a golden opportunity. He had already in January been strongly critical of Hornbeck's dismissal of the Japanese 'moderates', arguing that Japan was seeking an escape from the China Incident and that if the West was able to offer a feasible alternative to autarky it might make all the difference. On 1 January he had observed

Though every Japanese naturally desires the advancement of his country's fortunes, distinction must be made between moderates who favour gradual economic expansion through the control of

vital raw materials and the development of overseas markets as the
solution for Japan's organic economic ills and extremists who,
impelled by mystical fanaticism, aspire to world domination. . . .
Danger here is that too severe pressure from the United States . . .
might have more immediate effect of bringing the extremist
government into power to carry out re-orientation of Japan's
foreign policy.[46]

The settling of the *Asama Maru* crisis was taken by Craigie as proof
that he had been right in this judgement and he began to press for
progress, particularly in the field of trade relations. In addition, however, he noted that there was another possible avenue: co-operation
against the Soviet Union.

THE TEMPTATION OF AN ANTI-SOVIET ALLIANCE

The hostility between Britain and the Soviet Union had increased
markedly in the last months of 1939, in part due to Soviet trade with
Germany, but in the main because of the Russian invasion of Finland
in December. On 22 December, as a result of a report from Seeds that
the Soviets were more or less in a state of undeclared war against
Britain, Sir Orme Sargent, the Deputy Under-Secretary at the Foreign
Office, had asked the Chiefs of Staff to prepare a memorandum on the
contingencies that might lead to war with the Soviet Union.[47] The
Chiefs of Staff produced their report on 8 March 1940, and argued
that the most likely area for a Soviet advance was Afghanistan,
leading to a threat to India. In regard to East Asia the report noted

The fact that we are at war with Russia might . . . cause Japan to
pursue a more forward policy in the Far East to the detriment of
British interests. The extent to which Japanese action might cause
us embarrassment would depend on the attitude of the United
States. On the other hand, Japan might attempt to exploit the
situation by compromising with us in order to improve her position vis-à-vis Russia. Our diplomatic action should be directed to
bring about this latter course.[48]

Evidence from Japanese sources suggested that any such anti-Soviet
overture to Tokyo would find a receptive audience. As early as
January Craigie had reported that the invasion of Finland had dis-
credited the pro-Soviet faction in the army and that relations with
Moscow had once again deteriorated. This was also the impression
given by Shigemitsu, who in a series of talks with Butler did his best

to conjure up sinister images of Soviet plots and intrigue and to emphasize that Britain and Japan had a common enemy in Russia.[49]

By the end of February there were rumours that Japan was on the verge of proposing to Britain and France an anti-Soviet front in East Asia. On 26 February Craigie reported his belief that

> In the course of the struggle in which we are now engaged in Europe we already have to deal with the U.S.S.R. as a covert enemy and may soon have to fight her in the open. One of our natural allies in such circumstances would be Japan, who can ill afford to see the Soviet emerge enlargened [*sic*] and strengthened from the present struggle. Only our differences in regard to China and the strength of the somewhat artificial pro-German sentiment which has been generated here during the hostilities in China bar the way to a closer and more fruitful Anglo-Japanese collaboration in regard to Russian affairs.[50]

On 29 February he built on this by offering to do preparatory work in case anything came of the rumours circulating.[51] Such talk met with some interest within the Foreign Office, as there was by this point serious consideration by both France and Britain of a plan to cripple the Soviet economy and reduce oil sales to Germany by bombing the oilfield at Baku in the Caucasus. To some, such as Sargent and Sir Horace Seymour, who was now overseeing the Far Eastern Department, the idea of Japanese co-operation against Russia was vital and they urged that more should be done to bring Japan into line with Britain. Other officials, notably Cadogan and the Far Eastern Department itself, were more cautious as they recognized that Japan's price for co-operation would be an end to British support for China, which would have disastrous consequences for relations with the United States; they therefore believed that the issue could not be properly addressed until war had actually broken out between Britain and Russia. This view was supported by Halifax and even by Butler, who was worried about the effect of an anti-Soviet policy on the left's support for the war in Britain.[52]

A similar debate took place in the War Office where MO2 produced a paper entitled 'Japan as an Ally'. This memorandum strongly supported the case for an anti-Soviet alliance with Japan, although it did note that Japan's likely *quid pro quo* for such an arrangement, removal of recognition from Chiang Kai-shek's government, would lead to problems and that 'the Japanese are strange companions on a crusade against aggression and against atrocities on weaker peoples'. This report was in turn strongly criticized by MI2c, which took a line very similar to that taken by the Far Eastern Department, and in this they were supported by the upper echelons. In particular, the Deputy Director of Military Intelligence, Brigadier van Curtsem, noted that it might very well be that Japan would repeat its performance as an ally in the First World War, when it had spent its time expanding its interests in East Asia.[53]

While it was decided that Britain could not afford to propose an anti-Soviet alliance, this still left the question of whether Britain and Japan could pool their resources at a lower level. This issue was raised on 31 March when a Japanese journalist named Hashimoto suggested to Craigie that Japan and Britain should exchange information about the activities of the Comintern. Despite the similarity of this idea to the Anti-Comintern Pact, it met with some enthusiasm in the Foreign Office, Halifax indicating some interest and Butler minuting his approval, subject to the agreement of other departments.[54] MI2c also supported the idea as they believed that this plan would allow for the exchange of military intelligence about the Red Army, but they found themselves overruled by the Director of Military Intelligence (DMI), Major-General Beaumont-Nesbitt, who recollected that a similar arrangement had existed between Britain and Japan from 1926–9, and that Britain had brought the exchange to a close due to the lack of useful data received from their Japanese counterparts. The War Office therefore turned down the Japanese initiative on 24 April, but by this point the start of the Norwegian campaign and a lack of heavy bombers in the Middle East had anyway forced a postponement of the Anglo-French attack on Baku.[55]

TOWARDS A WAR TRADE AGREEMENT

The option of using the Soviet Union as a means of overcoming Anglo-Japanese antagonism was thus blocked; this left only two avenues, concessions over trade and a settlement of the problems at Tientsin. The difficulties over trade concessions in the first half of 1940 remained substantially the same as in 1939; Japan resented the curbs on German exports and was deeply concerned about restrictions on Japanese purchases of raw materials from the British Empire, while Whitehall was disturbed by the Japanese trade with Germany along the Trans-Siberian Railway and feared that concessions to the Japanese would only generate similar demands from other neutrals and thus undermine the effectiveness of the blockade.

The first major problem to arise in 1940 was once again over the issue of German exports; the Japanese had two ships, the *Tajima Maru* at Rotterdam and the *Muroran Maru* at Genoa, ready to sail for Japan in February carrying goods bought from Germany. On 11 January the Japanese asked that these ships be allowed through British contraband control, thus contravening the spirit of the agreement that had been reached on 15 December.[56] By early February Halifax, realizing the importance of maintaining momentum now that the *Asama Maru* crisis had been solved, was keen to meet this Japanese request and therefore put pressure on the MEW to compromise by using the argument that to make concessions over this issue could lead to Japan becoming more amenable over exports to Germany.[57] With the MEW's approval a deal was finally struck in a meeting between Halifax and Shigemitsu on 20 February at which the latter said that in future the Japanese would provide all the necessary documentation over payment and descriptions of goods. Nigel Ronald, now Head of the Foreign Office's General Department, who was also present at the meeting, hinted in return that, if Japan curtailed its trade with Germany along the Trans-Siberian Railway, Britain would be willing to compromise over German exports. Shigemitsu displayed a distinct interest in this proposal and observed that it could act as the basis for an agreement.[58]

The Foreign Office was encouraged further along this road in early March by the inadequate American response to Anglo-French overtures about economic warfare. In February a joint delegation, consisting of Frank Ashton-Gwatkin and the Economic Adviser to the French Ministère de Blocus, M. Rist, had, in line with the Cabinet's decision in January, been sent to the United States to discuss the plan for restricting the sale of ferro-alloys, but on arrival had found that Morgenthau was unwilling even to see them, let alone discuss the ferro-alloy issue.[59] With the situation in East Asia so unstable this response hardly encouraged Britain to show restraint in trade talks with Japan, and therefore pressure grew for negotiations which would touch on all aspects of economic relations.

This was not only a matter of interest for the Foreign Office; the MEW was also keen to begin talks. The latter had been encouraged to move in this direction first by evidence that Germany was building an extensive network in East Asia to arrange for the purchase and transport of vital commodities along the Trans-Siberian Railway, and second by the revelation that on 16 February a new German–Soviet trade agreement had been signed in Moscow.[60] A memorandum circulated by the MEW to the War Cabinet on 11 March suggested that the best way to tackle this problem was to extend contraband control to goods entering the Soviet Union and enforce this by intercepting ships heading towards Vladivostock, which would require the Royal Navy to increase its patrols in waters off Japan. The MEW indicated that to make the blockade of the Soviet Union complete it was essential to have the co-operation of the United States and Japan, and argued that in the case of the latter the most obvious way to force it to accept contraband control was to coerce it by temporarily rationing its supply of imperial raw materials and to promise advantageous quotas in the future if it complied with British economic warfare policy. The MEW memorandum was discussed by the War Cabinet on 14 March and its recommendations were accepted.[61] While this might suggest that a consensus had been reached and that these measures could now be implemented this was in fact far from the case, for while the MEW's policy rested largely on coercion, the Foreign Office still believed in the need to win over Japan by less confrontational means; the result was that a long delay took place before talks could start with Japan.

In particular, the two ministries clashed over whether Britain should be prepared to make concessions over German exports to Japan and whether Japanese merchant ships should be exempted from the contraband control system. In regard to the former, the Foreign Office was able to persuade the MEW to be more accommodating and on 27 March the War Cabinet accepted that concessions over goods from Germany could be offered to Japan.[62] Over the second issue, the Foreign Office, influenced by indications that the Gaimushō was extremely sensitive about the possibility of interceptions in Japanese coastal waters, took the position that, while they were not prepared to allow Japan to veto all interceptions in these waters, Britain should at least meet Japanese sensibilities by exercising restraint over searches. This argument was not accepted by the MEW, which saw any such compromise as fatally undermining the whole *raison d'être* for contraband control in the Pacific.[63]

While these interdepartmental battles raged, the introduction of contraband control was delayed until the issue could be discussed by a meeting of the joint Anglo-French Supreme War Council on 28 March. At this gathering the French agreed to the MEW's policy even to the extent of concurring with the interception of Japanese ships bound for Vladivostock.[64] The next steps were to inform Craigie of the Anglo-French plan and to square the United States, but before this could be done the picture was complicated by the raising of two further issues. The first was that on 27 March the Treasury informed the Foreign Office that it was necessary to negotiate a payments agreement with Japan, as the Japanese were continuing to run a balance of payments surplus with Britain and were selling off surplus sterling to buy dollars, thus helping to drive down sterling's value. The problem here was that the desire for a payments agreement ran contrary to the MEW's plan to restrict Japanese access to the British Empire's raw materials, since if Japan could not buy these commodities but continued with their present level of exports to the Empire the result would be that Japan would have even more excess sterling.[65] The second issue was that on 3 April Shigemitsu asked Halifax to allow another eight Japanese ships, which were mainly loading at Italian ports, to carry consignments of German exports to Japan.[66] This proposal meant that the issue of German exports was not just theoretical but had immediate relevance for Japan and thus much greater potential for use by Britain in achieving a *quid pro quo*.

The raising of these two issues increased the fear within the Foreign Office that the overtly coercive line favoured by the MEW was too blunt an instrument for dealing with the present situation. This belief was also in part the result of hints from Shigemitsu that Japan was keen to see an improvement of Anglo-Japanese relations. The Japanese Ambassador not only put over this view himself in his weekly meetings with Butler but also used another channel to put pressure on the Under-Secretary of State. On 27 March Arthur Edwardes wrote privately to Butler stating that Shigemitsu was very keen on negotiating a War Trade Agreement but could not say so openly as Shudō's initial proposals had been rejected by the British.[67] The hint was clear; if Britain put forward reasonable proposals it would find the Japanese responsive. The result was that on 5 April Butler wrote to Ronald Cross, the Minister for Economic Warfare, stating

> We accept the main line of reasoning, but do not see why a severe strain need be imposed on our relations with Japan. We have evidence of a predisposition on the part of that country to reach an agreement with us which will be satisfactory. They realise as well as we do the strength of our bargaining position in view of their need for raw materials and other commodities we can provide.
>
> . . . the Far Eastern situation cannot be divorced from the world situation, and we would not be happy were our relations with Japan to take a wrong turning as a result of our handling of the Japanese over this question.
>
> We have, over the past few months, affected a considerable

relieving of tension which has not been without its effect on our world position.[68]

The MEW, however, rejected this attempt to make the approach to Japan more conciliatory, and on 14 April a long telegram describing the intended agenda for the economic talks was finally sent to Craigie.[69] The latter was glad to hear that negotiations were finally to start; he agreed with the general aims, and had no objection to the talks taking place in London rather than Tokyo, but he did express a number of reservations about the methods suggested. In particular, he objected to the idea of any measures restricting the export of key commodities to Japan and warned the Foreign Office in the strongest possible terms that such a policy would have a disastrous effect, noting on 16 April that

> Negotiations should take place against the background that we still have a host of enemies in this country who are only waiting for some pretext to stem the current running in our favour and nothing would assist their campaign more than some drastic step calculated to divert to us the present ill-feeling against the United States. . . . Drastic action of this kind may well create such a storm here as to render impossible future negotiations along the lines you contemplate.[70]

Craigie also stressed that he still believed it would be a mistake to intercept any Japanese ships. These views had a considerable impact in London where they mirrored concerns expressed by the Australian Government to the Dominions Office. The combined weight of these arguments had the effect of forcing the MEW to climb down over the interception of Japanese ships and to agree to only a very limited curtailment of exports to Japan, which consisted of the maintenance of the current embargo on ferro-alloys and restrictions on sales of raw jute and jute bags from India and of rubber and tin from Malaya.[71]

Despite the growing consensus on the agenda there were still further delays, largely because of the need to consult the Americans. Lothian was insistent that Washington must be fully briefed before talks began in London in order to convince them that the talks were an essential element in introducing contraband control against the Soviet Union. To this end he requested that the MEW supply him with as many statistics as possible about the state of Soviet–German trade. The collation of this material took time and it was only on 4 May that Lothian finally reported Washington's approval of the British scheme.[72] The delay caused by the need to reassure the Americans caused irritation in Whitehall and to the Japanese, and to placate the latter it proved necessary to make some minor concessions over Britain's right to seize some of the cargo on the eight ships carrying German exports. A slight climb-down was communicated to Shigemitsu by Butler on 7 May at a meeting in which the latter also announced that Britain was now ready to begin the contraband negotiations. Three days later the first formal talk on trade took place between Shigemitsu, Cross and Leith-Ross and an *aide mémoire* setting out Britain's intentions in the contraband talks was handed to the Japanese Ambassador.[73] After six months' delay the negotiations had finally started.

EAST ASIA AND THE GERMAN OFFENSIVE IN WESTERN EUROPE

The terrible irony for Britain was that the date that the economic talks finally began, 10 May 1940, coincided, not only with the formation of the Churchill government, but also with the start of the German blitzkrieg into France and the Low Countries. Even before this the deteriorating fortunes of the Allied Powers in Europe had had an impact on the position in East Asia. As early as April the German assault on Denmark and Norway had led to the belief that Holland would be next and to questions about the status of the Dutch East Indies. On 17 April, amid rumours of Japanese interest in this subject, the United States had declared that any change in the status of the Dutch colony would endanger stability in the Pacific region.[74] The assault launched on 10 May which brought Holland into the European conflict put the question about the future of the Dutch colony into even sharper focus, but it also did more than that; the collapse of the French and British forces before the might of the German forces led to a renewed belief in Japan that alignment with Berlin was the way forward and that Japan should seek to take advantage of the power vacuum that was emerging in South-East Asia.

It was against this background that the talks about an economic agreement took place. The first meeting between the two main negotiators, Leith-Ross and the Counsellor at the Japanese Embassy in London, Okamoto Suemasa, took place on 14 May, when the former handed over the list of goods that Britain wished to see considered as contraband and Okamoto responded by making known the raw materials which Japan wished to import from the British Empire. The talk was held in a friendly atmosphere and seemed to fulfil the hopes that Shigemitsu had displayed the day before when he had told Butler that he believed that Anglo-Japanese relations were at last turning for the better.[75] This initial sense of optimism was assisted by another British concession over the eight ships, as Shigemitsu was informed by Butler on 15 May that Britain would agree to the sailing of two ships, the *Noto Maru* and *Najima Maru*, which were ready to leave from Genoa, and to consider a third, the *Nagara Maru*, sympathetically when it was ready to depart.[76]

The talks therefore started in a potentially fruitful atmosphere, but they soon began to lose their momentum; the problem was that the Japanese considered the British list of contraband goods to be too extensive and felt that the request that Japan should ban the re-export to Germany and the Soviet Union of *any* goods imported into the country was too wide and should only apply to items imported from the British Empire. The British were equally determined to compromise as little as possible over these vital issues and, in addition, the MEW found itself unable to agree to the Japanese list of desired commodities, in particular because they clashed with the commitment to act in parallel with the American ferro-alloy embargo. By the beginning of June, after another two meetings between Leith-Ross and Okamoto, it had become obvious that the talks were approaching stalemate and that the directives arriving from Tokyo were becoming more rather than less severe.[77] At first Shigemitsu tried to keep an optimistic attitude in his meetings with Butler and to play down the gravity of the debate in Tokyo, and on 12 June he told Butler that he was still hopeful about the economic talks. However, a more realistic assessment of the situation was given the next day when John Keswick of the MEW reported that Okamoto had told him that the news from Tokyo was not good and that he saw 'no hope at all of the full MEW demands being even discussed, they are far too wide'.[78] In this increasingly chilled atmosphere the contraband talks had no chance of success and after a last meeting on 28 June between Leith-Ross and Okamoto they were abandoned; it was decided in the interim to limit negotiations to arriving at a Payments Agreement.[79]

Despite the failure to attain a deal over contraband and Anglo-Japanese trade there was progress at this time in another area. The Tientsin talks, as stated earlier, had stalled in December 1939 due to Chinese opposition to the concessions that had been made over the silver issue and in particular to their objection to the Yokohama Specie Bank having any role in the sealing of the silver. It was only in mid-March, when Clark Kerr suggested that the British and Japanese Consul-Generals at Tientsin should seal the silver, a solution that excluded banks altogether, that progress was made.[80] On this basis a new consensus was reached by the middle of April and it was agreed that, although there would be an initial sum of £100,000 for flood-relief, the Japanese were entitled to request further sums in the future and that these applications would be reviewed by the British 'in the spirit which had led to conclusion of previous agreement'.[81] The apparent settlement of these problems meant that work could begin on drawing up final formulas over the silver, currency and police issues concerning Tientsin and, although there were further delays, an agreement was finally signed in Tokyo on 19 June; the problems that had brought Britain and Japan to the brink of war in 1939 were settled at last. Craigie felt that this was a great achievement and on 24 June he wrote to the Foreign Office saying

> it is undoubtedly a cause for satisfaction that in spite of Allied reverses the Japanese Government should have seen fit to carry the negotiations to their conclusion and the fact that they did so is good evidence that the present Government at any rate are not anxious to be stampeded by the press and by extremist opinion into a completely pro-Axis and anti-British attitude.[82]

If this was a genuine outburst of optimism from Craigie it could not have been more greatly misplaced; the signature of the Tientsin Agreement was the last conciliatory gesture to emerge from the now desperately fragile Yonai government, which was being buffeted from all sides with the demand that Japan should not 'miss the bus'.

A period was thus ending in which Britain and Japan had come closer to agreement than at any time since the summer of 1937. The start of the European war had forced Britain to minimize as far as possible its problems with Japan over China and instead concentrate on issues of mutual interest. Finally, however, the two sides had found it impossible to bridge the gap between them. The economic talks had failed because the needs of the concurrent British and Japanese war efforts were simply not compatible. Both countries had negotiated solely out of self-interest; Arita and Shigemitsu had striven to push Britain towards alleviating the effects of the economic blockade while the British had in turn pressed the Japanese to cut voluntarily a link with a vital trading partner. The common desire for improved relations was therefore buried under the fact that negotiation had revealed that compromise was impossible as the potential disadvantages involved were too great. This, however, was not all, for looming in the background throughout these months were other negative factors which hindered an understanding; for Japan there was the alluring image of alignment with a Germany that had successfully challenged the *status quo*, while Britain was held back by the disapproving countenance of the United States. And all of Craigie's warnings that an opportunity was being lost could not change the fact that in defeating Germany Britain needed America more than it needed Japan.

6 The Burma Road crisis
June 1940 to October 1940

To understand British policy towards East Asia in the period between June and October 1940 it is essential to realize that Britain was that summer at its lowest ebb. In Western Europe France, Belgium and Holland had all succumbed to the Nazi onslaught, German forces had reached the Channel and a battle for air supremacy raged over English skies between the *Luftwaffe* and the Royal Air Force. In the Mediterranean and in East Africa, Britain wrestled with the problems posed by Italian entry into the war and, in addition, had to deal with uncertainty over the future of the French fleet and the problem of how to restrain Franco's Spain. In the Atlantic a desperate battle raged between Germany's U-Boats and the overstretched resources of the Royal Navy as both sides sought to strangle the other's economy. Britain faced these problems to all intents and purposes alone; the Soviet Union remained wedded to the Nazi–Soviet Pact while the United States watched from the sidelines and waited to see if Britain had the resolve and resources to survive.

These events, which pushed British endurance to the sticking point, dominated the agenda of the newly appointed Churchill government; the threat to British interests in East Asia in the same period was an inconvenience that had to be neutralized by whatever resources were available, including appeasement if necessary. Japan, well aware of the temporary weakness of the European colonial powers in the East, was determined to take advantage of this opportunity to hasten the defeat of China and to increase its political and economic influence in South-East Asia, thus circumventing the potential American stranglehold over its economy. The result was the Burma Road crisis in which Britain capitulated to the Japanese demand for the closure of one of the last supply routes into China. However, to describe this whole period as the 'Burma Road crisis' is somewhat misleading, as it was not one crisis but a series in which it became increasingly clear to

Whitehall that Japan could not be appeased. Thus a period that began with a blatant act of appeasement ended with the first signs of a new determination to resist Japan.

THE BURMA ROAD CRISIS

On 11 June 1940, with the Tientsin agreement still not quite finalized, Craigie was summoned to the Gaimushō and told by Tani that, due to the Italian entry into the war, Japan believed that Britain should now withdraw its remaining gunboats and troops from China in order to avoid any clash with the small Italian garrison in Shanghai.[1] This was a repeat of a request that Japan had made at the beginning of the war in Europe, to which Britain and France had not even deigned to reply, and was, at first, not considered in London to involve any threat. However, it did not take long for events to become more serious. On 19 June Major-General Tsuchihashi Yūichi, the IJA's Director of Military Intelligence, told Colonel Mullaly, Piggott's replacement as Military Attaché, in an abrasive interview

> Situation is critical and there is now nothing to stop Japan from seizing either French Indo-China, Netherlands East Indies or Hong Kong or all of them . . . . United States are in no condition to prevent Japan from taking whatever action she likes in Western Pacific. Great Britain now has her last chance and if she takes it positive action by Japan may be averted. Japan's demands are:
> (1) Immediate closing of Burmese frontier with China;
> (2) Immediate closing of Hong Kong frontier;
> (3) Immediate withdrawal of British troops from Shanghai.
> Instant and decisive compliance with these demands is the only thing that may yet avert a declaration of war by Japan against Britain.[2]

These demands had been agreed to by Arita at a ministerial conference the previous day, at which it was also decided to demand that France close the border between Tonkin and Yunnan. Tani had presented this demand to the French Ambassador on 19 June, but had not approached Craigie because the Gaimushō wanted time to present the demands to Britain as requests and stress that this was a way in which improved relations could be achieved; they were thus outflanked by the more brutal approach of the Army.[3]

The timing of the Army's ultimatum was excellent since it could not have come at a more inconvenient time for Britain. By this stage the Allies in Western Europe were in disarray; on 10 June Italy had entered the war on Germany's side and on 16 June the French, to the dismay of the British, had requested an armistice from Germany. Consequently the initial Foreign Office reaction to the threat in East Asia was to inform Craigie that he should play for time and should warn Japan that siding with the unreliable Germans could be dangerous and might lead to further restrictions on Japanese access to British and American raw materials, a message that was also conveyed to Shigemitsu.[4] Craigie felt this response was unrealistic, as the danger was too great for Britain to rely on vague threats of its own, and on 22 June, in a long telegram which recalled his previous tirade of 18 June 1939, he implored the Foreign Office to change its East Asian policy in order to ward off any potential for conflict, observing

> I take it for granted that, short of any dishonourable yielding on principle, it is the policy of His Majesty's Government that everything possible should be done to prevent Japan from being drawn into the war on the side of her former Axis partners, but I am doubtful whether this can be achieved without the adoption of some more positive methods than have been adopted hitherto. In wider aspects of policy we have been content to rely on the United States which has favoured a purely negative policy designed so to wear down Japanese resistance that the army in Japan would be deposed from its paramount position. Whatever merit there may have been in this policy before the French collapse it is now certainly ineffective; long before it could produce results the whole face of things in the Far East may be changed by that very army at which the United States seeks to strike with such puny weapons.[5]

Craigie proceeded to espouse a plan to win over Japan, which consisted of the presentation to the Japanese government by Britain and America of a draft understanding that would include the following terms

(a) joint assistance to Japan in bringing about a settlement with the Chinese Government on the basis of Japan's restoration of China's independence and integrity.

(b) Japan formally to undertake to remain neutral in the European War and to respect full territorial integrity not only of the Netherlands East Indies but also of British and French and American possessions in the Pacific so long as the status quo of these territories is preserved.

(c) United States and members of British Commonwealth to give

Japan all financial and economic assistance and facilities in their power both now and during post-war reconstruction period.
(d) Allied Governments to receive full guarantees against re-export to enemy countries.
(e) Question of future settlements and concessions in China to be left in abeyance until the restoration of peace in Europe and China.[6]

This was certainly a radical and wide-ranging series of propositions designed to lay the foundations for a complete post-war settlement rather than merely to buy a temporary understanding. Craigie was, of course, not unaware of the problems arising from such a policy; he stated that he realized that any such proposals would have to be seen as originating from Japan rather than the West in order to avoid the accusation of appeasement, and recognized that this was not a policy which Britain could pursue alone, allowing the Americans to remain on the sidelines raining down criticism. Craigie felt, however, that the only alternative, if the United States was not willing to co-operate, was for Britain to put up a rearguard action in the Far East and hope that war could somehow be avoided; a conclusion which he reiterated three days later after receiving official confirmation from Tani that Japan desired to see the Burma Road closed.[7]

The seriousness of the situation meant that the United States had to be consulted and on 25 June Lothian was asked to enquire if Washington was willing to support Britain militarily should it refuse Japan's demands, and whether, if this was not the case, it would agree to joint Anglo-American mediation of the Sino-Japanese war. The American response was received on 28 June, when Lothian reported that Hull's attitude was that Britain should only give way over the Burma Road under *force majeure* and that no guarantee of support from the United States would be forthcoming. Over the peace issue Hull was equally non-committal, stating that though he did not object to the idea Britain should not expect joint or parallel action by the United States. The implication was clear; once again Britain was to be left to fend for itself in East Asia.[8]

In theory there was another option open to Britain and that was to use the Soviet Union as a counterweight to Japan. Since May, when a decision had been taken to send Sir Stafford Cripps as the new British Ambassador in Moscow, there had been a move in the Foreign Office to try to improve relations with Russia. However, this had from the first been a largely Eurocentric exercise. On 22 May Howe had prepared a brief for Cripps which stated that there was no desire for Anglo-Soviet collaboration in East Asia, since this might only have the result of pushing Chiang Kai-shek even further towards the Soviets and of encouraging the extremists in Japan to outbid Britain for Russia's friendship.[9] This distaste for the Soviet Union still remained in June, despite the seriousness of the crisis Britain faced. When on 24 June the Far Eastern Department was asked to advise on what Cripps should say about East Asia in his forthcoming meeting with Stalin, Ashley Clarke duly noted that the department felt that at this delicate time Cripps should avoid the subject of East Asia altogether; the Soviets would only be antagonized if they heard that Britain was considering mediation, and the merest hint of Anglo-Soviet co-operation would only make Japan more irreconcilable.[10]

One might expect from the above that the Foreign Office, faced with the threat of war in East Asia, with no chance of American support and no desire for Soviet involvement, would agree to Craigie's advice that Britain should comply with Japan's demands. However, this was not the case. Influenced by the views of Clark Kerr and Dr Quo, the Chinese Ambassador in London, the Foreign Office strongly opposed any closure of the Burma Road on the grounds that it would irreparably damage Chinese morale.[11] This was an important consideration, as the consequence could be either to drive China into the hands of the Soviet Union or to force it to make peace with the Japanese on unfavourable terms, thus freeing the IJA to pursue a policy of southern expansion. In addition, there was a danger that, despite the United States' unwillingness to help Britain, the sacrifice of principle involved in closing the Burma Road would alienate American public opinion, with repercussions not only in the Pacific but also in Europe. Another factor was the fear that Craigie might be exaggerating the danger from Japan, as it was believed he had done previously over the Tientsin and, to an extent, the *Asama Maru* crises.

These views were collated in a memorandum which Halifax presented to the War Cabinet on 29 June. The paper argued that Britain should not close the Burma Road, but make only the minimal concession of keeping trade along the road to the 1939 level of 21,965 tons per annum, and that over Hong Kong, it should be pointed out to the Japanese that, as the border was already closed due to the Japanese occupation of the area around Canton, the demand for an end to supplies for China was irrelevant. In addition, it was proposed that as a conciliatory measure the two battalions of troops stationed in Shanghai should be withdrawn and sent to Singapore. Finally, in line with Craigie's suggestion, it was proposed that a comprehensive peace settlement in the Far East should be sought.[12] On 1 July the War Cabinet approved the Foreign Office's recommendations, although New Zealand and Australia had to be consulted before the Japanese could officially be told of the British decision.[13]

Craigie was told of the War Cabinet's decision on 2 July. His response the next day was nothing short of apocalyptic; he warned that the Foreign Office was completely mistaken if it believed that the war in China meant that Japan did not have the resources for hostilities with Britain, and went on that he believed that, if the Japanese request was refused, the chances of war were over 50 per cent, that if war did take place Britain would in essence not be fighting for her own interests but for China's, and that he feared that Germany planned to use the crisis to influence Japan to enter the war against Britain. This was but the first of a barrage of telegrams Craigie was to send to the Foreign Office over the next few days.[14]

These warnings did not impress the Foreign Office, but did have the desired effect on the Chiefs of Staff, who were decidedly uneasy about the way the Far Eastern situation was developing. As early as 25 June, Admiral Godfrey, the Director of Naval Intelligence (DNI), had noted

> It is vital for us not to add the Japanese to our list of enemies. We have got to win this war in Europe and it seems obvious that all we can do in the East is to save what we can of our possessions and prestige and, if it is in any way possible, improve our relations with Japan.[15]

Since this had been written the European situation had deteriorated even further. On 3 July, as Craigie's telegram arrived in London, the Chiefs of Staff were waiting to hear whether the Royal Navy's bombardment of the French fleet at Mers el-Kebir had succeeded. The next day General Dill, the Chief of the Imperial General Staff, noted to his colleagues that 'in the light of events of the past twenty four hours' there was a 'possibility that we might find ourselves at war with France' and that this made it even more imperative for Britain to avoid taking risks in East Asia.[16] The situation was such that already, on 2 July, General Ismay, Churchill's Chief of Staff, had informed the Australian High Commisioner in London, Stanley Bruce, that Britain could not honour its commitment to despatch a fleet to Singapore to protect Australia and New Zealand, an undertaking that Churchill had cynically reiterated as recently as November 1939 in an effort to persuade the antipodean dominions to send forces to Europe.[17]

Against this strategic background the Foreign Office's arguments, dedication to principles and insistence that Britain could not afford to alienate the United States seemed irrelevant and dangerous. In contrast Craigie's proposals seemed to be the voice of common sense, not only because he warned of the potential crisis that could ensue from British intransigence, but also because he offered in his peace plan a potential long-term solution to the East Asian problem. To the overstretched British military such suggestions were very welcome, as it was obvious that the neutralization of East Asia would allow more of Britain's military power to be directed against Germany and Italy.

Influenced by these concerns the Chiefs of Staff prepared on 4 July a memorandum for the War Cabinet in which they outlined their recommendations. It stated plainly that Britain could not possibly risk a war in the Far East at the present time, that there was no fleet available to be sent to Singapore, and that war would mean the diversion of Australian and New Zealand troops to South-East Asia rather than the Middle East, where they were urgently needed to bolster Egypt against Italian attack. It concluded by urging that a peace settlement in the Far East be reached as soon as possible.[18] This memorandum was not greeted with much enthusiasm in the Foreign Office which, seemingly oblivious to the severity of Britain's military position, blamed the cautious line of the Chiefs of Staff on Craigie's unsubstantiated warnings.[19]

BRITISH APPEASEMENT OF JAPAN

In the War Cabinet meeting of 5 July Halifax clung to the idea that Britain should refuse to close the Burma Road and only agree to set a ceiling on the amount of goods. However, this plan for a limited compromise was undermined when Leo Amery, the Secretary of State for India and Burma, dismissed the idea which had been raised at the previous meeting of a strict rationing of supplies as hopelessly impracticable. This left Halifax and Amery supporting a line of no concessions at all over the Burma Road which contrasted sharply with the warnings from Craigie and the Chiefs of Staff. The deadlock was broken by Churchill, who said that he felt the United States ought to take more of the strain in the Far East, but that since it was obvious that this was not going to happen Britain would have to make a unilateral decision, and that he believed that in the present situation 'he did not think that we ought to incur Japanese hostility for reasons mainly of prestige'.[20] The War Cabinet therefore decided that the best policy was to let Craigie try to find a compromise over the Burma Road while gaining time and giving away as little as possible. It was agreed that he was not to surrender any British rights but only to give way under *force majeure*. The limitations on Craigie's freedom of action demonstrated that this was not a decision to accept the 'New Order in East Asia' or to bolster the position of the Japanese 'moderates'; it was instead a temporary measure to allow Britain a breathing space in East Asia and a direct result of the singularly dire strategic position of Britain in July 1940.

The War Cabinet's orders for Craigie to find a compromise reached him on 7 July and he immediately entered into talks with Arita, who showed interest in the British offer of good offices to seek a peace settlement with China but was displeased that Britain still refused to close the Burma Road.[21] On 9 July Craigie reported to the Foreign Office that the situation was still delicate and suggested that Britain should adopt a new negotiating position, in which it would agree to 'suspend the transit of war material through Burma Road for a period of three months (i.e. during rainy season)' in return for a Japanese promise to use this time to pursue a 'just and equitable peace'. Craigie saw many advantages in this proposal: it allowed Britain and the United States to push for a Sino-Japanese settlement; the actual loss of material to China would be negligible, as the Burma Road was largely impassable during the rainy season; and lastly Britain could very well be in a better international position by October and therefore able to resist Japanese demands to extend the agreement.[22]

On 10 July Halifax presented Craigie's proposal to the War Cabinet who, with the added incentive of Australian pressure for a more realistic policy to be pursued in the Far East, decided to approve negotiations on these lines. On 12 July Craigie presented the British terms to Arita who agreed to them in principle. The task then was to tackle details such as which goods were to be stopped, the rights of inspection of the Japanese Consul-General at Rangoon to ensure that Britain was complying fully, and how formally to tie the pursuit of a peace settlement to an agreement about the Burma Road. Over the next few days progress was made on the minutiae of the agreement, but Craigie's work was threatened on 16 July when the Yonai Cabinet fell from power due to the resignation of the Army Minister, General Hata Shunroku. It had been clear for some time that the Japanese government had been losing its grip on power and that the next Cabinet would be considerably more extreme, with Konoe once again as Prime Minister and possibly the fiercely pro-Axis Shiratori

Toshio as Foreign Minister. In such a situation Craigie decided to press for the signing of the agreement as soon as possible in order to avoid the reopening of the issues with a new government. With War Cabinet permission, on 17 July he and Arita signed the Burma Road agreement which banned the transport of war materials including petrol to China until 18 October.[23]

News of the agreement was greeted abroad with cries of dismay that the British Government had appeased Japan; criticism being particularly strong in China and the United States. In the former displeasure was chiefly directed at the peace initiative and it was widely held that the Burma Road had been closed to bring pressure on Chungking to make peace. This was ironic, because as Sterndale Bennett, the new head of the Far Eastern Department, noted, this part of the agreement had only been added to make Britain's surrender more palatable to outside opinion.[24] In Washington Hull's reaction to the agreement was to declare that the closure of the Burma Road and the Hong Kong border constituted 'unwarranted interpositions of obstacles to world trade', although he later declared that this criticism was directed against Japan for putting pressure on Britain. This comment was not well received in British official circles who knew that an important motive behind the agreement with Japan had been the lack of American support.[25] In addition, Hull did not endear himself when he remarked to Lothian on 15 July that, as the Burma Road would now be closed, it would be a good idea if the Foreign Office tried to persuade the Soviets to increase their aid to China in order to maintain pressure on Japan. This suggestion was met with some bemusement in London where it was an article of faith that any attempt to influence Soviet policy in East Asia was doomed to failure.[26]

This image of American inaction was soon, however, to change. On 19 July Lothian reported that he had met with three of Roosevelt's Cabinet, Treasury Secretary Henry Morgenthau, Army Secretary Henry Stimson and Navy Secretary Frank Knox, and had been told that they were considering the idea of introducing a ban on the export of American oil as a means of putting pressure on Japan and would be pleased to see Britain and Holland introduce similar restrictions.[27] In Whitehall this proposal was met with some trepidation for, although the American desire to take a tough line was welcome, there was still no evidence that the United States would be willing to step in militarily should such a provocative measure cause Japan to launch an offensive against the Dutch East Indies. Even Churchill, who sometimes exasperated the Foreign Office with his willingness to pander to Roosevelt's whims, recognized that this American plan was potentially dangerous. Luckily Lothian did not have to communicate these British doubts as, before the official British response arrived, Morgenthau was outwitted by the State Department and forced to accept only the introduction of licensing for exports of high-octane aviation fuels and high-quality scrap metal.[28] This was a cautious but significant move; the United States was beginning to stir itself from its lethargy.

A TIME FOR REFLECTION

Opposition in Whitehall to any precipitous initiatives was largely the result of continuing fears about Britain's military weakness in South-East Asia. In late July the Chiefs of Staff used the temporary calm in South-East Asia to consider a Far Eastern Appreciation drawn up by the JPC, which made clear the desperate plight facing British possessions in the region. It noted that, in the light of the present situation in Europe, it was extremely unlikely that a fleet could be sent to Singapore if war was imminent, that the defences in Malaya were woefully inadequate and that the situation could only be improved by reinforcement with substantial quantities of aircraft and men. It further observed that until such reinforcement had taken place Britain was in no position to resist Japanese encroachments into Thailand, French Indo-China or the Dutch East Indies.[29] This was a disquieting picture and made it clear that caution was the best option.

The report also raised a dilemma that was to trouble British strategic thinking until December 1941, which was what should Britain do if Japan attacked the Dutch East Indies, considering that Holland was already an ally in the fight against Hitler. To virtually all ministries, and initially to Churchill himself, it seemed axiomatic that Britain should give a guarantee of support to the authorities in Batavia, but the Admiralty were adamant that since Britain could do nothing to save the East Indies from capture by Japan it would be giving a hostage to fortune to give any definite commitment to the Dutch. The position of the Admiralty was reinforced by fears that the Dutch forces harboured Nazi sympathizers and that joint planning could therefore lead to British plans entering the wrong hands. After some discussion Churchill came to accept the Admiralty's argument and no guarantee of support was given to the Dutch East Indies. Nothing could more clearly have demonstrated Britain's weakness.[30]

In addition to dealing with the military issues arising from Japanese ambitions in South-East Asia, the Chiefs of Staff noted in their final report on 5 August that the paucity of British resources in the region made it essential for an effort to be made to achieve a general settlement in East Asia in line with the terms of the Burma Road agreement. This was a logical suggestion from their point of view, but the issue of a peace settlement was one which did not offer any easy answers. Before Craigie and Arita had signed the agreement over the Burma Road many British officials, including Lothian and even Clark Kerr, had displayed an interest in the idea.[31] On 14 July Craigie had, as a reaction to this, expanded on his original proposals. He began by stating his belief that a generous peace for China could only be achieved if the West was willing to make concessions to Japan. He then outlined what he saw as the grievances which Japan would raise in any general talks on East Asia, including the rejection of the racial equality clause in the League of Nations Covenant, the United States Immigration Act of 1924, the imperial preference policy decided at the Ottawa Conference of 1932, and the general refusal of credits to Japan. He declared that the most important initiative the West could take was to make trade concessions, particularly in the area of access to raw materials, which he held to be more vital to Japan than territorial aggrandizement. Again Craigie stressed that if there was to be any meaningful progress over these issues then it was vitally necessary for the Foreign Office to get in touch directly with the Americans so that joint proposals could be drawn up.[32]

By the time this telegram came to be considered opinion within the Foreign Office had begun to change. The fact that an agreement had been signed with Japan ending tension, albeit temporarily, over the Burma Road meant that for many observers the need for a wider peace had vanished. On 20 July Churchill noted to Halifax

> Don't you think we might go very slow on all this general and equitable, fair and honourable peace business between China and Japan? Chiang does not want it: none of the pro-Chinese want it: and so far from helping us round the Burma Road difficulty it will only make it worse. I am sure that it is not in our interest that the Japanese should be relieved of their preoccupation. Would it not be a good thing to give it a miss for a month or so and see what happens.[33]

The Far Eastern Department's reaction to Craigie's proposals was very similar, as they believed that discussion of peace terms would only inflame American indignation at Britain's lack of principles and also make any improvement of relations with the Soviet Union more difficult. However, this inactivity and the unwillingness to approach

Washington was not appreciated by Butler who, taking completely the opposite tack, believed that an East Asian peace settlement was essential if Britain was to avoid war with Japan. On 23 July Butler ordered work to begin on a draft peace proposal and when faced with further stalling by the Far Eastern Department noted in exasperation that 'we may well go to the grave chanting that we must be polite to the Americans, but we shan't save our civilization like this'.[34]

Under this pressure the Department finally put its views on paper and on 10 August sent a letter and memorandum based on Craigie's views to related government departments in order to elicit their attitudes to a peace settlement.[35] The memorandum noted the danger that an incident in China could lead to an Anglo-Japanese war and that therefore Britain ought to consider what type of settlement it would like to sponsor and what concessions it could make to meet Japan's desires. The answers to the Department's paper and Craigie's suggestions were not enthusiastic. The Dominions Office explained that Australia and New Zealand would never agree to concessions over immigration and the Colonial Office stated that an influx of cheap exports from Japan would only succeed in damaging the fragile economies of the colonies.[36] The Board of Trade and the MEW pointed out, as they had done on previous occasions, that to make any trade concessions to Japan would only result in the diversion of resources away from Britain, which would damage the war effort against Germany with no guarantee that Japan would be pacified, and that Japan might be encouraged to undertake further foreign adventures. In addition, the MEW attacked the very idea that the cessation of the Sino-Japanese war would benefit Britain.[37] Craigie's peace initiative thus failed to make any headway, but it was not only opposition within Whitehall that hindered it; it was also compromised by the continuing crisis in Anglo-Japanese relations.

SECOND CRISIS AND A CHANGE OF POLICY

The chances that Japan would collaborate in a general peace for East Asia had been fairly slim even under the Yonai administration, but the appearance of the Konoe Cabinet on 22 July with General Tōjō Hideki as Army Minister and Matsuoka Yōsuke as Foreign Minister made any co-operation even less likely; the only comfort that Britain could take was that at least Shiratori had not been appointed to head the Gaimushō. The choice of Matsuoka was ambiguous; he had led the walkout of the Japanese delegation from the League of Nations Assembly in February 1933 and been Chairman of the South

Manchurian Railway, was an ardent nationalist and, it was assumed, would pursue only policies that reflected Japan's self-interest. Shigemitsu, who was a close acquaintance of Matsuoka, was encouraged by his appointment, and Butler on 19 July reported the Ambassador as stating that

> M. Matsuoka would be a very good Minister for Foreign Affairs. He, Shigemitsu, was closer to M. Matsuoka than any other member of the Japanese Foreign Office, and had worked with him in the past. Japan's new Minister for Foreign Affairs had the advantage of appreciating the economic importance of the United States of America and Great Britain to Japan.[38]

However, a series of Japanese actions in late July and August soon showed that Shigemitsu's hopes were misplaced. Within days of taking power the Konoe government demonstrated its determination to introduce a more assertive foreign policy. On 1 August Matsuoka announced in a press release Japan's intention to set up a Greater East Asian Co-prosperity Sphere which would include the Netherlands East Indies and French Indo-China. At the same time rumours abounded that the Japanese were planning an economic mission to Batavia to press the Dutch into further concessions over commodity quotas for Japan. In Indo-China the pressure was even more palpable; the French Governor-General, Admiral Jean Decoux, had already agreed on 20 June to close the border with China, but in early August the stakes were raised when Japan demanded free passage for her troops through Tonkin province and the use of air-bases around Hanoi.[39]

In Anglo-Japanese relations the lull before the storm was extremely short. On 27 July a British subject was arrested for spying, another seven being detained the following day. By 1 August fourteen Britons, all well-respected members of the British community, were in custody; some even held the position of Honorary Consul for other countries such as Sweden and Greece. The orders for these arrests originated with the Military Police, the *Kempeitai*, and may have been directed at curtailing the activities of the SIS harbour-watchers who reported on the movements of Japanese and German shipping.[40] The situation was made worse on 29 July with the news that the first man to be arrested, Melville Cox, who had replaced Captain Malcolm Kennedy as Reuters's correspondent in Tokyo, had fallen to his death from a third-floor window while in custody. The first reaction was to suspect foul play, but although it soon became clear that Cox had committed suicide it was certain that this had been brought about by the terrible conditions in which he had been kept and the incessant questioning to which he had been subjected. The situation caused Kennedy, who by this stage was working at the GCCS's wartime site at Bletchley Park, to note in his diary on 29 July that he was very lucky not to have been in Japan himself and to reflect that

> Whether or not he (Cox) and the others are guilty, the fact 10 have been arrested and other arrests are threatened wd. seem to indicate that Japan is either making, or considering, plans for action against this country and is therefore taking precautionary measures to prevent well-informed Englishmen from passing on information.[41]

The outrage felt in Britain at the arrests was even more intense than that over the Burma Road issue because, as in the case of the Tientsin crisis, the incident involved the welfare of British nationals overseas, always a sensitive subject for the general public. In addition, the calls for a tough British response were influenced by the fact that this crisis followed so shortly after Britain had appeased Japan in the hope of achieving an easing of tensions and that the concessions had been shown to be worthless. The result was that the arrests forced Britain to conclude that the policy of conciliation towards Japan had run its course.

The significance of the arrests can be seen in that they did not simply influence opinion in London but also deeply affected Craigie, who was outraged by events which he saw as a deliberate attempt to intimidate Britain, an impression reinforced by information from a secret source that the arrests had been ordered by General Tōjō.[42] Craigie's initial reaction was to insist on 30 July that no attempt be made to settle the dispute by negotiation but that Britain should prepare to take reprisals; such as the progressive detention of Japanese in Britain, India and the South-East Asian colonies, the ending of all negotiations in progress, and economic reprisals. This change of attitude on Craigie's part came as a welcome sign to the Foreign Office and directly influenced the War Cabinet's decision on 1 August to arrest in retaliation ten Japanese subjects who were already under suspicion of spying.[43]

Craigie's advice led to a fundamental reassessment of British policy. The first issue raised was that of the remaining British garrisons in China. This matter had been left in abeyance during the latter half of the debate over the Burma Road as there was no desire for Britain to make too many concessions. The arrests caused the issue to be reopened and on 6 August the War Cabinet decided to withdraw the troops.[44] More important was the question whether economic reprisals should be taken against Japan. On 14 August an interdepartmental meeting was held at the Foreign Office to discuss the introduction of unobtrusive measures and a letter was then sent to each department asking them to draw up their own suggestions.[45] During this interval it was also deemed necessary to consult Craigie about this issue and on 14 August a telegram was sent to Tokyo which starkly set out the options open to Britain

> If . . . Japan is now determined to embark upon her programme of southward expansion . . . then it seems that we are faced with two alternatives: either to stand idly by and watch the situation deteriorate until we ourselves are in serious danger, or to adopt some sort of reprisals short of war which would retard the pace of Japan's advance and so gain valuable time. In the latter event our object would be to try to convince Japan by example that aggression does not pay, and that, though she may gain control of territories, the resultant loss of goodwill . . . will, on balance, only increase her economic difficulties even if it improves her strategic position.[46]

It then asked Craigie whether he believed Japan could sustain total war without the benefit of its extra-East Asian trade and whether it was willing, in order to gain control over Indo-China and the Dutch East Indies, to run the risk of a temporary loss of trade with those colonies.

Craigie's response to this enquiry was very carefully balanced. His position, once the initial furore over the arrests had died down, was that Britain had to discontinue its policy of conciliation but at the same time not move into a position of outright hostility. This meant that he approved of a tough stand over current negotiations and agreements, but deprecated the idea of severe economic sanctions which he held would only lead to war. Craigie's opposition to an excessively coercive policy was influenced not merely by his conviction that Japan would react violently to economic sanctions, but also by his belief that the wave of extreme nationalism sweeping Japan was due only to the momentarily enthralling prospects offered by the power vacuum in South-East Asia, that this phase would pass once Britain had shown that it could stand up to Germany, and that the 'moderates' would then reassert their influence.[47]

Craigie's advice was heeded during August and no moves were made to put pressure on Japan apart from the retaliatory arrests and the refusal to allow the Japanese ship *Nagara Maru* to carry a consignment of Italian mercury to Japan.[48] There was, however,

one issue that required immediate attention, and that was to decide
whether or not Britain should continue with the Burma Road agreement. There was in late August a general consensus in London that,
as Japan had not honoured their part of the deal, Britain should
reopen the Burma Road on 18 October, but that this should be done
without any fanfares so that Japan would not have any grounds for
taking retaliatory action. It was also agreed that in the interim
British defences should be improved and efforts be made to ensure
American support so that a reasonable deterrent to Japanese retaliation existed. In Tokyo Craigie had come to the same conclusion and
on 30 August he recommended that the Burma Road should be
reopened when the agreement expired. Craigie's approval for the
reopening of the Burma Road was greeted with satisfaction, and
was referred to in a Foreign Office memorandum to the War Cabinet
on 2 September which outlined the case for reopening and led to a
decision to prepare the climate for a safe abrogation of the Burma
Road agreement.[49]

AMERICA FLEXES ITS MUSCLES

The prospect of reopening the Burma Road was made far easier by
the appearance of a tougher American stance towards the 'aggressor'
nations and a greater willingness to co-operate with Britain. The latter
was evident in late August when an American military delegation
arrived in London for secret talks, nominally on arms standardization.
In practice the conversations ranged further and on 31 August
Brigadier-General Strong, the leading American army representative,
offered to exchange intelligence information about Japan with
Britain, informing his British counterparts that American crypt-
ologists had broken the Japanese diplomatic code.[50] While this
boded well for the future, a move of even greater significance
occurred on 3 September when the Destroyer for Bases agreement
was signed, an action which symbolized Washington's determination
to support Britain in its fight against Nazi tyranny. In addition, by
mid-September Cordell Hull was talking of further sanctions against
Japan and of a joint declaration with Britain, Australia, New Zealand
and Holland to uphold the *status quo* south of the Equator. This new
American drive towards co-operation reversed one of the key factors
that had forced Britain to sign the Burma Road agreement in the first
place and suggested that a decision to reopen could be taken without
too great a concern about Japanese retaliation.[51]

To some, such as Vansittart and Craigie, the American attitude towards Japan seemed excessive, as it could all too easily lead to a confrontation which would divert the resources of the United States away from the main enemy, Nazi Germany. Churchill, however, held a different view, believing that any American move away from isolationism was to Britain's advantage, and when in a telegram Craigie opined that it was only 'likely' that Britain would enter an American–Japanese war, the Prime Minister sent a sharp note to Halifax stating

> This shows the very serious misconception which has grown in Sir R. Craigie's mind about the consequences of the United States entering the war. He should surely be told forthwith that the entry of the United States into war either with Germany and Italy or with Japan is fully compatible with British interests.
>
> That nothing in the munitions sphere can compare with the importance of the British Empire and the United States being co-belligerent, that if Japan attacked the United States without declaring war on us we should at once range ourselves at the side of the United States and declare war upon Japan.[52]

This was a significant message, as it indicated quite clearly that Churchill had begun to see the problems in the Pacific as a possible back door for American entry into the war in Europe. All Britain had to do to encourage this tendency was to follow the American lead.

The need for a tough American stance was also shown by a series of events in September which demonstrated that Japan was still seeking to expand its influence in South-East Asia and that it was veering ever closer to the Axis Powers. On 11 September it was officially announced that an economic mission led by Kobayashi Ichizō, the Minister for Commerce and Industry, had been sent to Batavia to discuss closer economic relations with the Dutch. At the same time Japanese pressure on France to allow Japan military bases in Tonkin continued to mount. On 19 September the continuing intransigence of Admiral Decoux led his opposite number, General Nishihara, to issue an ultimatum that Vichy either accept Japan's terms or face war. On 22 September Decoux finally capitulated and signed an agreement to allow 25,000 troops free passage into Tonkin province and four air-bases to be allocated for use by the Japanese.[53] This act of intimidation led the United States to announce on 26 September its intention to expand the embargo on goods to Japan by banning the export of all scrap metal and of all petroleum that could be processed into aviation fuel.[54]

Within Britain the new wave of Japanese expansionism led to the end of the investigation by the Foreign Office into the possibility of an East Asian peace settlement. On 18 September Butler minuted that there was no point presenting a British plan for peace while the new Konoe government remained so bellicose. Despite this, on 25 September John Sterndale Bennett, the new head of the Far Eastern Department, did produce a document encapsulating the views of the interested government departments. The memorandum observed that not only was it difficult because of their activities in South-East Asia to offer Japan favourable concessions at the present time, but that, as long as the war with Germany was in progress, it was hard to see what Britain could do to alleviate Japan's position without damaging its own war effort. The paper did not end there, for it also noted that for the long term the opposition within the dominions to Japanese immigration, the impracticability of dismantling imperial preference solely for the benefit of Japan, and the impossibility of giving any cast-iron guarantee of Japanese access to raw materials meant that it was difficult to see how Japan in its present aggressive state could be satisfied. In describing this predicament Sterndale Bennett wrote

> The pressure of events may conceivably bring about the downfall of the military party and a return to the wiser policy of economic expansion by conciliation and negotiation. But so long as Japan believes she can attain strategic and economic security by force or threat of force, she is unlikely to be satisfied with offers which will only partly meet her requirements. To employ a metaphor, she believes she can found a company ('The New Order in Greater East Asia'). We on the other hand are only prepared at the very utmost to offer her a few more shares in a company already existing.[55]

This was a revealing comment, for while it was obvious that Britain would not wish to make concessions in the face of Japanese aggression it suggested that the former had precious little to offer even if Japan were to become more conciliatory. And if the *status quo* power was not prepared to work for equality of opportunity Japan had just as much to gain from unilateral expansionism as it did from multilateral negotiations, if not more.

BRITAIN AND ECONOMIC SANCTIONS AGAINST JAPAN

On 27 September before the Foreign Office had had time to mull over the significance of the American sanctions, news arrived that a

Tripartite Pact between Germany, Italy and Japan had been signed in Berlin. The Pact, which pledged that each signatory would go to war if either of the other parties was involved in a conflict with a third power, was obviously aimed at the United States and designed to deter Washington from entering either the European or East Asian conflicts by threatening America with a war on two fronts.[56] As far as Britain was concerned it meant that Japan was now allied to a power which was raining bombs on London; nothing could have proved more convincingly that appeasement of Japan had become pointless.

The signing of the Tripartite Pact was the culmination of the series of crises in Anglo-Japanese relations which had begun on 11 June. There was now patently no reason for Britain not to reopen the Burma Road and on 3 October the War Cabinet decided, as a means of expressing Britain's displeasure, to announce earlier than necessary the decision not to renew the Burma Road agreement. On 8 October Parliament was informed that the road would open in ten days' time.[57] However, the fact that Japan had so obviously tied itself to the enemy camp demanded sterner action than a mere repudiation of this agreement, and continued evidence of Washington's new-found will, including a proposal from Hull on 30 September that Britain and the United States should begin staff talks, provided inspiration for the introduction of a new tough policy.[58]

While waiting for military co-operation with the United States to begin, the most obvious means of retaliation against Japan was to increase the restrictions on trade, which also had the advantage that it would keep Britain in step with Washington. By September the review of sanctions policy begun by the interdepartmental meeting on 14 August had been completed. The most extreme response had come from the MEW which on 5 September recorded that it had always disliked the Foreign Office's leniency towards the Japanese, that it had reluctantly agreed to follow this lead for political reasons, but that now those motives had gone

> it would do little harm to adopt a stiffer attitude towards Japanese requests wherever the merits of the case justify it. We would suggest that henceforward we should treat each case on its own merits, and not attempt to give the Japanese unduly favourable treatment for political reasons.[59]

This view was supported by the Treasury which in its letter to the Foreign Office on 25 September called for action against Japanese exports as a way of hindering Japan from accumulating sterling.[60] However, opinion on the utility of sanctions was not universally in favour. The Board of Trade felt that it was possible to be overoptimistic about their possible effect. On 15 August Richard Pares of the Commercial Relations and Treaty Department minuted in the wake of the interdepartmental meeting the day before

> It is not very easy to see what the Foreign Office have in mind . . . . Apparently they hold the theory that it would be possible to devise a certain type of pin-pricking policy which the Japanese extremists would recognize as a sign that our resistance to their advance was stiffening, without either being able to put a finger on any positive act of injustice on our part or being goaded to regard us as committing acts of hostility, and so to declare war against us. I do not believe such a policy could exist in practice – we should be sure to do too much or not enough. [61]

While obviously in line with the Board of Trade's traditional dislike of sanctions, this was a prescient statement and hit on a very important problem that Britain was to face over the next few months, namely, what level of sanctions was appropriate if the motive was deterrence rather than outright dislocation of Japan and at what point would restrictions become provocations. The feeling in the Board of Trade, for Pares' minute was approved by his seniors, was that caution was the bèst course of action, but in this they were to be virtually a lone voice. [62]

Faced with a virtually united call for action Cadogan decided that a new interdepartmental meeting was necessary. Sterndale Bennett pointed out, however, that the chaos engendered by the crises in July and August showed that it was essential for a more formal body to be established to oversee and co-ordinate British policy towards East Asia. [63] The result was that on 2 October the War Cabinet approved a proposal from Halifax for the establishment of a Far Eastern Committee (FEC) to be chaired by Butler. In proposing the establishment of this Committee Halifax noted that its policy should be based on the idea that 'in the near future there might be several ways in which we should be able to cause inconvenience to the Japanese without ceasing to be polite'. [64] This clearly set down the parameters of British policy; the aim was to deter so that a war in the East could be avoided, rather than to force a confrontation. The result was that discussion of economic sanctions rested not on the need to bring Japan to its knees, but instead, as Butler put it later in a report for the War Cabinet, to have 'the double object of preventing the Japanese from assisting our present enemies and from building up stocks themselves'.[65] On 5 October the FEC held its first meeting and began to consider what measures should be introduced.

By the beginning of October Britain had thus come a long way from the surrender it had meekly been forced to accept in July. The obvious failure of the Burma Road agreement and the marked shift in the attitude of the United States meant that by the early autumn British policy had substantially changed. There was a new confidence in Whitehall that Britain could now afford to call Japan's bluff and a consensus existed that Japan could only be deterred if Britain remained resolute. The remarkable fact about the development of this new line was that, for virtually the first time since June 1937, there was a consensus amongst the most influential departments over which approach to take. Renouncing the idea he had espoused since September 1939 that compromise was essential to keep Japan out of the European war, even Craigie was willing to accept this policy of resistance. He noted in a telegram to the Foreign Office on 11 October that

> The pro-British faction has been driven still further to ground by the recent espionage campaign against the British community and is now powerless to exert any influence whatsoever. Japanese foreign policy will continue to be dominated by the extremists until such a time as the Axis powers meet with a decisive reverse in Europe or until the peril of an unwanted war with the United States becomes so great that a decisive change in popular opinion begins to make itself felt.[66]

However, this newfound strength had shallow roots, Britain could only afford to be tough with Japan if, first, the United States stood firmly by its side, and second, it could reinforce its own military position in Malaya and Singapore, and there was no guarantee that these conditions could be met. In addition, if the aim was to avoid war the new policy had to be flexible and responsive to changes within Japan. The danger with the nature of the Burma Road crisis was that it seemingly taught the lesson that Japan was irreconcilable, so that there was never to be any point in negotiating. That was an unfortunate conclusion and in 1941 would contribute to the opening of hostilities.

7 Confrontation
October 1940 to June 1941

It is tempting to portray the fourteen months from the reopening of the Burma Road to the start of hostilities in the Pacific as a period of close co-operation between Britain and the United States to contain the threat of Japanese expansionism. However, any such impression would be largely false; it was in reality not until the spring of 1941 that the Anglo-Saxon partners began to forge a joint policy of sorts and even then there was no guarantee of American involvement should an Anglo-Japanese war break out. This meant that the period between October 1940 and June 1941 remained one of acute concern in Whitehall about East Asia, since Washington continued to lag behind while Britain turned its back on conciliation and started to construct a policy of deterrence. This was a dangerous policy for Britain to pursue, but the Burma Road crisis and the signing of the Tripartite Pact had shown that there was precious little choice: if war with Japan were to be avoided the only possible policy was to walk the tightrope of deterring Tokyo from a further southern advance while not acting so harshly as simply to provoke such an offensive.

These months therefore saw the introduction of limited sanctions against Japan, the use of propaganda to undermine its confidence and encourage divisions with Germany, and a slow increase in British forces in the region. All of this was done in the belief that the United States would eventually catch up and that it would then, as the senior partner, ensure that the policy of deterrence that Britain had begun would become a firm barrier against Japanese aggression. There were, however, two problems with this approach. First, there was a dangerous underestimation in Whitehall and Malaya of the likelihood of a Japanese attack and a belief that, if they did attack, it would pose a nuisance rather than a direct threat to the Empire, which led to a naïve belief that only a bare modicum of military force was needed to keep the Japanese at bay. Second, there was an inadequate understanding of the effect of sanctions on Japan, where the increasing restrictions on access to raw materials only strengthened the insistence of the IJA and the IJN that expansion in South-East Asia was necessary for the survival of the Japanese Empire. The result was that British, and later American, policy, only served to encourage Japan to become more reckless.

THE MIRAGE OF ANGLO-AMERICAN CO-OPERATION

The immediate task facing Britain in October 1940 was how to take advantage of the new co-operative trend in American policy. In terms of sanctions, this meant constructing a programme of economic restrictions which could be co-ordinated with Washington. On 11 October the FEC's Sub-Committee on Economic Matters met to consider a MEW memorandum which recommended that, in the light of the Tripartite Pact, Japan should be defined as a 'dangerous destination' and that therefore exports to that country should be limited to normal trade levels, that a gradual restriction of sales of strategic materials should be introduced and that an embargo be placed on the export of key commodities. The Sub-Committee decided to accept these proposals and to define normal trade as consisting of 75 per cent of the 1939 figures, but in so doing emphasized the need for an integrated policy of restrictions against Japan which could be uniformly applied throughout the Empire rather than following what were perceived as the haphazard methods used by the United States. On 18 October the full FEC agreed to this policy and decided that the dominions and India should be asked to follow suit. A telegram was sent the next day to Lothian instructing him to inform the State Department of the British decision, to state the desirability of American introduction of a similar programme, and to ask whether it would be possible to hold talks over collaboration in this field.[1]

The American reaction to this overture was disappointing; on 23 October Nevile Butler, the Counsellor at the Washington Embassy, reported that the State Department, although welcoming the tightening of British restrictions, felt that formal talks could not take place until after the Presidential election in November.[2] This apparent retreat from the forward policy that had been espoused in late September was also evident in the sphere of defence. Hull had already on 9 October informed Lothian that staff talks could not be held until after the election, and this was followed by a marked reluctance on the American part to discuss the British idea that a

USN squadron should visit Singapore to display Anglo-Saxon solidarity.[3] The result was that the autumn of 1940 saw only slow progress towards Anglo-American co-operation rather than the rapid pace preferred by Britain.

Despite this setback, Britain continued with its policy of introducing further economic measures against Japan, and by 28 November the FEC was able to note that India and all the dominions, bar Australia, were coming into line with British licensing policy, that iron and steel scrap exports had been stopped and that supplies of Indian manganese to Japan had been drastically reduced.[4] However, British activity did not just rest on embargoing vital exports from the Empire to Japan; it also saw action in other fields. In particular, efforts were made to co-ordinate restrictions with the Dutch on the grounds that there was little point in the Straits Settlements curtailing its exports of rubber and tin to Japan if the Japanese were simply able to replace these materials with imports from the Dutch East Indies. In fact it was the Dutch who made the first move in this field. On 31 October Hubertus Van Mook, the Director of Economic Policy in Batavia, informed the Dutch Colonial Ministry in London that, as it appeared that Japan had gained control over Indo-China's rubber crop and could therefore afford to re-export substantial supplies of the commodity to Germany, it was vital for the East Indies and the Straits to co-ordinate their quota policies. This proposal won the approval of both the Foreign Office and the MEW and on 27 November the Anglo-Netherlands Committee on Economic Affairs held its first meeting and officially agreed on the need to draw up a joint policy.[5]

Another area of interest in the battle to curb Japan's imports and its re-exports to Germany was South America. Evidence began to reach the MEW in October and November that Japan's purchases of commodities from this region had markedly increased, with a special emphasis on Brazilian castor oil and rubber, Chilean copper and iodine, Peruvian cotton and molybdenum, and Bolivian wolfram. There was naturally a suspicion in Whitehall that these goods were predominantly destined for re-export to Germany, which was desperate for these commodities, and it was therefore considered essential for Britain to take action.[6] One possible tactic was to engage in pre-emptive buying and this was the method chosen to deal with the Chilean iodine problem; Britain agreed to pay £60,000 to Chile for the iodine and then persuaded Santiago to stop exports to 'dangerous destinations' for the next six months.[7] Another British device was to increase the number of interceptions of Japanese merchant ships under the contraband control system. During

December at least two Japanese ships, the *Kanto Maru* and the *Ana Maru*, were stopped at Cape Town and commodities such as casein, rutile, bort and mica were impounded.[8]

The lack of American co-operation was, however, a severe drawback because, although Britain could afford to seize Japanese cargoes travelling via the Cape, it could not set up contraband control in the Caribbean or the eastern Pacific for fear of offending American sensibilities, and this was the route taken by the merchant ships carrying the most important of the commodities, the rubber from Brazil. Also, if increasing importance were to be given to pre-emptive buying then it was obvious that the United States was far better placed financially than Britain, but Washington showed a marked reluctance to act. This, added to the fact that the United States still lagged behind Britain in the range of goods put under licence, meant that the British restrictions on Japan could only have a limited effect. In a FEC report to the War Cabinet on 17 December, which described current American policy as an 'improvisation', Butler noted on the subject of British sanctions

> The screw will have to be applied, more or less firmly, in proportion as the Japanese control their wayward tendencies, or as our hand grows stronger in Europe and the Middle East, or as the United States Administration interests itself more in the Far East.[9]

Even so Britain had come a long way since October 1940.

Defence was another area in which Britain continued to plan for the future, in the hope of eventual American co-operation. In October it was decided to establish a unified command in the East under Air Chief Marshal Sir Robert Brooke-Popham who was appointed Commander-in-Chief Far East. Meanwhile in Singapore an Anglo-Australian conference made progress on the preparation of British defences and recommended an increase in the number of battalions in Malaya from seventeen to twenty-six, stressing too the need for more aircraft. This was, however, a fairly piecemeal approach which failed to satisfy the Foreign Office, who were concerned that Britain's continuing military weakness was acting as a spur to Japanese expansionism. Prompted by Butler, Halifax wrote on 23 November to the First Lord of the Admiralty, A.V. Alexander, urging him to send a naval squadron to Singapore. This plea met with some sympathy, but Alexander was forced to point out that, despite the recent British success over the Italian fleet at Taranto, the Royal Navy was so overstretched that it could not afford to send out any forces to the East, and noted that the only 'real deterrent to Japanese aggression in the Far East' was 'the willing and open co-operation of the United States'.[10]

This view had the general support of Churchill and the Chiefs of Staff, who saw the Pacific and East Asia as an American responsibility. The Prime Minister in particular was convinced that to send reinforcements to Malaya to defend it against a potential enemy, Japan, rather than use those forces against actual enemies, Germany and Italy, was a dangerous indulgence. Underpinning this attitude was the fact that Churchill was much more sanguine than his subordinates about the chances of deterring Japan and even played down the possible effect of conflict if it should break out. On 22 November in a note to Alexander he observed

> Should Japan enter the war on one side and the United States on ours, ample naval forces will be available to contain Japan by long-range controls in the Pacific. The Japanese Navy is not likely to venture far from its home bases so long as a superior fleet is maintained at Singapore or Honolulu. The Japanese would never attempt a siege of Singapore with a hostile, superior American fleet in the Pacific.[11]

The corollary of this was that he felt that the Japanese knew they could not win such a war and would therefore not attack.

THE SOVIET UNION AND CHINA

The failure of Washington to live up to the promise of September 1940 was not the only problem that Britain faced in East Asia at this time, for events in the region were moving apace. One particularly disturbing development was that it appeared that the strengthening of German–Japanese ties might lead the Russians to pursue a more conciliatory line towards the Japanese. There were two possible ramifications to such a policy. First, Russia might curtail its supplies of munitions to China, which would have serious implications for the latter's ability to resist the Japanese; second, that the Soviet Union might sign a non-aggression pact with Japan, which would lower tensions along the Soviet–Manchukuo border and free Japan to pursue expansion in the south. These were both frightening prospects for Britain and in the period immediately following the signing of the Tripartite Pact, while rumours abounded that Soviet supplies to China were dwindling, an effort was made to persuade Moscow to stand firm in its East Asian policy.

The Soviet response was distinctly chilly. On 4 October Cripps met with Molotov only to be told by the latter that the Tripartite Pact did not change anything and would not lead to any shift in Soviet policy. Cripps felt, however, that beneath this veneer the Soviets were in reality considerably alarmed by their predicament, and, after hearing gossip among the diplomatic corps in Moscow that a Soviet–Japanese pact was in the offing, he affirmed to London his belief that only a concerted effort to win Russia's confidence could prevent its conclusion.[12] With the Foreign Office's approval and with an eye also on European issues, Cripps on 22 October tackled Molotov's deputy Vyshinsky on the subject of Japan, and warned him of the dangers that might arise from a Chinese collapse. He also sought to demonstrate Britain's desire for co-operation in East Asia and Europe by offering *de facto* recognition of Russian sovereignty over the Baltic States, an offer that went beyond his Foreign Office instructions. Vyshinsky's reaction was, however, typically dismissive; he rejected the idea that a Soviet pact with Japan was imminent and took little notice of Cripps's attempted bribe.[13] It thus became obvious that there was no prospect of influencing Russia – a situation that was not helped by the failure to establish fuller co-operation between Britain and the United States – and this underlined the need for Britain to take a tougher stand in South-East Asia in an effort to ward off further Japanese penetration.

The uncertainty over the Soviet attitude had other repercussions. On 19 October Chiang Kai-shek, citing his fear of an end to Russian support, pressed Clark Kerr for greater British assistance and, specifically, for staff talks to establish a common defence against Japanese aggression; on 4 November he went even further and openly asked for a Chinese–American–British alliance, a new loan of £200–300 million and the supply of a thousand planes per annum. These requests were described by Chiang as essential if Chinese resistance were to continue into 1941, and in support of his argument he again noted the unreliability of the Soviets and pointed to his concern that China's deteriorating economic position was allowing the CCP to increase its support.[14] It was recognized in London that this was one of Chiang's habitual attempts to squeeze more support from Britain, but the very real danger that Moscow might stop its arms supplies and withdraw its advisers made the situation more serious than usual. In addition, Chiang found an unwitting ally in the shape of Ribbentrop, who in mid-November, in the wake of Molotov's visit to Berlin, warned the Chinese Ambassador that China was faced with its last chance to make peace with Japan; a threat that was promptly brought to Britain's notice.[15]

In London, China's plight and the possible cessation of Soviet support led to a belief that Britain had to do more to assist, and a number of initiatives were set in motion. The most significant was that on 10 December it was announced that a loan of £10 million was to be given to China. In addition, it was decided to despatch Brigadier Dennys, formerly of MI2, to Chungking as the new Military Attaché with authority to discuss possible collaboration should Britain find itself at war with Japan, and to allow the Chinese to relocate the Loiwing aircraft factory to India.[16] Although these two measures were kept secret, the change in British policy was marked, and in part can be explained by reference to similar measures of support for China from the United States; Washington was clearly supposed to be impressed by Britain's largesse. There were though strict limits to how far Britain was prepared to go: on 9 December, when Clark Kerr was told about the decision to provide a loan, he was also informed that Chiang's proposal for an alliance had been rejected on the grounds that

> An alliance without the participation of the United States scarcely seems likely to offer political advantages commensurate with the disadvantage that it might simply furnish Japan with a pretext for further aggression. This would not serve our interests in view of our commitments in the struggle in Europe.[17]

Britain's new-found enthusiasm for the Chinese cause was not an outburst of morality or altruism; the simple fact was that Britain could not afford to risk a Chinese collapse which would allow Japan to expand south.

THE THAI PROBLEM AND THE FEBRUARY 'WAR-SCARE'

The continuation of Chinese resistance was particularly important in the light of events in South-East Asia. By the autumn of 1940 the situation in the region was increasingly complex, for the fall of France had not only inspired Japanese pressure on Indo-China, it had also led Thailand to make territorial claims on the French colony. This irredentism provided Japan with the opportunity not only to put its 'New Order' principles into action by claiming its right to intervene in the dispute, but also to use its intervention to expand its influence over the two countries and thus gain a firm foothold in the region without having to resort to war. To the Foreign Office this raised the prospect that Japan would be able to edge closer to Singapore and at the same time gain control of the rubber and tin produced in Thailand and Indo-China. Obviously this had to be resisted, but the question was how to proceed.

The problem facing Britain was that supporting either side in the Thai–French dispute had its disadvantages: to back France might irrevocably drive Thailand into Japan's orbit, while support for Bangkok would only weaken French resistance to Japanese encroachment into Indo-China and secure the colony's rubber for re-export to Germany. A solution could possibly be achieved if Britain backed Thailand and used a British embargo on exports to Indo-China to force Vichy to restrict its sales of rubber and rice. In November the latter initiative was put into action, but any effort to win over the Thais was hindered by the unwillingness of the United States to take any sort of lead in the dispute apart from stating that to satisfy Thailand's claims would be tantamount to appeasement. Britain was therefore put in a very difficult position, hindered by Washington from making a diplomatic intervention and too weak militarily to dampen down the growing tensions.[18]

As had been the case so often before, the result of British weakness was that policy was left to drift and no concerted effort was made to contain the crisis. Finally, on 28 November a Thai–French war broke out. Almost immediately the two combatants were subjected to intense pressure from Berlin and Tokyo to accept Japanese mediation. In London, this was interpreted as a clear indication that the Tripartite Powers were determined to establish Japanese dominance over the region, and raised the disturbing possibility that Japan might synchronise its action to coincide with a German offensive in Europe. These fears were reinforced by increasing evidence of German–Japanese collaboration, such as the announcement that Japanese naval and military missions were to travel to Europe and that General Ōshima, who had been relieved of his post in Berlin following the Nazi–Soviet Pact, was to be re-appointed as Ambassador to Germany. In addition, there were reports suggesting that Japan was giving assistance to German commerce-raiders in the Pacific, which had not only been attacking Allied shipping but had also bombarded the Australian-mandated island of Nauru. Perhaps most threatening was that intercepted Japanese consular telegrams had revealed that Japanese consuls in ports such as Alexandria in Egypt were passing on information about British naval and military movements to Tokyo where it was presumed that this material was being handed to the Germans.[19]

Early in 1941 the crisis in South-East Asia began to approach a climax. During January, while the Foreign Office tried forlornly to persuade the State Department that the situation could only be saved by joint Anglo-American mediation, Japanese pressure on the combatants to make peace under Japan's auspices markedly increased. The Thais, with little success on land or sea, saw the Japanese offer as a way of retrieving the situation and agreed to mediation. The Japanese then began to hint to the French that serious consequences would arise if they continued fighting. Not surprisingly considering the lack of support from the United States, Vichy quickly acquiesced, and on 29 January armistice talks began in Saigon. Simultaneously the Japanese military and naval presence in the region began to escalate. This build-up had been approved in Japan at a Liaison Conference on 19 January and was designed to intimidate the Thais and French into making peace and to force them to agree to Japan's desire for closer political, military and economic ties.[20]

The British were well aware of these diplomatic and military developments. Through the use of radio direction-finding equipment and traffic analysis at Singapore the FECB was able to follow the deployment of Japanese naval forces into the South China Sea and the Gulf of Thailand, which included indications that Japan was beginning to operate in the vicinity of Cam Ranh Bay, the best anchorage in Indo-China.[21] To this was added disturbing decrypts of telegrams sent from Tokyo to the Japanese Consul-General in Singapore which included one, intercepted on 20 January, that was summarized as stating that

> future intelligence and propaganda policy will be 'mainly directed southwards in order to secure supplies of war commodities'. Promotion of agitation, political plots, propaganda and intelligence (particularly naval and military) must be expedited and intensified so that new order in greater East Asia may be expedited.[22]

In addition, decrypts of telegrams passing between the Japanese Minister in Bangkok and Tokyo clearly demonstrated the Japanese interest in bases as a *quid pro quo* for assistance in mediation. Important information was also received from the Dutch intelligence community in Bandung, with whom co-operation over Japanese cyphers and the activities of local Japanese agents had begun only recently. These indications of impending crisis were reinforced by a number of bellicose speeches by Matsuoka in January, which included the assertion that the European colonial empires of South-East Asia fell within the Greater East Asia Co-Prosperity Sphere.[23]

The accumulation of evidence hinting at some imminent advance by the Japanese meant that Britain obviously had to make some sort of response. However, the problem was deciding what sort of threat Britain was faced with, what exactly Japan's intentions were and when a strike was likely to take place. On 5 February the JIC synthesized the evidence from all available sources and concluded

> Japan will take advantage of her role as mediator in the dispute between Thailand and French Indo-China so as to gain naval, military and air bases which would enable her to threaten Malaya, the Netherlands East Indies, North Borneo, and possibly Burma. Of these objectives we believe that she will probably select, in the first instance, the Netherlands East Indies, and that she intends to move against this territory in the near future.[24]

The situation therefore did not at this point suggest to London any imminent attack on British territory, but there was some concern that Japan might be preparing for a future offensive, which would be timed to coincide with a new German offensive in Europe or even an invasion of Britain. Overnight, however, the British assessment of Japan's timetable changed and a report drawn up the next day by the Chiefs of Staff noted that new information indicated that a direct threat to British interests was possible.[25] The source of this drastic reassessment was an operation run by the SIS to bug the telephones at the Japanese Embassy in London. On 5 February the operator responsible for translating the telephone conversations within the Embassy reported that staff had been ordered to cut off all fraternization with British officials and be prepared to leave Britain at short notice: this was followed the next day by news that 'some kind of action' was expected shortly.[26] These reports suggested, and were certainly interpreted in Whitehall as indicating, that a Japanese offensive was far closer than originally thought and that the target of Japanese aggression was not only to be the Dutch but probably British territories as well.

Now that the nature of the threat was apparent the British had to decide how to approach the crisis. Obviously the forces in Malaya were insufficient to resist Japan and reinforcement in strength was impossible, therefore war had to be averted and to do this Britain had to deter. One way that Britain could signal its resolve was to increase the severity of its economic sanctions, but this was felt to be too provocative. Indeed, there was a deliberate move towards caution at this point as Britain made the interception of a Japanese ship, the *Asaka Maru*, dependent on American approval.[27] This left only two weapons: propaganda and diplomacy. The strategy decided upon was to use these two methods to build up an atmosphere of crisis and to stress Britain's apparent readiness to resist any advance, in the hope that Japan might be deterred not only from war with Britain but also from pressing its claims for military bases on Thailand and Indo-China.[28]

The propaganda campaign was based on using the media to print and broadcast reports that war with Japan was thought to be imminent; an activity which was co-ordinated by a sub-committee of the FEC. At the same time rumours were circulated that Britain was preparing to resist a Japanese attack; one rumour which reached the Japanese Embassy was that the Royal Navy was preparing to send a squadron to Singapore.[29] At the diplomatic level there were two aims; first, to persuade the United States to exert diplomatic pressure on Japan, and second for Britain itself to browbeat Japan. The former also offered a useful opportunity to bring to Washington's attention the increasingly tense climate in South-East Asia and thus pave the way for a more forward American policy. An approach to the Americans was made both through Roosevelt's close confidant, Harry Hopkins, who was at this time in London on a mission to report on British morale, and directly to Roosevelt by Halifax, who by this time had passed the post of Foreign Secretary to Eden and become Ambassador to Washington. In these talks the Americans were urged to understand that war with Japan would dangerously overstretch British resources and could threaten the trade routes in the Indian Ocean.[30]

The initial diplomatic move by Britain against Japan came on 7 February when Eden called Shigemitsu to the Foreign Office to protest against recent Japanese policy. The talk began with Eden stating that, since Matsuoka had entered the Japanese Government, Anglo-Japanese relations had steadily worsened and had come to a new low with the Japanese mediation of the Thai–French dispute. He noted that Craigie had forwarded evidence of widespread rumours in Japan that a crisis was expected during the next few weeks and asked if there was any substance to this. Shigemitsu was taken aback by this sudden outburst and tried to convince Eden that the situation was not as serious as the latter had made out.[31]

It may appear from the above, considering what Britain knew of the activities at the Japanese Embassy, that Shigemitsu was displaying the most flagrant duplicity in this interview. In fact, he was genuinely surprised by Eden's protestations; the impression gained in British circles of an atmosphere of crisis in the Japanese Embassy had all along been the result of bad intelligence. The agent responsible for the information was a foreign journalist who knew only colloquial Japanese, and it appears that he either accidently mistranslated conversations or, as MI2c later thought more likely, deliberately distorted them to exaggerate his own importance.[32] However, it was only in May 1941 that MI2c came to this conclusion and throughout the course of the crisis this source was assumed to be reliable. Other indicators could have shown from the start that Japan did not intend war in the immediate future, the most obvious being that the Japanese merchant fleet had not been called back into home waters, but this information was only relayed to other departments on 12 February by the DNI when the decision had already been taken to use the propaganda weapon.[33] The British therefore laboured for about a week under the false premise of an imminent assault.

By 15 February the sense of imminent crisis in London began to pass. To some degree this was due to the protestations of innocence, and bewilderment at British brinkmanship, of Matsuoka, who held a talk that day with Craigie. A more important factor was that evidence of a Japanese retreat was provided by further reports arising from the interception of the Japanese Embassy's telephone conversations. Information obtained from the embassy suggested that a telegram that had been expected had not arrived and that the Japanese were climbing down.[34] These signs were reinforced by evidence from another source – decrypts of the Japanese diplomatic code. The British had been able to get some decrypted material from the United States in January, but in early February an American intelligence mission arrived in Britain with permission to hand over a Purple machine to the GCCS at Bletchley Park. On 15 February it appears that this source provided Britain with news that Matsuoka intended to visit Europe in the near future, which Churchill interpreted as an indication that any attack on British territory had been postponed. The belief that the crisis had passed was fortified over the next few days by a number of BJs confirming that no attack was planned.[35] One decrypt from Tokyo to the Consul-General in Sydney, was summarized by the FECB as stating

> All talk of impending crisis in Far East is nothing more than British propaganda aimed at winning over American public opinion, checking Japan's southward advance and hindering improvements of her relations with Thailand and Indo China; no action by Japan is indicated.[36]

The apparent decision by Japan to postpone the next phase of its southern advance was believed in London to be a triumph for the policy of publicizing Japan's activities and putting pressure on the United States. However, this was a rather dangerous lesson for Britain to draw from the crisis because what the British authorities did not know was that the pressure exerted by the Western powers had only led to Japanese indecision because of the internal divisions within Japan itself. In particular, splits had appeared within the IJN over the issue of whether to use military force to seize bases, with moderates such as Admiral Yamamoto Isoroku, now the Commander-in-Chief of the Combined Fleet, still convinced that any action which might provoke the United States should be avoided. British ignorance of the internal debate in Japan was, of course, not altogether surprising, and, even if Craigie had reported it the Foreign Office would probably, on past form, have doubted its significance. The result nevertheless was that Britain took away from this crisis the false belief that Japan could be deterred from further military action by propaganda.[37]

TOWARDS ANGLO-AMERICAN MILITARY CO-OPERATION

The 'war-scare' was an important watershed in Anglo-Japanese relations; it was the last crisis that Britain had to face more or less alone, and the manner in which it resolved itself had important ramifications for the balance of power in East Asia. The chief effect was that it finally pushed the United States into taking the lead in the region and co-operating more fully with Britain. As indicated above, this had been one of the major British aims in publicizing the Japanese threat, and progress was made in a number of fields, the most welcome being military relations. During the crisis the long-promised Anglo-American staff talks had begun in Washington. At first the negotiations had been rather strained, as the head of the British delegation, Admiral Bellairs, had disregarded Churchill's instructions and tried to use the 'war-scare' to press the Americans to station their Pacific fleet at Singapore. This earned him a sharp rebuke from the Prime Minister, but once this issue was removed from the agenda the talks began to make progress and led to an agreement that, in the event of the United States being at war with both Germany and Japan, priority would be given to offensive operations in Europe and to defence in the Pacific.[38]

Following from this, it was agreed that it would be useful to hold a conference in Singapore, with delegations from the British Empire, the Dutch East Indies and the United States, to discuss a regional defence plan. The conference duly opened on 21 April and made significant progress, but its discussions were qualified by one important flaw; though the participants could roughly agree on military matters, there was still no political guarantee that any one of them would go to war with Japan for the others. Without such an arrangement the conclusions reached by the military planners were at the most of tentative significance. The British were still at this stage reluctant to give any commitment to the Dutch, even though Eden and Leo Amery, the Secretary of State for India, had pressed Churchill on this during the 'war-scare'.[39] Indeed, an Anglo-Dutch–Australian defence conference had taken place in Singapore in late February without any mention of the political angle. One possible solution to this was the idea, which originated in the Foreign Office, of an Anglo-American–Dutch joint declaration which would warn Japan that any further advance would be treated as a matter of great concern. In early March, much to the surprise of Halifax, this proposal was received favourably by Cordell Hull, with only the proviso that it should not be termed an 'unqualified threat'. Unfortunately Hull's enthusiasm was short-lived; in May he began to shy away from the prospect of joint action and nothing came of this initiative, even though the British were well aware from the BJ source how disturbed Matsuoka was at this prospect.[40] The 'war-scare' had thus motivated the United States to take a more active role in East Asia, but that did not yet mean that Washington was ready to agree to the establishment of a 'trip-wire' which, if crossed, would ensure a military response.

To the frustration of many British policy-makers, Churchill did not help the situation by his continuing unwillingness to press Roosevelt to commit more American resources to the Pacific theatre. The Prime Minister believed that the sheer military potential of an Anglo-American–Dutch bloc was enough to deter the Japanese, who were, he often stated, by nature a cautious people, and that therefore neither Britain nor the United States should be diverted from the primary task: the defeat of Hitler. When faced in April with a demand from the visiting Australian Prime Minister, Sir Robert Menzies, that more resources be allocated to Malaya, Churchill's response was to say that

> everything indicated a slackening of tension in the Far East. It was most unlikely that Japan would enter the war in the next three or four months, and it would be foolish to send further reinforcements to Malaya in the near future. He quite appreciated Mr Menzies' anxiety, but the completion of the defences of Malaya must be subordinated to more pressing needs elsewhere.[41]

In addition, Churchill was convinced that Britain could not afford to lecture the United States on its responsibilities. As he saw it, the overriding necessity was to get the Americans into the European war and he held that anything Roosevelt did to commit the United States further should be welcomed. A prime example of this attitude came on 30 April at a meeting of the Defence Committee, when Churchill, in opposition to Eden, Cadogan and the First Sea Lord, Admiral Sir Dudley Pound, stated that Britain should forward its agreement to an American plan to move a large part of the Pacific Fleet to the Atlantic. To the Foreign Office and the Admiralty the American proposal seemed dangerous as it would weaken the deterrent to Japan: to Churchill the military value of the plan was secondary; he saw only the political expediency of agreeing with the American President.[42]

A slightly more promising field for collaboration between Britain and the United States was the sharing of intelligence information. At the highest level Churchill was well aware of how intelligence could, if judiciously used, be instrumental in influencing American attitudes. In the context of the war against Germany this meant allowing Washington to receive some material from the Enigma source, while in East Asia, where the Americans were already reading the Purple material, he made use of the information garnered from the bugging of the Japanese and Thai Embassies in London. For example, a letter from Churchill to Cadogan on 21 February noted the importance of forwarding to Roosevelt a digest of telephone conversations between two diplomats, one Thai and one Japanese, on the subject of Japanese–German plans in South-East Asia.[43] At the local level there was growing co-operation between the FECB and the American intelligence centre at Cavite Bay in the Philippines. On 14 March the head of the FECB informed the Admiralty that he had given Britain's partial solutions of the Japanese Army's transport code book and the Air Arm cypher to his American counterparts and on 23 March he indicated his approval of the stationing of two US Army personnel with the FECB. The co-operation did not end there, for in May these two intelligence centres began to pool their resources in the decryption of the IJN's operational code, JN–25B.[44] Another success was that SIS arranged to receive through their New York office information gathered by the American consul in Vladivostock.[45] However, the most significant breakthrough came on 31 May when the American Military Attaché in London, General Lee, forwarded a request from the War Department for a full exchange of data with the British authorities in the Far East. The JIC naturally accepted this invitation and on 11 June a telegram was sent to Brooke-Popham and Admiral Layton, the Commander-in-Chief China Station, authorizing them to begin complete co-operation with the United States over intelligence material, only excluding that derived from Special Operations Executive (SOE) and SIS sources.[46]

Although it was possible to collaborate in the field of exchanging special intelligence, there was less of an opening in two other areas of intelligence activity: subversion and black propaganda. The leading British protagonist of subversion was SOE's Oriental Mission, which was established in Singapore in April 1941. Its prime objective was to hinder German activities in the region, which included plans for sabotaging the Trans-Siberian Railway, but it also had to make preparations for the possibility of war with Japan. This led to the establishment of organizations in Thailand and Indo-China which were supposed at the first sign of Japanese aggression to indulge in sabotage, such as in Thailand the destruction of tin mines and in Indo-China attacks against Japanese ships using Cam Ranh Bay. To what extent these plans were co-ordinated with the Americans is unclear, but certainly Eden in May 1941 asked Halifax to suggest co-operation in this field.[47]

Propaganda was possibly an even more sensitive area. As early as October 1940 the JIC had approved the use of 'rumours' to intimidate Japan and to drive a wedge between it and Germany, and this, of course, had been the policy used, with apparent success, during February 1941.[48] In the wake of the 'war-scare' even greater emphasis was put on propaganda. A series of weekly meetings was held at the Ministry of Information to direct official sources, while the Inter-Services Security Board and the JIC were responsible for the 'rumours' campaign. British government restrictions make it difficult to follow this policy but certainly on 28 April a detailed policy was put up to the JIC and on 12 May two 'rumours' were proposed; the first was that the USN at the first sign of trouble would blockade Japan, while the second described German aims in Asia as clashing with those of Japan, particularly in regard to the control of commodities in the Dutch East Indies.[49] However, the problem in this field was that 'rumours' such as the former, which involved speculation on American activities, had a potential for backfiring and thus met with opposition from the American Department in the Foreign Office. This was no doubt a hindrance, but despite this problem it was possible for SO1, the branch of SOE responsible for black propaganda, to place material in American newspapers. One particular success was a series of articles beginning in July on the activities of the German fifth column in Japan which Craigie later reported as having an effective result.[50]

TIGHTENING SANCTIONS

Despite the progress made over military planning and intelligence collaboration, these advances did not forward the policy of restraining Japan; the only active way to achieve that remained economic sanctions. It was in this field that Britain felt the greatest frustration at American tardiness. The British complaint against the United States was that Roosevelt seemed to envisage sanctions against Japan as a punishment for specific acts rather than as part of a coherent, unified policy. The result was that American measures inconvenienced, but failed to weaken, Japan. The British concept of economic warfare was very different. To the MEW and the Foreign Office trade restrictions were a weapon to use to incapacitate one's enemies and to manipulate wavering neutrals. The whole purpose of British policy had been to restrict supplies to Japan in order to limit its ability to go to war and its capacity to re-export to Germany; American lethargy meant that even by early 1941 neither of these aims had been achieved, in fact Japan had been able to send goods to Germany while simultaneously building up its own stockpiles.[51]

The perceived underachievement in this field meant that Whitehall was determined to rectify the situation by increasing Japan's difficulties in South-East Asia and putting greater pressure on Washington. In regard to the former, Britain began to tighten the noose around Japan in a number of areas. One area of initial success was that in December 1940 the French Governor, Admiral Decoux, was driven by the British embargo to send one of his officers, Captain Jouan, to Singapore to engage in talks with the British authorities. This led to the conclusion of a trade agreement under which Britain ended its restrictions in return for a French commitment to restrict its exports of rubber to Japan and to sell rice to Singapore and Hong Kong. Unfortunately this achievement was short-lived, for the Vichy regime was unable to resist Japanese and German pressure for access to its rubber crop and by May, with reports that 40,000 tons of rubber were to be allocated to the Tripartite Powers, it was clear that the agreement had been fatally undermined.[52]

The eventual failure in Indo-China was, however, balanced by success elsewhere, notably the progress made in the collaboration with the Dutch. On 14 January the Anglo-Dutch Committee on Economic Affairs agreed that a maximum figure should be set for exports of rubber and tin to Japan, that the authorities in Batavia would try in their trade talks with the Japanese to push their quota as low as possible, and that the British would make up the balance. Subsequently a figure of 42,000 tons of rubber and 4,000 tons of tin was set.[53] However, when it became clear that the rubber in Indo-China was more or less under Japanese control the British and the Dutch agreed to reduce these quotas drastically; by May no rubber was being exported to Japan from Malaya and in Batavia that month's licence was reduced to a mere 728 tons.[54] In addition to the agreement over rubber and tin, the British also sought more generally to bolster Batavia's resolve in its talks with the Japanese trade delegation that had been present in the Dutch East Indies since September 1940. On 25 February an agreement was reached between the MEW and the Dutch Colonial Ministry which drew up a proposed annual quota of exports from the colony to Japan for a whole range of commodities. Also the British assisted by supplying the Dutch authorities with information derived from the BJ source about the Japanese terms.[55]

However, the struggle to deny Japan raw materials from South-East Asia was meaningless if the United States continued to be lenient towards Japan and therefore, while the screws were tightened in Malaya and the Dutch East Indies, Britain began to exert pressure on Washington for a tougher stance. The feeling in Whitehall was that in particular the Americans had to be persuaded to co-operate in clamping down on German and Japanese imports from Latin America, which were a matter of growing concern. In January 1941 a mass of evidence emerged on the extent of this trade; most worrying were the revelations that Germany had purchased $3 million of rubber from Brazil and that it was also showing great interest in Chilean copper.[56] This led to a concerted effort to convince Washington of the need to introduce contraband control in the Caribbean. In a talk in January Nevile Butler tried to persuade Welles that this was an essential move, and that the interception of two or three Japanese ships would bring this trade to a stop, an effort echoed in London when Dalton met Harry Hopkins.[57] The State Department was, however, adamant that this proposal was unacceptable as it would alienate the South American states; instead they suggested on 30 January the establishment of an inter-American control scheme at the Panama Canal. Whitehall was not impressed by this gesture as it was thought that it would take an age to establish controls acceptable to all parties and therefore on 7 February Halifax was instructed to tell Welles that though Britain was grateful for this proposal it wished, while the terms were negotiated, to start, as a temporary measure, contraband control off Jamaica.[58]

The American reaction to this threat was completely unexpected; on 19 February Welles revealed to Halifax that two days earlier he had proposed to the east coast governments of South America that they should establish export licence controls and that the United States would contribute by large-scale pre-emptive buying of their commodities.[59] The initial Foreign Office reaction to this proposal was disappointment that once again Welles had evaded the interception issue, but in the MEW its true significance was quickly realized; one official noted on 24 February

> We have long been asking the Americans to cooperate in preemption in South America, but if Mr Welles means what he says, this is cooperation beyond our wildest dreams, and if our proposal to intercept ships in the Caribbean only drives the Americans to carry out this scheme, it will be an immense achievement.[60]

Evidence over the next few months did suggest that Welles was sincere. By April Halifax was able to report that American copper companies in Chile had cancelled Japanese contracts, and that Washington had agreed to pre-empt Japanese purchases of wolfram from Bolivia and to buy up virtually all of Brazil's strategic materials. On 14 May this last move was formalized when an American-Brazilian agreement was officially signed. This in turn encouraged British co-operation and by July Britain had contracted to pre-empt molybdenum from Peru and wool from a variety of South American states. Another Japanese market was slowly but surely being whittled away.[61]

Progress was also made in the spring of 1941 in persuading the United States to expand its export licensing programme. In March and April a large number of commodities were added to the American list and finally on 29 May the United States made the very significant move of extending the export control system to include the Philippines.[62] In addition, both Britain and the United States began to introduce restrictions in the field of shipping. As early as November 1940 the Foreign Office had proposed to the Americans that pressure on Japan could be increased by denying Japan the use of non-Japanese tankers for transporting oil. This plan was based on information that Japan consumed some 5,500,000 tons of oil per annum, but only produced 500,000 tons from indigenous sources and had only enough vessels to carry 4,000,000 tons per annum; therefore a tanker embargo would cause an annual shortfall of

1,000,000 tons, and thus force Japan to draw upon its oil stockpile. It was hoped that in this way Japan could be undermined without risking the volatile situation that might arise from a complete embargo on oil sales. Typically the American response was to prevaricate, and it was only in March, after Britain had unilaterally withdrawn all its tankers from the Pacific and put the export of oil drums under licence, that the Americans followed suit.[63] It was not only oil-tankers that were affected by such measures; in March the British introduced bunker-controls for Japanese shipping to ensure that vessels only had enough fuel to take them to their next port of call and two months later the United States established its own controls.[64]

The overall effect was that by June 1941 the Western trade embargo of Japan had become a powerful and debilitating weapon. On 18 June a MEW memorandum for the FEC summarized the developments in the field of economic sanctions since October 1940, noting the growing scale of the restrictions, the expansion of co-operation with the United States and the Dutch and the steady easing of Japan out of South American markets, and concluded

> The Japanese are, it may be hoped, finding it more and more difficult to avoid drawing on their reserves. In every part of the world they are meeting with obstruction ultimately caused either by British or United States action. . . . While it would be foolish to claim that they are as yet seriously weakened, it would be equally foolish to deny that they are becoming increasingly alarmed.[65]

The MEW seemed very content with its work.

The gathering strength of the restrictions on Japan did not, however, please everyone. One voice of discontent was Craigie's. He had always viewed sanctions with caution and, though not opposed to their use, did feel that Britain had to be judicious in their implementation. He first expressed his concern in March 1941 when Vice-Minister Ōhashi complained to him about a Canadian decision to put licence restrictions on the export of wheat. Craigie took this complaint very seriously and noted to London that for Britain to engage in the restriction of food exports to Japan was a dangerous enterprise liable to make the country even more pro-German. Craigie felt particularly uncomfortable because the official line was that restrictions were only designed to preserve vital raw materials for the war effort and to prevent the re-export of commodities to Germany, and not as sanctions against Japan.[66] However, this explanation seemed completely inappropriate in relation to the

Canadian wheat and led Craigie to believe that the economic sanctions policy was in urgent need of rationalization.

As a result on 30 April he sent a memorandum to London, drawn up with his Canadian and Australian colleagues in Tokyo, which attempted to set out clearly the aims of British policy and the methods appropriate to that task. The memorandum began by suggesting that Britain should differentiate between sanctions designed to deter Japan from further expansion, and those to be introduced as reprisals against any further Japanese *fait accompli*. In relation to the first group Craigie warned against the use of overly provocative measures, and with the case of Canadian wheat in mind stressed that it must be made clear to Tokyo that

> provided that Japan does not go further in her policy of southward expansion or in seeking a privileged position in Eastern Asia, there is no intention of interfering with the available food supply and raw materials for internal consumption in Japan or for supply of Japan's normal peacetime industry.[67]

In terms of the second group, Craigie proposed that, at the first sign of trouble, Britain should give a 'slight turn of the screw'. Thus Japan would be made aware of the cost of further expansion and then, if it still proceeded to advance, firmer action should be taken but in the clear realization that this could lead to war. Craigie felt that this delineation would provide Britain with greater flexibility in its sanctions policy and allow for stricter co-ordination within the Empire, and he concluded by noting that the best deterrent to Japanese expansion was to make sure that Tokyo knew the potential price of further adventures.

The reaction in the Foreign Office and the MEW to Craigie's memorandum was that the issues it raised, such as co-ordination, had been dealt with already in the FEC, and that the difference he postulated between the two types of sanctions was artificial and unconvincing. John Troutbeck of the MEW noted in relation to the latter

> The only limitation to our action should be the danger of forcing Japan to violent reactions, and that danger remains whether Japan makes a move or not. . . . [W]e must get away from this false antithesis of a comparatively good Japan and a possibly bad Japan. Japan is already bad, and our whole policy is based on this obvious fact.[68]

Another disagreement with Craigie's thinking was over his assertion that Britain should not restrict supplies of foodstuffs or raw materials designed solely for Japanese consumption. The Foreign Office told Craigie of their reservations in a telegram on 21 May which informed him that the issue was not as clear cut as he thought since some Japanese imported foodstuffs were used to replace exports to Germany.[69] This issue was particularly relevant because Britain had begun within the last month or so to restrict exports from its Pacific islands and North Borneo to Japan of copra (the source of coconut oil), which was used as a cooking agent. This was part of an attempt to force Japan to turn to soya bean oil and thus cut back its exports of the latter to Germany, which was woefully short of fats. Craigie, however, was still not convinced that such restrictions were either necessary or desirable because there was the danger that they could be presented by the Japanese government as clear evidence of the West's attempts to force Japan to its knees and thus justify retaliation.[70] On 3 June he displayed his continuing disquiet in a telegram to the Foreign Office, in which he noted prophetically

> To extend restrictions on Japanese imports to an extent that would force Japan to draw on her reserves on any considerable scale would at present be liable to produce those very reactions we wish to avoid. The elements here in favour of violent measures would be able to point out that we had in fact embarked on a policy of withholding normal current supplies from Japan, and that it was therefore essential to secure those supplies from sources outside our control.[71]

His words fell on stony ground. On 12 June the FEC considered his 30 April memorandum but dismissed his ideas as outdated.[72]

PUBLIC AND PRIVATE INITIATIVES FOR PEACE

Craigie was not the only figure who was disturbed at the apparent drift towards confrontation; in London Shigemitsu shared the same concerns. Ever since the signing of the Tripartite Pact he had attempted to stop the move towards confrontation. In pursuit of this aim he had tried in his talks with Butler in the autumn of 1940 to argue that Japan's relations with Germany only mirrored the support that the West had given to China, and hinted that the withdrawal of British support for Chiang Kai-shek could lead Japan to draw away from the Axis. However, Shigemitsu's sentiments seemed to bear little relation to the threats emanating from Matsuoka or to Japan's actions in South-East Asia, and his overtures were therefore disregarded by the Foreign Office.[73]

With the previously sympathetic Butler now taking a hard line, Shigemitsu increasingly turned to other channels as a means of influencing the British government. In September 1940 he had with Halifax's approval held two meetings in private with Lord Lloyd, the Secretary of State for the Colonies, and Lord Hankey, the Chancellor of the Duchy of Lancaster. The intermediary in this liaison was Major-General Piggott, who was still endeavouring to establish an Anglo-Japanese *rapprochement*. At the first meeting on 11 September there was only the most general of discussions, but at the second on 25 September Shigemitsu put forward a concrete plan. His proposal was one that the Japanophile group in London had been espousing ever since April, which was that a British Cabinet Minister should go to Japan as the head of an official mission with the aim of improving relations and countering German influence. Lloyd and Hankey found this idea appealing, but before they could act events were overtaken by the Tripartite Pact.[74]

Shigemitsu, however, remained keen to pursue this line and on 20 November he held a further meeting with the two Ministers. At this lunch Lloyd suggested that, instead of an official government mission to Japan, it might be possible to send one led by Hankey under the auspices of the British Council, of which Lloyd was president. Shigemitsu expressed considerable enthusiasm for this idea, and it was agreed that Lloyd should enquire at the Foreign Office to see if this was acceptable.[75] He subsequently wrote to Halifax on 4 December laying out the plan, but the latter's reply was not favourable. It noted bleakly that such a mission

> might be welcomed by those whose views are suppressed and unheard and who may be on our side, but, merging as it would into the political field, it would risk being misunderstood as a gesture designed to conciliate those who every day take steps to prejudice ourselves and our interests. . . . I am convinced that it is only by showing a combined firm front that we shall restrain the extremist elements from extreme measures.[76]

This was hardly an unexpected response, but it, and the death of Lord Lloyd in February 1941, effectively brought these talks to an end.

Shigemitsu next entered the picture as the postman in a rather bizarre correspondence between Churchill and Matsuoka in February to April 1941. The first letter in this series was sent by the Japanese Foreign Minister on 15 February in response to the 'war-scare', and was, in Eden's absence, passed to Churchill. This note, after protesting at Britain's warlike posturing, set the tone for Matsuoka's half of the subsequent correspondence, consisting largely of vague axioms, its only substantial proposal being a totally unacceptable plan for Japan to mediate a European peace settlement. This lack of substance did not come as any surprise to the Foreign Office, but Churchill saw the letter as an opportunity to bring home to Matsuoka the consequences of a Japanese alignment with Germany and on 24 February handed his reply to Shigemitsu.[77]

Over the next month the Japanese Ambassador shuffled back and forth delivering and receiving the two parties posturing communications. His exposure to the clear disparity in viewpoint between the two correspondents, his close contact with Churchill, and his frustration at Matsuoka's failure to take notice of his, Shigemitsu's, telegrams, led the Ambassador to propose to Hankey and Butler in late March that he should meet Matsuoka while the latter was in Europe.[78] This idea was seized upon with some enthusiasm by the two British Ministers, who both wrote to Churchill requesting permission for Shigemitsu to get a priority-passage flight to Lisbon from where he would rendezvous with Matsuoka in Berne. The Prime Minister also saw the benefit from such a meeting, as it was clear from the BJ decrypts that Shigemitsu had what Butler referred to as 'a proper view of the British war effort and the state of Europe'. In addition, Churchill was keen for Shigemitsu to deliver to Matsuoka his latest letter, which sought to overawe the Japanese Foreign Minister by pointing out such matters as the huge disparity in iron and steel production between the Anglo-Saxon bloc and Japan. Therefore on 31 March Churchill persuaded the War Cabinet to agree to provide a flight to Lisbon.[79] Unfortunately, however, disaster struck; Matsuoka changed his schedule and the meeting never took place.

With his plan for a mission to Japan blocked and unable to meet and influence Matsuoka, Shigemitsu could only rest his hopes on the last talks still in progress between Britain and Japan, the payments agreement negotiations. These had their origins in the collapse of the trade agreement discussions in June 1940. It had been decided then that talks should continue over the possibility of a payments agreement between the two countries. At that point, and in the light of a decision to end sterling convertibility, the Treasury had offered Japan very favourable terms for an agreement. The proposal was that the financing of Anglo-Japanese trade in the future should be based on a Japanese special account in London with a minimum balance of £3 million, that Britain would commit itself to converting into gold 10 per cent of the daily sterling payments into the account, and that if, after three months the balance was over £3 million, another 10 per cent would be converted.[80]

In August, due to the lack of a Japanese response and the arrests crisis, Britain withdrew the clause referring to the three monthly conversion payments. However, there was still silence from Tokyo, and on 31 October the FEC approved a proposal to remove all promises of gold for Japanese sterling and to restrict Japan to using sterling to finance the purchase of goods from the Sterling Area, thus turning the original offer into a simple clearing agreement.[81]

This new draft was handed over on 16 November, and soon precipitated a Japanese response. This, however, was not a reply based on the 16 November proposals, but one that expressed general agreement with the terms offered in August. It also included a number of amendments, of which the most important was a proviso that

> no unreasonable prohibitions or restrictions shall be imposed on exports from the British Empire to Japan, in other words, that the export of commodities from the British Empire to Japan shall be facilitated to the utmost possible.[82]

This made it clear that the new Japanese enthusiasm for these talks was not because they felt that a payments agreement had an intrinsic value of its own, but rather that it might act as a means to overturn Britain's economic restrictions. Shigemitsu was very keen for the Treasury to accept the Japanese draft and in the winter of 1941 pressed for a positive response. Any optimism he had was, however, sadly misplaced; the British interest in a payments agreement had dwindled with the increase of restrictions on trade with Japan, which had curbed the flow of sterling into Tokyo. The British were also wary of signing an agreement because of the uncertainty of the foreign reaction, and in a meeting of the FEC on 8 May it was agreed that any such deal would raise the spectre of appeasement.[83]

The decision to end the talks was communicated by Butler to Shigemitsu at a meeting on 16 May. In response, Shigemitsu asked whether an agreement could be concluded if the Japanese dropped the clauses in their draft linking it to a commitment to withdraw restrictions and settled instead for a verbal agreement over the latter issue. In support of this proposal the Ambassador told Butler that 'he found in the Payments Agreement the only opportunity for maintaining discussion of any sort between our two Governments in a period of crisis'.[84] This was, of course, grasping at straws and Butler was unable to agree to any such proposal. Shigemitsu's bitter reaction to this latest setback, and to British policy in general, was evident in a further talk with Butler at the end of the month, when he stated that British 'economic policy towards Japan was vindictive'.[85]

Frustrated on every front, Shigemitsu received the final humiliation in May 1941 when Matsuoka ordered him to return to Japan. The Foreign Office, however, still hoped that he could help Britain's cause and great efforts were made to fête him before his departure. He met once more with Churchill, a farewell luncheon was arranged at the Foreign Office on 9 June which was attended by Eden, Butler and Lord Moyne, the Secretary of State for the Colonies, and on 17 June his departure was marked by an officially inspired editorial in *The Times* praising his efforts for peace. Whether he could make any impact in Tokyo was though a moot point for the storm clouds were gathering.[86]

JAPAN TURNS SOUTH

While Britain and the United States concentrated on the tightening of their trade restrictions on Japan, the situation in South-East Asia continued to deteriorate. Although the threat that Japan would seize bases in Thailand and Indo-China had receded after the war-scare, the Japanese were still involved in mediating between the two combatants. Britain was able to follow the progress of these tortuous negotiations through the BJ source and material received from the Americans; it also received evidence, partly from intercepts of Vichy telegrams, of Japanese efforts, including secret arms deliveries, to win over the Thai government of Pibul Songgram. In addition, economic negotiations had begun between Japan and Thailand, with Japan showing great interest in cornering the market in Thai rubber.[87] All this activity meant that the debate between London and Washington over how best to treat Bangkok continued. The Americans remained deeply suspicious of any concessions to the Thais, but the Foreign Office, under the influence of the British Minister in Bangkok, Sir Josiah Crosby, believed that the Thais, who were dissatisfied with the territorial gains made under Japanese arbitration, could still be pacified by economic bribes. On 22 May the FEC agreed that Britain should supply Thailand with oil in return for Thai rubber and tin, thus denying these commodities to Japan; a policy set in motion with limited American support in June.[88]

Although Britain was, for the moment, able to hold the line in Thailand, events elsewhere threatened to undermine the fragile *status quo*. The most disturbing development came on 13 April when it was announced that Matsuoka and Molotov had signed a Soviet–Japanese Neutrality Pact in Moscow. This boded ill for the future, for if Japan was reassured about the security of Manchukuo from Soviet attack then it would be free to concentrate on expansion to the south.[89] Allied to this was evidence both from BJs and from comments made by Japanese officials that the country was becoming increasingly concerned about the threat to its economic livelihood; both in Singapore and in Tokyo complaints about British restrictions were made by Japanese officials.[90] The most obvious manifestation of this disquiet came in relation to the continuing economic negotiations in Batavia with the Dutch. By the end of May 1941 it was clear that these talks were close to collapse, and that this could only lead to a further worsening of Japan's economic position. On 22 May, in anticipation of this event, Matsuoka asked Craigie if it would be possible to use Britain's good offices to rescue the talks. Craigie did not support Matsuoka's proposal, but, discomforted by present British policy, he did indicate to the Foreign Office that this situation raised an opportunity for Britain and the Netherlands to make a joint enquiry to the Japanese about the quantities of each commodity that they wished to import and whether they were willing to give a guarantee against re-export.[91] The Foreign Office reaction to this idea was little short of apoplectic; the lesson of the past was that talks only encouraged Japanese aggression, and Craigie's idea was rejected outright. Indeed restriction on Japanese access to the Dutch East Indies was considered to be a step forward, as it meant that the pressure on Japan would increase even further.[92]

There was some awareness in British quarters that this latest set-back could lead to an escalation of tensions, particularly as Matsuoka appeared to blame Britain for the collapse of the talks, but there was little concern that war was imminent and Churchill continued to maintain that Japan would only make a dramatic move if Britain suffered a major reverse in the European conflict.[93] This was a grave underestimation of the gravity of the Japanese situation. Increasingly in Japan, once it was clear that the Dutch talks had collapsed, there were calls from within both the IJA and the IJN for a renewal of the southern advance in order to secure access to the strategic raw materials on which the 'self-existence of the Japanese Empire' depended. At a Liaison Conference on 16 June the Army Chief of Staff, General Sugiyama Gen, with the support of the Navy Chief of Staff, Admiral Nagano Osami, insisted that south Indo-China must be occupied by the end of July so that Japan would have the option of a military advance later in the year if the present level of economic pressure had not ceased.[94] This was the beginning of the final phase in the path to war and the kind of development that both Shigemitsu and Craigie had feared would arise from the economic stranglehold that was developing around Japan. For as they had warned London, the policy of sanctions was not deterring the Japanese extremists from action – it was instead provoking them to launch new adventures that would greatly increase the prospects of conflict.

8 Conflict
June 1941 to December 1941

June 1941 is often seen as one of the most crucial months of the twentieth century for it was at this point that Hitler unleashed Operation Barbarossa, the event that was eventually to lead to his downfall and to Soviet post-war dominance over Eastern Europe. The German invasion of the Soviet Union was, however, not an episode which affected only European affairs; it also had important ramifications for East Asia and the Pacific region. The significance of Barbarossa was that it, more than any other event, helped to complete the polarization of the international system into two rival camps; the 'fascist' states and their opponents. Now that Stalin was a victim of Nazi aggression it automatically followed that he was a 'friend' of the democracies and that the latter should do everything in their power to ensure the continuation of Russian resistance.

Unfortunately for Japan this meant that, besides the Western powers' existing fears for the security of South-East Asia, they also became concerned that the 'treacherous' Japanese would strike against Russia's maritime provinces at the first sign of Soviet collapse and thus assist Germany in its task. This meant that more than ever Britain and the United States felt that Japan had to be deterred from belligerency and the most logical way to achieve this was to immobilize it through economic asphyxiation. Washington took the lead in this process and, though there were mumbles of discontent in Whitehall at the lack of subtlety in American policy, no word of criticism was allowed to reach Roosevelt. After months of British manoeuvring the Americans were at last taking a lead in the Pacific, and there was a fear that the slightest sign of recalcitrance on London's part would hurt this fragile relationship. However, any hope that a policy of deterrence would succeed in deterring Japan was misplaced; faced with the West's challenge to all its achievements since 1931, and indeed to its Great Power status, the Japanese had no recourse but to plan for war.

JAPAN'S ADVANCE INTO SOUTH INDO-CHINA

The initial reaction in Japan to the outbreak of the German–Soviet war was one of confusion. Suddenly the Konoe government was faced with a radically changed world, in which Hitler was demanding that Japan follow his lead and strike north to take advantage of Russia's dilemma. Certainly such action appealed to some within the IJA who had always desired a confrontation with Russia. Others, however, saw little advantage in turning north, a move which they felt would do next to nothing to assuage Japan's economic problems, and instead continued to press for the occupation of south Indo-China.[1]

The debate that raged in Tokyo after Barbarossa was not lost on foreign observers and there was much speculation about which direction Japan would take. Craigie's reaction was to speculate that the situation was so confused that it was worth Britain's muddying the waters even further by slightly relaxing the economic restrictions on Japan in an attempt to wean the Konoe Government away from the dire influence of Germany. Certainly the start of the Russo-German War offered a legitimate excuse for such action, as the conflict had made negligible the chances of Japanese re-export of goods to Germany due to the closure of the Trans-Siberian route. However, the FEC remained opposed to any relaxation of sanctions because this would interfere with their policy of forcing Japan to draw on its stockpiles of raw materials, and also because there was no guarantee that, in the case of a quick Soviet defeat, the Trans-Siberian Railway would not once again come into operation as a route linking East with West.[2]

The opposition to any conciliatory measure was also influenced by British knowledge of Japanese intentions towards south Indo-China. Through the reading of the BJ intercepts it was obvious that seizure of bases was being planned. As early as 21 June the Admiralty informed the FECB in Singapore that

Japanese Govt: considers it essential to obtain without delay further information for the establishment of air bases in Southern Indo China and freedom for Naval and merchant ships to use harbour in that area.

Berlin is being asked to obtain Vichy's consent to these facilities.

Berlin is to be told that Japan has of course no southern ambitions but only wishes to protect Indo China against British aggression and the De Gaulle movement. Japan intends to obtain these facilities with or without Germany's assistance.[3]

On 25 June the DMI, Major-General Davidson, reported to Dill, that the JIC had discussed Japan's intentions and had come to the conclusion that Britain should try to deter any move into south Indo-China, and that the best way to achieve this was to 'open up a vigorous Press Campaign against Japan; such action has already succeeded once in January/February of this year – and may succeed again'. Dill acted on this briefing and on the same day persuaded his fellow Chiefs of Staff to adopt this line as policy.[4]

Despite the reports on Japanese interest in south Indo-China, British policy was left in a state of limbo because it was still, at the end of June, difficult to tell whether Japan would forsake the opportunity to strike north to concentrate on southern expansion. Confirmation that Japan intended to continue with the southern move was received on 4 July when a Japanese telegram to Berlin, forwarding the decisions reached two days earlier at an Imperial Conference, was intercepted by Bletchley Park. This decrypt revealed that Japan still intended to obtain bases in south Indo-China while the situation in Siberia was to be carefully monitored.[5] Once this information was received it was necessary to consider what action Britain should take if Japan carried out this next move. On 7 July the War Cabinet discussed a number of recommendations submitted by the FEC, which included a moderate tightening of sanctions and abrogating the 1911 Commercial Treaty with Japan. The need to take some action in response to further Japanese expansion was recognized but, in line with the FEC's advice, a harsh policy was rejected and instead the comparatively muted actions recommended to them were approved. In this decision they were influenced by the general consensus that had developed in the meeting that

the general situation did not justify us in taking strong deterrent measures to prevent further Japanese encroachments. Our policy must be, for the present, to take appropriate counter-action after each encroachment, calculated to play on Japanese reluctance to come into the war against an unbeaten and still formidable power.[6]

This policy followed the line Britain had taken towards Japan since October 1940, that is, incremental pressure designed to weaken but not provoke. However, on this occasion the favoured British response was undermined by the American reaction to events in South-East Asia. On 9 July Welles told Halifax that he had advised Roosevelt to introduce a complete economic embargo of Japan should the latter make another move, and that this should be done without any fore-warning to Tokyo.[7] In the Foreign Office there was considerable disquiet about this American initiative and on 13 July Eden observed to Halifax

> while we are reluctant to discourage the United States from strong measures provided they are prepared to face the consequences, we feel that such an embargo imposed at one blow . . . would face the Japanese with only two alternatives, either to reverse their policy completely or to exert maximum pressure southwards.[8]

The next day Halifax communicated this concern to Welles who dismissed the possibility that Japan might retaliate by noting that the IJA was too concerned with the situation in the Soviet Union and China.[9]

Whitehall was not reassured by this response; in particular there was apprehension in British circles over the American opposition to a warning. On 14 July Leith-Ross, who had been one of the major figures in forcing other departments to accept economic restrictions on Japan, noted to Dalton that it would be far easier to deter Japan from moving into south Indo-China by spelling out the consequences of such an action than it would be to prise them out afterwards through sanctions.[10] On 15 July the Chiefs of Staff approved and forwarded to Churchill a memorandum by the JPC which opined that war with Japan must be avoided and that the best deterrent would be a joint declaration by Britain, the Netherlands and the United States. Churchill, however, did not share his subordinate's concerns and indeed did not even seem to understand the issues involved. On 16 July he informed Eden and Ismay that he was still convinced that Japan would not declare war and that even if it did Britain would find the United States by its side.[11] This was hardly a response to the question of whether or not to issue a warning, but it meant that the JPC's proposal was sidelined.

There was also some concern about the necessity of introducing a complete embargo. On 17 July Welles indicated that the American intention was to freeze Japanese assets in the United States and on 21 July an even clearer picture was produced when the Assistant Secretary of State, Dean Acheson, informed Halifax that the plan was to use the freezing order and a wholesale licensing of exports, including petroleum exports, to bring all trade to a close, and that dollars and licences would only be provided for specific transactions.[12] This was in marked contrast to the measured policy agreed by the War Cabinet and the serious implications of the proposed move were immediately understood. Sigismund Waley of the Treasury noted succinctly to Sterndale Bennett, '[in] short, the effect of freezing Japanese assets would be to suspend economic relations and thus to declare economic war'.[13] The chief concern was over the possible embargo on oil sales to Japan. Petroleum had been the one commodity which the MEW, a 'hawk' in so many areas of policy, had always treated with due sensitivity. A Far Eastern Department official had noted as late as May 1941, when the MEW had expressed disapproval of an American proposal for the restriction of oil sales to Japan to 'normal' levels, that

> MEW are still addicted to the indirect method, (tankers and containers) except where aviation spirit is concerned, + are apprehensive of the consequences of a rationing policy. They appear to contemplate without any misgiving the prospect of Japan continuing indefinitely to take from America as much oil, except aviation spirit, as she can lift in her tankers.[14]

The new United States policy did not brook such timidity and there was fear that it might lead to unfortunate consequences.

Despite these misgivings, Britain was not in a position to overturn the State Department's lead. On 20 July Eden forwarded a memorandum to the War Cabinet which demonstrated Britain's dilemma

> A complete embargo in the literal sense of the stoppage of all current trade between the United States and Japan . . . would be likely to force the Japanese to choose between two grave alternatives, namely, completely to reverse their pro-Axis policy, or to proceed with their southward move to the point of war with the Netherlands East Indies and ourselves in an endeavour to obtain control of sources of raw materials. Even a complete embargo on oil *might* have this effect. . . . At the same time I cannot conceal from my colleagues the dangers inherent in our lagging behind the United States Government in dealing with Japan, *a fortiori* in our actually attempting to dissuade them from firm action. The risk of creating another Simon-Stimson incident and of seriously weakening the ties between us and America is real.[15]

Eden's conclusion from this was that, although it did not suit British interests to act so harshly against Japan, parallel action to that of the

United States had to be taken, and that as an insurance policy Britain should try to tighten defence co-operation in South-East Asia by seeking a cast-iron guarantee from Washington and itself provide a guarantee to the Dutch. The War Cabinet agreed that there was no alternative but to follow the American example and decided that, if Japan occupied south Indo-China, its assets within the Empire would be frozen and all remaining trade brought under licence. However, the Dutch guarantee was once again rejected on the grounds of British military unpreparedness and no decision was made over the need for an American military commitment.[16]

FOLLOWING THE AMERICAN LEAD

On 25 July, two days after Vichy capitulated to Japanese demands, Roosevelt announced the American freezing order and this was quickly followed by a parallel British decree. In Tokyo the reaction was one of stunned amazement. On 26 July Craigie reported that the Japanese government, despite periodic warnings from Grew and himself, had not expected anything other than the usual protests, and that this naïvety had been exacerbated by the recent political crisis, in which the Konoe Cabinet had resigned in order to purge Matsuoka from the Gaimushō and then reconstituted itself with Admiral Toyoda Teijirō as Foreign Minister. Toyoda tried to rectify the situation by insisting to Craigie and Grew that his appointment was a sign that Japan wished to improve its relations with Britain and the United States, but his efforts were in vain.[17]

One problem was that Britain was in a desperately insecure mood. This was in part due to pressure from Australia for a firmer line with Washington, but also to confusion over American intentions in regard to its sanctions policy; by 31 July it appeared that the State Department might be more lenient than first expected.[18] Britain's sense of insecurity made some sort of American security commitment even more urgent and on 1 August Eden, prompted by the Australians, pressed Halifax to seek an assurance of support from the Americans and to stress to the State Department the economic importance of the Dutch East Indies and Malaya to the Allied war effort.[19] In addition to this general concern, British anxiety was also raised by fears that Thailand might become the next object of Japanese aggression. On 2 August an SIS report noted that the American Military Attaché in Bangkok had information that the Japanese were once again pressing the Thais for naval and air bases and on the same day the JIC produced a memorandum entitled 'Japan's Next Move' which

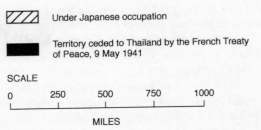

Under Japanese occupation

Territory ceded to Thailand by the French Treaty
of Peace, 9 May 1941

SCALE

0   250   500   750   1000

MILES

South-East Asia c., 1941

predicted that Japan might attempt an occupation of the Kra Isthmus.[20] The obvious answer to this threat was for the British forces in Malaya to initiate a pre-emptive seizure of the isthmus, an operation which Brooke-Popham had been planning since the spring, but this raised the problem that it might lead to an Anglo-Japanese confrontation which would not necessarily involve the Americans. Britain was thus in a dilemma; it could not afford to acquiesce to Japanese control of southern Thailand without compromising the security of Singapore, but at the same time it could not afford to fight Japan single-handed.

In the face of continuing American inaction over Thailand the Cabinet Defence Committee met to discuss the options open. Its analysis of the situation took place without Churchill, who on 3 August boarded HMS *Prince of Wales* on the way to his first summit with Roosevelt at Placentia Bay. In three meetings between 5 and 8 August the Committee decided that Britain should not take any action that could lead to war with Japan without a firm guarantee of American support and that therefore occupation of the Kra Isthmus should not take place nor any unilateral warning to Japan be issued unless this was assured. As a result of these deliberations on 9 August the Deputy Prime Minister, Clement Attlee, informed Churchill that he should try to persuade Roosevelt to agree to the presentation of parallel warnings to Japan against any further aggression. This recommendation was supported by telegrams from Menzies to Churchill which warned of the serious effect that the fall of Thailand would have for the security of Singapore.[21] The result was that at the Placentia Bay summit Churchill worked hard to prise an agreement to parallel action from Roosevelt. On 12 August Churchill was able to inform Attlee that the President had agreed to a warning to Japan that any advance in the region of the south-west Pacific, including Thailand, would lead to conflict.[22]

The success was soon shown to be short-lived. On 17 August Roosevelt met the Japanese Ambassador to the United States, the former Foreign Minister Nomura Kichisaburō, and delivered an admonition which had been considerably watered down by the State Department. The document stated that, if Japan made a further advance, the United States would take whatever steps necessary to defend its interests, a considerable climbdown from the terms agreed at the summit.[23] If this was not disappointing enough there was also continuing confusion about the extent of American economic restrictions against Japan. On 18 August Ashley Clarke of the Far Eastern Department noted that although Anglo-Japanese trade, including oil and Indian cotton exports, had come to a standstill the Americans were

> apparently prepared to allow quantities of these commodities [oil and cotton] to go to Japan on approximately the same scale as in recent months, except that some of the higher grades of petroleum products will be excluded. The whole question is whether Japan can obtain dollars to pay for them and in particular whether the United States will release dollars from Japanese assets frozen in the United States for this purpose. We await a definite answer on this.[24]

Eden was astonished at this report, which suggested that Britain was in the perilous position of being more advanced than the United States in the scale of its economic restrictions against Japan.[25] However, this was not the only danger, for on 17 August Halifax cabled from Washington that Nomura had proposed to the President the idea of a summit between the latter and Konoe at which the two men would solve the differences that existed between their respective countries.[26]

The idea of American–Japanese talks had been disturbing the Foreign Office for some time. Meetings between Hull and Nomura to discuss mutual problems had begun in March but had only officially come to Britain's notice on 17 May when Hull briefed Halifax on them (there is a possibility that Britain might have had prior knowledge of the talks through the BJ source). Despite Hull's claims that he intended to be circumspect in his discussions with the Japanese Ambassador, the Foreign Office were gravely concerned at the prospect that Japan might use the talks to divide Britain and the United States. On 21 May Eden had told Halifax of these doubts, and instructed him to reiterate to Hull the Foreign Office's conviction that only a policy of firmness would detach Japan from the Axis and that the Japanese intended the talks to act as a trap. When Halifax communicated these views to Hull on 24 May the latter's reaction was apoplectic; he interpreted Eden's warning about Japanese duplicity as an insinuation that he was being naïve even to engage in talks.[27] Eden was forced to send an apology to calm the Secretary of State's wounded pride, but this did not mean that the Foreign Office was reconciled to the wisdom of Japanese–American talks. Even though there was a realization that nothing further could be said to the Americans on the subject, there was still a belief that such conversations were not in Britain's interest. Suspicion had been kept alive over the next few months by the lack of information from the

State Department on the content of the talks, but this reached new heights when news of Konoe's summit proposal reached London.

Eden was obviously in no position, considering the events of May, to lecture Hull on the dangers of this path, but there was some uncertainty about how Roosevelt would react to this latest overture. At the Placentia Bay meeting the President had attempted to put Churchill's mind at rest about the talks with Nomura, stressing that he saw them as a means of gaining time in order to improve American defences in the Pacific, but with the toning down of the warning to Japan it was unclear to what extent the United States could be relied upon. These fears about the talks in Washington were also evident in Chungking and on 8 September Clark Kerr reported that Dr Quo, who had recently become the Foreign Minister, was worried that Britain and the United States would betray China. Churchill recognized that by forwarding these Chinese complaints to Washington he could indirectly indicate his own forebodings about the Hull–Nomura talks, and on 10 September he instructed Eden to take action along these lines.[28] Even using this tactic it remained difficult to gain any information on how the talks were progressing and on 14 September the Counsellor at the Washington Embassy, Sir Ronald Campbell, reported to Eden that he was sceptical about the utility of pressing Hull, noting pessimistically

> there seems to be a real danger . . . that he [Hull] may be drawn forward on to dangerous ground, and encouraged to believe that a genuine settlement can be achieved when, in fact, he may merely be playing into Japanese hands. Thus he may, for example, be led to accept an interpretation of his principles which, ostensibly for the purpose of saving Japanese face, were capable of almost unlimited exploitation by the Japanese.[29]

MISGIVINGS IN TOKYO: INFLEXIBILITY IN LONDON

While the Foreign Office were disturbed that the Americans might be hoodwinked by the Japanese, the concern in the British and American embassies in Tokyo was rather different. Both Craigie and Grew were convinced that Matsuoka's dismissal and the subsequent proposal from Konoe for a summit with Roosevelt showed that the 'moderates' were once again exercising influence, and that the United States and Britain should respond positively to their overtures. Important in this calculation was the return of Shigemitsu to Japan in late July. On 29 July the former ambassador told Craigie that he had been pleasantly surprised on his return to find that the situation within the country was not as desperate as he had feared and that there was no desire for war with Britain. This impression was confirmed by a series of talks that Craigie held with Toyoda in August in which the latter, though critical of Britain, emphasized his hopes for a peaceful settlement.[30]

The apparent revival of the 'moderates' led Craigie and Grew to believe that a 'carrot and stick' approach to Japan was the best way to achieve an understanding, but this did not seem to be the view of London or indeed Washington. On 3 September Roosevelt responded to Konoe's summit proposal by stating that, before any meeting could take place, Japan must commit itself to accept the 'Four Principles' – respect for territorial integrity, non-interference in internal affairs, equality of opportunity in trade and non-disturbance of the *status quo* except by peaceful means – which Hull had outlined at the start of his talks with Nomura and show a willingness to compromise over its policy towards China and its links with the Axis.[31] This was at cross-purposes with Konoe's original plan which, due to the necessity to present the Army with a *fait accompli*, had been drawn up on the basis that there could be no preconditions, as this might provide an excuse for the IJA to prevent any meeting between the two leaders. Konoe's desperation for a meeting was increased further when, at an Imperial Conference on 6 September, it was decided that if talks had not been concluded by early October then Japan should be ready to go to war before the end of that month. This was a tight deadline, and that day Konoe invited Grew to dine secretly at his house and there expressed orally his acceptance of the 'Four Principles' and his belief that a meeting with Roosevelt could turn the corner.[32]

In addition to the pressure on Grew, the Gaimushō also tried to strengthen their diplomatic offensive by bringing in Craigie, in the hope that Britain could be persuaded to use its influence to encourage Washington to take a less rigid stance. On 8 September Shigemitsu held a secret meeting with Craigie, at which he assured the latter that the moderates were beginning to regain control and that the link with the Axis was steadily growing weaker.[33] Influenced by this and by his own conversations with Grew, Craigie forwarded to the Foreign Office on 9 September the contents of a telegram which the American Ambassador was sending to the State Department. Grew had written in this note that he believed that Konoe and Toyoda were sincere in their wish for peace, but that they were hindered by the rest of the Japanese Cabinet and that therefore the United States should try to encourage the peace process by explaining to the Japanese

people the advantages which would accrue from a policy of friendship with the democracies. Craigie noted in his telegram his complete
agreement with this approach but observed that neither he nor Grew
were suggesting any relaxation of sanctions.[34]

This communication did not impress London; the Foreign Office
was adamant that if there was going to be any conciliatory gestures
then they should come from Japan. One of the key factors behind this
opinion was a belief that the Japanese government was beginning to
realize the extent of its dilemma and was considering how to retreat.
This impression was in part a result of the latest Japanese diplomatic
overtures in Washington, but it was also supported by evidence from
the BJ source. In particular decrypts of both Japanese and Italian
telegrams revealed that Japan was seeking to withhold the details of
the talks in Washington from its Tripartite Pact partners. On 29
August Churchill was shown a telegram from a worried Ōshima to
Toyoda which demonstrated that the Japanese Ambassador in Berlin
had virtually no information on Nomura's instructions.[35] A reply duly
came from Toyoda but it noted, in vague terms that were hardly likely
to reassure Ōshima, that Amō Eiji, the Vice-Minister for Foreign
Affairs, had recently told the German ambassador in Tokyo that

> The object of the Three-Power Alliance was the restoration of
> peace and this has been announced by the Governments of the
> other countries. The Japanese–American talks had this for their
> object, and were therefore not essentially opposed to our Axis
> diplomacy.[36]

In addition to this, there were hints from Italian cables that the
Japanese were becoming increasingly concerned that events in the
Atlantic could drag them into the European War; on 12 September
Bletchley Park decrypted a telegram from the Italian Ambassador in
Tokyo which noted the anxiety caused by an encounter between an
American destroyer, the USS *Greer*, and a German U-boat.[37]

Another vital factor was the perception that Japan was still in two
minds over whether to strike north or south. Military intelligence
showed that throughout August and September a steady build-up of
Japanese troops was taking place in Manchukuo; a weekly résumé for
the War Cabinet on 18 September reported that the Kwantung Army
now probably outnumbered the Soviet Far Eastern Army.[38] Many in
both the War Office and the Foreign Office felt that a Japanese attack
on its traditional enemy was more likely than a further move in
South-East Asia, but that Japan would not strike north until the
German onslaught had caused a Soviet collapse. This led to the

belief that the course of the war in Europe was far more likely to determine Japan's decision than the extent of the economic sanctions ranged against it and that therefore there was no point in making concessions.[39]

The perception that Japan was undecided about its future policy led Eden to take a reasonably bright view of the future, and on 12 September he sent to Churchill his assessment of the current situation and of Craigie's recent telegrams; he noted optimistically

> It is clear that the Japanese are hesitating but this better mood has only been brought about by the contemplation of the forces that may possibly confront them. Russia, the United States, China and the British Empire, to say nothing of the Dutch, is more than this probably over-valued military power is prepared to challenge. Our right policy is, therefore, clearly to keep up the pressure. . . . We are now engaged in examining Craigie's telegrams. It is important that we should not be too forthcoming to Japanese approaches, even through Shigemitsu. We want the Japanese to feel that we are in a position to play our hand from strength.[40]

Eden then proceeded to observe that Britain could not in any case seek to advise the Americans and that in fact the most positive move Britain could make to influence the situation was to send some naval reinforcements to Singapore, an idea that Churchill had already raised with the Admiralty. In the next few days the Foreign Office's uncompromising line was reinforced by reports from Washington that the Americans had after all introduced a virtually complete embargo on trade with Japan, which reaffirmed the need for Britain to keep its nerve and to stay in step with the United States. On 18 September a telegram was sent to Craigie informing him that the time was not right for making concessions to the Japanese.[41]

However, the pressure on Craigie from the Gaimushō was still intense and at the end of September an increasingly desperate Toyoda, assisted by Shigemitsu and Amō, urged the British Ambassador to press the Foreign Office to use its influence with Roosevelt.[42] Under this barrage Craigie, on 30 September, wrote a telegram to London in which he expanded on his conviction that there was a real prospect that an understanding could be reached. He noted, however, that the American insistence on slow, precise talks was proving counter-productive, and argued that if Washington persisted with this policy 'it bids fair to wreck the best chance of bringing about a just settlement of Far Eastern issues which has occurred since my arrival in Japan'.[43] Once again Craigie's words failed to elicit a positive response in the Foreign Office. The overriding reason was the conviction that any attempt to interfere in the talks in Washington would anger Hull but, in addition, Sterndale Bennett noted on 1 October that, despite Craigie's passionate argument, it was very difficult to see how in practical terms Japan could be weaned away from the Axis without sweeping concessions from the West.[44]

An example of the gulf between Japan and the Anglo-Saxon powers was evident in the Japanese response to the Atlantic Charter that had been drawn up by Roosevelt and Churchill at the Placentia Bay meeting. This document committed the democracies to the ideals of free trade and of free access to raw materials. One might assume that, considering Japan's economic plight, the Konoe government would have welcomed the apparent intention of Britain and the United States to move away from protectionism, but in fact the reception in Japan was far from enthusiastic. The general attitude of the Japanese press was that the Charter was designed simply to reinforce American and British dominance over the world economy and that it offered Japan very little. After all, the Anglo-Saxon states were merely reiterating principles which they had previously professed to hold in the 1930s and that decade had seen both powers follow a policy of high tariffs and quotas on Japanese goods. These criticisms were mirrored by Japan's diplomats. On 8 September Shigemitsu observed to Craigie that the tenets of the Charter seemed to contrast strongly with the policy that Britain and the United States were currently pursuing towards Japan.[45] A week later Amō took Japan's resentment even further and observed caustically to Craigie

You . . . have now lived in Japan some years, and I believe you have observed the condition of the people in their daily lives; I wonder if you think these people are really adequately compensated for their capacity and effort. Though they work from morning to night, still they are only barely at the level of subsistence, whilst virtually every Englishman, working less than the Japanese, enjoys a life of relative ease. In a word, whilst the Japanese are in a life and death struggle, the English give their thought to how they may live more luxuriously.[46]

It was thus clear that to Japan the Atlantic Charter was no more than an exercise in hypocrisy and, as the terms of the document were close to those espoused in Hull's Four Principles, it suggested that there was little likelihood that a permanent mutually acceptable understanding could be reached.

PROPAGANDA AND DETERRENCE

There was, however, by this stage another reason why the Foreign Office felt that it could refuse to countenance any effort at conciliation and this was the marked improvement which was beginning to take place in the military position of the Western Powers. Already at the Placentia Bay summit the American Joint Chiefs of Staff had indicated to their British counterparts that they were going to reverse their policy of a merely minimal defence for the Philippines, and by early October thirty-five B-17 Flying Fortress bombers were either stationed at or in transit to Clark Field on Luzon. On 11 October Halifax wrote a personal letter to Churchill in which he reported on a conversation he had had with Roosevelt about the effects of this deployment and also noted that Henry Stimson, the Army Secretary, had demonstrated with the use of maps that the B-17s would be capable of hitting targets in Formosa.[47]

The American build-up was mirrored by a similar expansion of forces in Malaya. The situation there had changed considerably since the February 'war-scare' with the arrival of substantial numbers of troops. There was still a problem with aircraft as the figure of 336 front-line planes that had been recommended in the Far East Appreciation of July 1940 had still not been reached, but numbers were slowly rising. There was a reasonable hope that the situation would continue to improve, as more modern aircraft such as Baltimores, Mustangs and Beauforts were to be assigned to the Far Eastern Command when production delays had been overcome in the United States and Australia.[48] On 1 October Brooke-Popham and the Commander-in-Chief China station, Admiral Layton, sent a joint telegram to the Chiefs of Staff which noted the progress that had been made, and recorded that they too felt that Japan was hesitating and was torn between the desire for southern expansion and the temptation of striking against the Soviet Union. They therefore recommended that the Admiralty should give serious consideration to the stationing of one or two battleships at Singapore, an action they felt would have considerable deterrent and propaganda value. The propaganda motive was important for Brooke-Popham as over the last couple of months he had sent a number of telegrams to the Chiefs of Staff criticizing the propaganda campaign against Japan for its ineffectiveness and in particular its failure to stress British preparedness for war.[49]

It was also recognized in Whitehall that the sending of a powerful naval squadron to Singapore could prove to be a very potent propaganda tool. It would act as a deterrent to Japan, while at the same time reassuring the antipodean dominions and demonstrating to the American public that Britain was willing to defend its interests in the region and was thus a worthy ally. On 10 October the Chiefs of Staff sent a telegram informing Brooke-Popham that the issue was under consideration and agreed that it would have 'considerable propaganda value'.[50] However, the problem was deciding what kind of force should be sent east; an issue which had been under debate since August. The Admiralty favoured stationing a number of Britain's oldest battleships in the Indian Ocean where they could act as a deterrent to Japanese raiders and provide a covering force for convoys. Churchill and Eden disagreed with this cautious stance; they instead preferred to send a small, fast squadron to Singapore which would include one of Britain's latest *King George V*-class battleships, on the grounds that such a force would have a considerable political impact as well as being able to menace Japanese convoys and thus more convincingly deter any Japanese advance into the region. The telegram from Singapore added to the immediacy of finding a solution but was not the spark which led to the final debate, instead it was a change in Japan that was to galvanize the policy-makers.[51]

On 16 October news came from Tokyo that Konoe had resigned as Prime Minister. This provoked Eden to note to Churchill

The fall of Konoye's government is an ominous sign. Though the complexion of the new Cabinet is not yet announced, we must expect the constitution of one more under the influence of extreme elements. The Russian defeats must inevitably be having their effect upon the Japanese appetite. There is nothing yet to show in which direction they will move, if any. But it is no doubt true that the stronger the joint front the A.B.C.D. Powers can show, the greater the deterrent to Japanese action.

In this connexion you will recall that we discussed some little time ago the possibility of capital ship reinforcements to the Far East. The matter has now become more urgent, and I should be glad if it could be discussed at the Defence Committee tomorrow afternoon.[52]

The Committee duly met on 17 October and Churchill endeavoured to persuade his colleagues of the wisdom of sending a fast squadron to Singapore. The Prime Minister received strong backing for his proposal from Eden and Attlee who both noted the political significance of despatching a modern vessel. No decision was taken at this

meeting due to the absence of Pound, but a second meeting with the
First Sea Lord present was held on 20 October. Pound argued as
strongly as he could against Churchill's plan, but finding himself in a
minority suggested a compromise under which HMS *Prince of Wales*
would proceed to Cape Town in South Africa and that a final decision
on its destination would be made on its arrival. On the same day
Churchill, somewhat ignoring Pound's proviso, wrote to Roosevelt
assuring him that a 'considerable Battle-squadron' would be available
for use in the Indian and Pacific Oceans before Christmas.[53] The
Prime Minister and Eden had thus achieved an important victory
which was designed not only to bolster Britain's position in South-
East Asia but also to encourage American resolve.

THE ARRIVAL OF THE TŌJŌ CABINET

The need to keep the United States up to the mark was particularly
important in the light of the establishment on 17 October of a new
government in Japan led by the former Army Minister, Tōjō Hideki.
Tōjō had a reputation as an ardent nationalist and his appointment
suggested that Japan was close to a decision for war, but the question
still remained – war against whom? The fact that Tōjō had strong
connections with the Kwantung Army and was known as a
Russophobe gave rise to an initial belief in many quarters that war
with the Soviet Union was imminent. This was certainly the view of
Maisky, who on 17 October urged Eden to issue a stern warning with
the United States against any Japanese move north. The Foreign
Office shared these fears and on the same day warned Halifax that
recent Russian reverses against Germany might tempt Japan to invade
the maritime provinces and that therefore there was a need to consider
what more could be done to deter Japan and to discover what the
United States intended to do if the Soviet Union was attacked.[54]

Before this enquiry could be addressed to Hull, the Foreign Office
learnt that the Secretary of State was, in direct contradiction to
Britain's policy of tightening the screws on Japan even further,
contemplating a barter agreement with Japan under which the United
States would exchange its cotton for Japanese silk. This news raised
all the latent fears in British circles that the talks in Washington could
lead to Hull making a disadvantageous compromise settlement; on 19
October Churchill minuted on his own copy of the telegram that this
was tantamount to appeasement. The Foreign Office concurred with
this judgement and on 21 October Eden told Halifax to advise Hull
against this course of action, but this was hardly necessary as fears in

Washington about a Japanese attack on Russia had already led to its burial.[55]

However, the belief that a Japanese–Soviet war might be imminent was short-lived, for by the end of October concentration was diverted to the build-up of Japanese forces in south China and Indo-China. On 30 October the weekly résumé of Japanese movements produced for the War Cabinet noted that since 18 October 12,000 troops had landed in Haiphong and that it appeared that Japan might be planning an expedition from Tonkin and Canton against Kunming in an effort to cut the Burma Road. The next day this impression was reinforced by an American intelligence report which stated that Japan intended to invade Yunnan on 2 November. This was a serious matter, for the Chinese had already, due to Barbarossa, seen their supplies from the Soviet Union plummet, and it was predicted by MI2c that there was a danger that Chinese resistance might collapse if they lost the only supply route linking them to Britain and the United States.[56] On 1 November a panic-stricken Chiang Kai-shek sent cables to Churchill and Roosevelt about China's plight, stressing his fear that an attack would take place in the next few days. He also insisted that China could not hope to survive this assault unless it had a promise of air support. In Whitehall Chiang's plea met with some concern: if China were to fall this would free a large number of Japanese troops who would then be able to strike against South-East Asia, but it was equally apparent that Britain could not unilaterally assist China lest it involve itself in war with Japan without bringing in the United States. The only possible course was therefore to try to persuade Roosevelt to assist the Chinese and on 5 November Churchill urged the President to give a direct warning to Japan about any advance into Yunnan. Roosevelt was, however, not convinced and on 9 November informed Churchill that he seriously doubted whether Japan was ready to attack Kunming and that he believed that as this stage further reinforcements would have a greater deterrent effect on Japan than more warnings.[57]

By the time Roosevelt's telegram arrived in London the fear of an imminent attack on Yunnan had to some degree passed, although it was still seen as a possibility for the future. The view within the War Office was that Japan was consolidating its position in Indo-China and that it would take at least another month before any attack was launched on Yunnan, and that in any case the Japanese offensive would be hampered by the harsh terrain.[58] This sense of complacency was also evident in higher circles. On 12 November Churchill turned down a request from Earle Page, the Australian Minister to the War

Cabinet, for more aircraft to be sent to Singapore, and brusquely told him that he was sure that he

> would recognise that it would be a grave strategical error to move forces to the Far East – possibly to remain inactive for a year – which were now actively engaged against Germany and Italy. . . . A policy of spreading our resources to guard against possible but unlikely attacks might be fatal.[59]

At the same meeting Eden told his colleagues that it was his conviction that Japan's next move would be directed against the Soviets, the Thais, the Dutch or the Burma Road, in other words any target other than Britain or the United States. It was still felt that Japan planned an incremental advance to improve its position but did not plan to risk war against the Anglo-Saxon powers, an impression which was fostered by reports received on the whereabouts of the IJN. Intelligence information received around this time showed that the Japanese navy had not taken up positions from which to threaten Britain or the United States. On 9 November the FECB at Singapore informed the Admiralty that Y intelligence (information derived from radio signals, possibly JN–25B) had revealed that the majority of the Japanese Combined Fleet, including five aircraft carriers, was still at Kure in Japan.[60] As long as this remained so there was no danger of Japanese attack.

CRAIGIE'S LAST SORTIE

This appreciation of Japanese intentions was not shared by Craigie. On 30 October Craigie gained the impression in a talk with Tōgō Shigenori, the new Foreign Minister, that the time left in which to secure a settlement was growing dangerously short and on 1 November, in a spirit of some desperation, he drafted a long telegram to London warning of the consequences should the talks in Washington fail. He began by noting his concern that in effect the United States was negotiating on behalf of Britain as well when in fact the two countries' interests in East Asia were markedly different and then turned his attention to the method that the Americans had used up to this time in the talks. He observed critically that

> little attention seems to have been paid in Washington to Japanese psychology and to the facts of the international situation here, which forbid so sudden and drastic a change in policy as the United States Government appear to demand. Feeling is being

worked up in both the United States and Japan to such an extent
that an explosion could occur at any time. This might take the
unpleasant form of a direct attack on British territory, from which
Japan might hope to achieve the first results before the ponderous
machinery of the United States Government had had time to
project the United States into active participation of the war.[61]

The potential for an attack on Malaya, he held, demonstrated the
importance to Britain of receiving a much fuller account of the talks
from Washington. In conclusion he noted

> Every act of the United States Government and ourselves in
> reinforcing our military position in the Far East, and the imposing
> of economic sanctions for specific misdeeds, has been excellent
> and salutary: but I have always recommended that simultaneous
> steps should be taken to convince the Japanese Government and
> people that there is a better way out for their country than a resort
> to arms, and that the door to it remains always open; in particular it
> is important to convince the Japanese that there is no truth in the
> repeated German assertion that a democratic victory would reduce
> Japan to the status of a third-rate power. It is in this latter direction
> that American diplomacy has seemed to me to be a little lacking in
> vision. In particular I feel that about the worst mistake that we and
> the Americans can make at this juncture is to underestimate the
> strength and resolution of this country and its armed forces, in the
> event – perhaps now not far distant – that it may feel itself driven
> to desperation.[62]

This comprehensive analysis of the current situation was followed
over the next few days by further telegrams from Craigie adding extra
emphasis to the points he had already made. Most significantly he
noted on 6 November that he was no longer convinced that Japan
would avoid war with the United States at almost any cost.[63]

Again, however, these pleas from Craigie failed to have the desired
effect in London, since the Foreign Office remained convinced that it
must adhere to its current policy and maintain a 'firm and united
front' with the United States. In addition to the continued reluctance
to press Hull over his talks with Nomura, this inflexibility was due to
serious doubts about the sincerity of Japan's negotiating position. On
6 November the Foreign Office was informed by Craigie that the
Gaimushō was sending the former Ambassador to Germany, Kurusu
Saburō, to assist Nomura and make one last determined effort to
reach a settlement, but there was little evidence to suggest that any

settlement suggested by Japan would be acceptable to Britain.[64] A telegram from the Italian ambassador in Tokyo to Ciano decrypted on 11 November revealed that Kurusu had been instructed to promise no further Japanese advances in return for a removal of the blockade and that, in addition, 'America would have to stop sending assistance to CHIANG KAI SHEK and instead would have to advise him to make peace'. This sentence, which Churchill underlined in red on his copy, had the same effect as the earlier fear of an attack on Yunnan; if Chinese resistance ended, the security of South-East Asia would be imperilled whether there was an American–Japanese understanding or not. In addition, other decrypts demonstrated that Japan's previous caution in its dealings with Germany had come to an end and that Tōgō had agreed to the revision and renewal of the Anti-Comintern Pact.[65] In the light of this Eden informed Craigie on 15 November that

> The maintenance of our present policy admittedly involves a risk of war, though with a good prospect of active American participation. With the Japanese in their present mood there is no alternative for us except appeasement which is of course what the Japanese are hoping for. But there can be no assurance that concessions to Japan, which would have to be made certainly at the expense of China, and probably of others, would stave off the risk of war. On the contrary Japan would then be confirmed in the conviction that aggression pays, and would be ready to resume her southward thrust at the first opportunity, perhaps when we are being hard pressed at home. We should find that we had merely bought a short respite at the cost of forfeiting both the respect and material assistance of our friends.[66]

Craigie's final foray into the maelstrom of Anglo-Japanese relations thus failed, once again, to elicit a positive response.

TOWARDS A *MODUS VIVENDI*?

By the middle of November it became evident that the deployment of Japanese forces was beginning to change. On 15 November the Deputy Director of Military Intelligence at Singapore informed the War Office that SIS operatives in Indo-China had reported a marked increase in activity in Cambodia which suggested that the intended target was now Thailand. The next day further evidence arrived to support this conclusion in a BJ in which the Gaimushō instructed the Japanese Ambassador at Vichy to press the French authorities to agree to a revision of the Nishihara–Martin agreement of September 1940 which would allow Japanese troops to operate south of the Red River. Two days later the JIC produced a memorandum which concluded that, if the talks in Washington failed to produce a settlement, the Japanese would seize bases in Thailand, including the Kra Isthmus, preparatory to an assault on Malaya or the Dutch East Indies.[67] On 21 November the feeling of impending crisis was reinforced by a BJ intercept of a telegram from Tōgō to the Consul-General in Hong Kong stating that, if the Washington negotiations failed, 'one may expect a sudden change in that part of the international situation which revolves around Japan'. It then stated that in these circumstances Japan would seize British and American concessions and interests in China.[68]

In this atmosphere of uncertainty the talks in Washington took on a new importance. It was obvious that they were the only thing that stood in the way of a further Japanese advance and that the latter could only be deterred if the negotiations achieved some progress. This calculation led the British government to change slightly its attitude towards the talks, a shift that was also influenced by Kurusu's arrival in the United States. On 18 November Kurusu held his first talk with Hull and suggested that Japan should withdraw from south Indo-China in return for a slight relaxing of the American embargo. Although Kurusu had no instructions to make such a proposal and was subsequently ordered by Tōgō to withdraw it, this idea proved attractive to the Foreign Office, and on 21 November Halifax was informed that such a deal might be worth making as long as it did not involve any abandonment of China.[69]

However, on 22 November Halifax was told by Hull that a new proposal had emerged from the Japanese camp. This second plan was not as liberal as that originally espoused by Kurusu but was on similar lines. It proposed that Japan and the United States should promise not to make any armed advance into South-East Asia, that Japan would withdraw its troops from south Indo-China, and that the United States would restore its commercial relations with the Japanese and supply Japan with a 'required quantity of oil'.[70] The agreement thus differed from the Kurusu initiative in that it required a more extensive lifting of the blockade and that it prohibited further American reinforcements from entering the region. Although these stipulations were considered objectionable, Hull told Halifax and the Dutch, Australian and Chinese ambassadors that the idea of a temporary agreement lasting maybe three months was attractive, he outlined in rough a counter-proposal under which Japanese agreement to remove the bulk of its troops from south Indo-China would lead to a slight relaxation of the American embargo, including the supply of some low-grade oil for civilian purposes, and noted that he would welcome the comments of the other governments concerned.[71]

In London Churchill received the news of a possible stalling of Japan with some enthusiasm and noted to Eden the next day that he would be happy to see a slight relaxation of the embargo in return for the stabilization of the situation in South-East Asia for three months, a view he reiterated to the War Cabinet. The Foreign Office was a little more circumspect, recognizing that real security could only come if the American *modus vivendi* was made watertight. Therefore on 24 November Eden told Halifax that he should inform Hull that as far as the British government was concerned the latter's counter-proposal did not go far enough. In particular, the Foreign Secretary emphasized the absolute necessity for the United States to push for an assurance that all Japanese military personnel and equipment, not just 'troops', be removed from south Indo-China and that Japan promise not to make any further advances in China. In addition, it was recommended that American economic concessions should be strictly limited and should not include any oil. These terms were communicated to Hull on 25 November but received an unenthusiastic reception, as Hull believed that they were too rigid, and in particular that to include provisions about China would doom the *modus vivendi* to failure.[72]

While Hull was disappointed at the qualified British response to his scheme, in London scepticism about the American approach to the Japanese was mounting. In the early hours of 26 November, Eden recorded in his diary, he arrived at the Foreign Office to be met by Sterndale Bennett, who gave him a 'message' about the American-Japanese talks. It is not clear what this refers too but it seems likely that it was the formal *modus vivendi* proposal which Hull had handed to Halifax the previous evening. Eden then noted that both he and Sterndale Bennett 'feared that Hull was giving away too much' and therefore Eden set off to see Churchill who agreed that there was a need to send a 'telegram to R from Winston about Chinese reactions'.[73] A cable was speedily despatched; it read

Of course, it is for you to handle this business and we certainly do not want an additional war. There is only one thing that disquiets us. What about Chiang Kai-shek? Is he not having a very thin diet? Our anxiety is about China. If they collapse, our joint dangers would enormously increase. We are sure that the regard of the United States for the Chinese cause will govern your action.[74]

This terse message has been interpreted by a number of historians as 'the needle that broke the camel's back', in that Hull recorded in his memoirs that it was this communication which persuaded him to drop the *modus vivendi*. The corollary of this accusation has been that Churchill's action was misguided since the failure to pursue a temporary settlement doomed the Washington talks to overall failure and thus contributed to the outbreak of the Pacific War. Churchill and the Foreign Office, it is said, made this error because they did not know that the *modus vivendi* was the last round in the Washington talks and because they had taken the lesson from the 1930s that appeasement did not pay.[75]

To understand why Churchill, with Eden's implicit approval, sent this message to Roosevelt it is necessary, as the historian Waldo Heinrichs has done for the administration in Washington, to consider what influences were exerting themselves on the British government. The first factor to note, as Heinrichs has stressed, was that in the last week of November the titanic struggle in the Soviet Union was reaching a climax with German troops poised to strike at Moscow; for example, on 24 November a summary of special intelligence from the Admiralty's Operational Intelligence Centre noted that German troops were now placed just fifty-two miles north-west of the Russian capital.[76] This is important because Churchill was in no doubt that a Russian surrender would lead Germany to turn westwards once again to extinguish British resistance. It might be thought that such a danger actually argued in favour of a temporary settlement in East Asia, but this is to miss a vital point. If Japan were diverted from a southern advance it might instead strike north against the Soviet Union, greatly aiding the German cause.

The second point to consider is the continuing British fear that a Chinese collapse would allow Japan to concentrate all its forces in South-East Asia. A number of books have challenged Churchill's sincerity in mentioning his concern for China in his note to Roosevelt on 26 November. While it is true that an overview of Churchill's life would not detect an abiding interest in China, the attention shown to Chiang Kai-shek's plight in late November was not a new departure but rather, as Akira Iriye has pointed out, a continuation of a policy that the Foreign Office and Churchill had followed throughout the late summer and autumn. This was, of course, not altruistic, it was quite simply a fear induced by the

potential consequences of Chinese collapse. It is worth noting here
that, as well as many other indications of Chinese disquiet about the
modus vivendi, on 26 November Churchill was shown a telegram
from the Chinese Ambassador in Russia to Chungking which recommended that, if the Americans made an agreement with Japan, then
China should seek its own radical settlement with Tokyo, although it
is unclear if the Prime Minister saw this information before his cable
was sent to Roosevelt.[77]

The third factor is the intelligence that filtered through into British
hands in the period between 20 and 25 November. Certainly the
military and naval intelligence received was disturbing; there were
further reports from the FECB which documented the build-up of
Japanese forces in south Indo-China, an upsurge of Japanese sub-
marine activity near Hong Kong and the Spratlys and off Rangoon,
and evidence that the Japanese merchant fleet had in the main been
brought back into home waters, all of which supported the possibility
that Japan was on the point of reactivating its southern advance.[78]
The diplomatic intercepts were also revealing. On 25 November a
telegram from the Gaimushō to its representatives in Europe was
decrypted; it noted

> For our part, we are doing our utmost to reach a compromise, but
> we cannot make any further concessions, and the outlook is not
> bright. Should the negotiations break down, that part of the
> situation in which the Japanese Empire is involved will be
> critical.[79]

The admission that Japan was not in a position to make any concessions was hardly a sign that the talks in Washington were on the verge
of a breakthrough and suggested that, as in Britain's previous negotiations with Japan, compromise was a one-way street. It also
revealed, as had earlier BJs, that Tokyo saw the current talks as the
final round; there could have been no illusion on this account in
London.

Even more significant was that also on 25 November the British
had in their possession an intercepted telegram which indicated
sinister intents on Japan's part; the message read

> On 19th NOV. Tokyo told Chargé d'Affaires in London that the
> international situation is tense. When diplomatic relations are on
> the point of being severed, following phrases will occur in the
> middle and end of Japanese Broadcast Service in the form of a
> weather report.

   (1) With U.S.A. The words–HIGASHI NO KAZE AME (easterly wind rain)

   (2) With SOVIET. Words–KITA NO KAZE KUMORI (north winds cloudy)

   (3) With Britain, including invasion of THAILAND. Words– NISHI NO KAZE HARE (westerly winds fine)

On receipt books are to be burnt.[80]

Unfortunately, due to the excessive secrecy of the British government over security matters, the impact of this message cannot, over fifty years later, be assessed, indeed the currently released records do not even indicate if this decrypt was shown to the Prime Minister, but it is hard to believe that such a cable, with its reference to the severing of diplomatic relations, was not distributed at the highest level and that it would not have raised fears of war. One of the most potentially disturbing aspects of this telegram was that war with Britain and war with the United States were treated as two separate entities; could this have provoked a fear that Japan was still trying to drive a wedge between the two countries? That Japan was using the talks in Washington as a camouflage for its aggressive intentions and would strike against Britain no matter whether an agreement was reached or not? This is speculation but it is nevertheless a possibility that the message was seen as having that connotation and therefore would have reinforced the belief in London that it was too late to talk of mutual compromise: one must remember that at this time there was still no guarantee of American support should Japan attack British territory.

The situation in late November was a complex one and the dangers very great. There was a chance that, if events went drastically wrong, Britain could find itself alone in a war against Japan, with the possibility in the near future of a renewed threat of German invasion. In these circumstances it may feasibly have been considered safest to continue with the policy of a hard line towards Japan, and to urge caution on the United States to forestall its being mollified by false assurances. It must be remembered that, while America was still at peace, Britain was fighting a war to the death and could not afford to take risks. One must therefore be careful to put Churchill's role in undermining Hull's *modus vivendi* in context, it was not an arbitrary act of vandalism nor anything as simple as the result of a revulsion of appeasement – it was an act taken under specific circumstances and for sound reasons.

THE FINAL DAYS

Hull's decision to drop the idea of a *modus vivendi*, and his subsequent reiteration of the previous American negotiating position to Nomura and Kurusu on 26 November, meant that to all intents and purposes the Washington talks had come to an end. It was obvious with the collapse of the conversations that Britain and the United States would have to wait for Japan's next move. The difficulty was in working out where Japan would strike. This problem was well illustrated in a telegram on 28 November from Admiral Layton to the British naval liaison officer in Batavia, which noted in relation to a report on a possible Japanese attack on Borneo

> Reports giving Japanese object as being Malaya, Thailand, China, Burma Road or Siberia constantly being received point out to CZM [Dutch authorities] that report quoted by you was only one of many. Latest reports give an attack on South Thailand without warning on 1st December.[81]

As noted above it still seemed that the most likely move was a Japanese advance into Thailand. A mass of intelligence material supported this conclusion, one of the most significant indications being a report on 26 November from the American Consul in Hanoi, who had been informed by the Vichy authorities that the Japanese intended to attack the Kra Isthmus on 1 December.[82] Military and naval intelligence seemed to support this assertion, as it was clear that the build-up in south Indo-China was continuing and that troops experienced in amphibious operations were being moved south from the Shanghai and Canton areas. In addition, there was evidence from the American naval intelligence centre at Honolulu that the Japanese Second and Third Fleets were being organized into a special task force which included four *Kongo* class battleships and four aircraft carriers and that this force was heading towards the ports of Takao in south Formosa (present day Kaohsing) and Bako in the Pescadores.[83]

Although this concentration of forces around Formosa might be construed as indicating an attack on Malaya, this was not considered likely in Whitehall. On 28 November a JIC memorandum noted that the danger of air-attack would very likely deter Japan from direct amphibious operations against Malaya or the Dutch East Indies, and that the most likely scenario was a Japanese seizure of the Kra Isthmus followed by a period of two or three months in which the Japanese would improve communications and aerodromes in south

Thailand preparatory to an attack on the British.[84] This judgement was influenced by the widely held belief that the Isthmus was water-logged at this time of year which would make any advance into Malaya virtually impossible and that the monsoon would complicate any amphibious operations attempted in the Gulf of Thailand. The impression that any advance would stop in Thailand was reinforced by information from the BJ source. Two telegrams, intercepted on 26 and 28 November, from the Italian Minister in Bangkok indicated that his Japanese colleague, Tsubokami Teiji, was convinced that invasion was imminent. Moreover, a Japanese telegram shown to Churchill on 28 November showed that the Thai Prime Minister, Pibul Songgram, was weakening, and had told Tsubokami that he wished to see Japan predominant in the region.[85]

The threat to Thailand still meant that precautionary measures had to be taken in case hostilities should ensue. On 29 November the AWAKE telegram which ordered the finalization of defence prepara-tions was sent from the Colonial Office to Sir Shenton Thomas, and the next day an interdepartmental *ad-hoc* committee chaired by Sterndale Bennett began to meet in Whitehall.[86] However, the most important issue raised by the concern over Thailand was whether or not Britain should pre-empt a Japanese occupation of the Kra Isthmus by launching Operation Matador. There was some doubt about the wisdom of such an action, as there was a danger that it might push Thailand irrevocably into the Japanese camp and alienate American public opinion by making Britain the aggressor. Even more import-antly, there was the possibility that the operation might lead to a clash with the Japanese while Britain was still without any firm guarantee of support from the United States, and over an issue which was hardly likely to galvanize the American public in Britain's favour. The result of Whitehall's deliberation over this issue was that the Chiefs of Staff informed Brooke-Popham that he could not initiate the operation without their express orders.[87]

The uncertainty over the Thai situation made it imperative for Britain to have some clearer knowledge of what act would lead to an American declaration of war against Japan. It was, however, difficult to confront Roosevelt with such a bald demand; Churchill and Eden therefore used a more subtle approach, and on 30 November the Prime Minister proposed to the President that another warning to Japan was necessary in order to show the Tōjō government that any incremental advance would lead to a wider war. The attempted manipulation of Roosevelt proved to be unnecessary, for the President was already thinking along these lines; on the next day

Roosevelt told Halifax that in the case of a Japanese attack on British or Dutch territory 'we should obviously all be together', and indicated that if Japan attacked Thailand he would support a British move into the Kra Isthmus.[88] This was welcome news, but Churchill still remained cautious about how far Britain should commit itself to any definite course of action until Britain had a more specific guarantee. This not only applied to the launching of Matador but also to the question of whether Britain should itself give a guarantee to the Dutch. Churchill noted to Eden on 2 December that his own feeling was that an attack on the 'waterlogged' Kra Isthmus was less likely than an invasion of the Dutch East Indies but that in the case of the latter Britain 'should do nothing to prevent the full impact of this Japanese aggression presenting itself to the United States as a direct issue between them and Japan'.[89] However, by 4 December this hesitation was swept away. In part this was a response to a clarification and indeed expansion of the American guarantee by Roosevelt to Halifax in which the President made it clear the guarantee meant American armed support and that he supported a British pre-emptive seizure of the Kra Isthmus if Japan attacked another part of Thailand. However, it is also probable that once again intelligence information contributed to this change. Evidence from the BJ source showed that the Japanese Embassies in London and Washington had been ordered to destroy their cypher machines, a sure sign that war was impending, while a decrypt of a telegram from Tōgō to Ōshima noted that the talks in Washington had broken down and that an armed clash with Britain and the United States could occur 'sooner than is expected'. This material might very well have reassured the Prime Minister that Britain and the United States would be mutually affected by any Japanese action.[90]

At a War Cabinet meeting that day it was finally agreed that a British guarantee of the Dutch East Indies should be granted and in addition it was decided that permission should be given to Brooke-Popham to launch Matador on his own initiative if he believed that the Japanese were about attack Thailand, and in particular if he had evidence that they planned to land at Songkhla, the main port on the east coast of the Kra Isthmus.[91] The evidence did not take long to appear. On the morning of 6 December a RAAF Hudson reconnaissance plane caught sight of a Japanese convoy passing into the Gulf of Thailand.[92] Logically this should have been enough to persuade Brooke-Popham to give the order for British troops to move into the Kra Isthmus and thus be in a position to resist any Japanese landing. The position, however, was not as simple as that. The problem still remained that the existence of a Japanese convoy three hundred miles out to sea from Songkhla did not unequivocally demonstrate that a landing was imminent. On 6 December a series of meetings discussed Japanese intentions, but was forced to conclude that it was still unclear whether the intended target was Bangkok or Songkhla.[93] This uncertainty was reinforced by evidence from BJs which hinted that Japan and its Thai supporters were deliberately trying to force Britain to infringe Thailand's sovereignty and by confusion over where Pibul's loyalties lay. In addition, there was at this point a debate over whether it would be wise to give Thailand a guarantee in order to bolster its resistance against Japan and it would hardly in such circumstances have been politic to infringe its sovereignty. The result was a consensus that Britain would have to wait for a clearer signal of Japanese intent before taking any pre-emptive moves and that it should continue to avoid making any precipitant action which might have politically disastrous consequences.[94] A bemused First Sea Lord was left to note to the head of the Admiralty delegation in Washington

> At the moment we are all wondering what the Japanese are going to do. I think it is quite possible that the arrival of the PRINCE OF WALES at Singapore may have made them hesitate for a moment, as surely it will necessitate their sending an escort of capital ships with any expedition to the South and they may not feel inclined to do this.[95]

At the time this letter was sent the information that the battleship *Kongo* was escorting one of the convoys had not reached London. The British squadron had caused concern in Japanese quarters but it had not deterred.

The difficulty with the British indecision was that it made Matador become ever more impractical. The operation had always been designed as a pre-emptive action and it was planned that it would take thirty-six hours between the order for an advance into Kra being issued and the arrival of British troops in Songkhla. As time passed and the convoy disappeared under cloud cover in the Gulf of Thailand it became increasingly clear that, even if it did become apparent that the Japanese planned to land on the Isthmus, Matador would take too long to achieve its objectives and that Japanese troops would be in Songkhla before the British. On the afternoon of 7 December (Malaya time) Brooke-Popham reluctantly informed the Chiefs of Staff that he had decided that in these conditions Matador could not be launched.[96] A similar conclusion had been reached by Churchill who, after receiving a telegram from Halifax indicating Roosevelt's support for an attack on the Japanese convoy, told Eden and the Chiefs of Staff at noon GMT on the same day that

> I assume COS position is that we do all in our power both to forestall and prevent a Japanese descent upon the Kra Isthmus by attacking any expedition obviously making in that direction, if we have the strength and the time, but we should not actually move into Singora [Songkhla] unless either Siam has been previously violated, or a Japanese landing on the Kra Isthmus is imminent. Sea or air power would have the advantage of not prejudicing us with the Siamese.[97]

The problem with this plan was that it was almost as impractical as Matador given that the convoy was still obscured from view. At 2300 hours (Malaya time) on 7 December Brooke-Popham was forced to admit to the Chiefs of Staff that, although a torpedo-bomber squadron was now stationed on the airfield at Kota Bharu in north-east Malaya, weather conditions in the Gulf of Thailand were still too poor for adequate aerial reconnaissance and the convoy's location was still unknown. The next message from the Commander-in-Chief Far East was sent at 0500 (Malaya time) on 8 December; it began ominously with the word CANNAMORE, the code indicating that Japan was making a move that would demand military countermeasures, and continued 'Following for Chiefs of Staff. Landing is being attempted at Kota Bharu'.[98]

The war with Japan had begun but it was not necessarily the war Britain had expected, for at the same time that Japan had launched its attack in South-East Asia it had also struck against the American naval base of Pearl Harbor in Hawaii. There has recently been some speculation about whether in fact Churchill knew that this latter assault was going to take place, and that he might deliberately have failed to forewarn the Americans in his desire to inveigle them into conflict with all three Tripartite Powers. This assertion has been challenged by a number of scholars who have levelled a number of pertinent criticisms, such as the fact that there was no guarantee that Roosevelt would use the Japanese attack as an opportunity to declare war on Germany and that in the end it was Hitler who, on 9 December, declared war on the United States much to the President's and Prime Minister's relief. Also it has been noted that evidence from contemporary diaries directly contradicts the idea that the British government was aware of a possible attack on Pearl Harbor. For example, Malcolm Kennedy, who was still working in the Japanese section at Bletchley Park, noted in his diary on 7 December his surprise over the Japanese attacking the United States in this manner, while the diary of General Sir Alan Brooke, the new CIGS, shows that on 6 and 7 December he spent hours in meetings discussing with colleagues 'all the various alternatives that might lead to war and trying to ensure that in every case the U.S.A. would not be left out'. His comment on hearing of the events in Hawaii was 'All of our work of the last 48 hours wasted! The Japs themselves have now ensured that the U.S.A. are in the war'.[99]

On top of this there is even more conclusive proof that Churchill could not have known of the intended attack; this evidence is contained in an Admiralty internal history of the NID's wartime activities written immediately after the war had concluded. This document, written only for internal consumption, states quite categorically that 'We had not penetrated the Japanese plan to attack Pearl Harbor'. It notes that on 1 December 1941 the NID's assessment of the distribution of Japanese aircraft carriers was that four were with the special task force that was forming around Formosa while another four were estimated to be in Japanese home waters; in fact six aircraft carriers were at this date in the north-west Pacific sailing towards Honolulu. The document also notes that the FECB did report on 4 December the presence of two aircraft carriers at Saipan in the Marianas Islands, but that this was the furthest east that such vessels were ever located and that, as these ships were still at a distance of 3,000 miles from Hawaii and for escorts could only rely on the Japanese Fourth Fleet, a motley collection of obsolete cruisers and destroyers, they posed little danger. The paper concludes by noting

intelligence cannot be entirely relied on to get an inkling of an opponent's major intentions, unless a large volume of Special Intelligence is available; ordinary low grade W.T. may be 'spoof' designed to mislead, as we mislead [sic] the Germans before Neptune and Overlord.[100]

This document, while significant in itself, is also reinforced by some of the raw intelligence released in the Public Record Office. Reports in late November indicated a number of possible locations for the Japanese aircraft carriers. Carriers were reported at various dates to be in Cam Ranh Bay, in the Japanese mandated islands and in the Japanese home waters, but never in the north Pacific.[101] On 3 December the NID noted tantalizingly on a telegram containing information from the American intelligence base at Cavite Bay in the Philippines that the Admiralty had accounted for the location of all IJN heavy units, and although they failed to give any details, it is noticeable that they did not contradict the American assessment that 'all-known 1st and 2nd fleet carriers are in Sasebo–Kure area'.[102] The evidence would therefore suggest that the Admiralty did not have prior knowledge of the attack on Pearl Harbor, and if this was the case neither would Churchill.

What is certain, however, is that the British bluff about how strong its defences in the East had become had been well and truly called. On 9 December the ships that constituted Churchill's floating propaganda exercise, the *Prince of Wales* and *Repulse*, were sunk by Japanese aircraft. In the next few months the Japanese pushed down the Malayan peninsula and on 15 February 1942 Singapore surrendered. The nation that Churchill had characterized as being essentially cautious had delivered a hammer-blow to the complacent British Empire.

9 Conclusions

The course of Anglo-Japanese relations from 1936 to 1941 is a complex and ultimately tragic story. The former allies descended from acrimony to confrontation and finally to conflict. In trying to understand why this took place one can see that the path of events that eventually led to the outbreak of war between Britain and Japan on 8 December 1941 can be divided into a number of phases that deepened the mutual rivalry and shut the door to reconciliation until the only recourse was war.

From the start of the period under scrutiny it can be seen that there were a whole range of issues separating Britain and Japan, such as the differences over trade, the naval rivalry and the controversy over Japan's links with the Axis, but underlying all of these, at least initially, was the issue of China. Britain and Japan may have liked at times to suggest that this was a moral divide, but in essence it was about power and in particular power over the commercial destiny of China. With the start of the Sino-Japanese war this conflict over whether China was to be an adjunct of the Japanese Empire or a market dominated by British capital became more intense, particularly in the autumn of 1938 when Japan renounced the Nine Power Treaty and declared its intention to establish a 'New Order in East Asia'.

The clash of interests over China was dangerous in itself but the problem was exaggerated further by the growing polarization of Europe between the Anglo-French and Axis blocs. Japan's flirtation with Germany in 1938–9 increased Whitehall's suspicions about Japan's intentions while the IJA's desire to push the government in Tokyo into open alignment with Berlin led it to challenge Britain's position in China, a process that culminated in the Tientsin crisis. The danger in these years was such that some in Britain, particularly in the Treasury, argued that the best course was to seek an understanding with Japan, but this flew in the face of weighty practical objections. One of the key restraints on any policy of appeasement was the involvement of the United States and the Soviet Union in East Asian affairs. The American role was crucial in denying Britain flexibility. Washington hung over Britain's East Asia policy like some Victorian morality painting warning of the dire consequences of veering from the road of righteousness. There was a clear understanding in London that any attempt to arrive at a deal with Japan at the expense of China or any undercutting of the sanctity of the Nine Power Treaty would have serious repercussions in the United States which would threaten Anglo-American co-operation not only in East Asia but also in Europe. Britain knew that in a war with Germany it would at the very least need the benevolent neutrality of the United States, and this perception of the necessity to assure American support grew ever greater as the threat to Britain grew ever closer. The Soviet Union was also important, largely because it was the chief supplier of *matériel* to China. This benevolence was deeply disturbing to Whitehall as there was a belief that the Russians, almost as much as the Japanese, desired to see Britain pushed out of China, and it was one of the factors that led Britain by the end of 1938 to stop any pretence of neutrality and give greater assistance to China.

An opportunity to break away from this escalation of tensions came in August and September 1939 with the Nazi–Soviet Pact and the start of the war in Europe. The conflict with Germany made it necessary for Britain to try to assure itself of Japan's neutrality, while Japan was at the same time faced with diplomatic isolation and was increasingly desperate to extricate itself from the war in China. It seemed to some that this new situation raised the possibility of a *rapprochement* and that it could be cemented by basing any understanding on the common antipathy towards the Soviet Union. However, the nature of Britain's conflict with Germany made an understanding more rather than less difficult to achieve. Britain could not pursue its policy of economic warfare, one of the major weapons in its armoury, without placing restrictions on the ability of neutrals to trade with the Reich, and also could not fight the war without increasing markedly its control over, and appetite for, imperial raw materials. Both these requirements had a severe effect on Anglo-Japanese relations and squeezed ever harder Japan's already limited access to raw materials. The failure of the war-trade talks in May and June 1940 was a clear indication that the aims of the two countries were fundamentally opposed. Britain was asking Japan to sacrifice its links with Germany but itself refused the obvious *quid pro quo*, which was that the British government should sever its links with Chungking. In talk after talk Shigemitsu emphasized to Halifax and Butler that this was a crucial obstacle to any Anglo-Japanese understanding, but the bait was never taken. Chinese resistance was seen as a check on Japan's ambitions, and in addition it was clear that Washington would make no allowance for the fact there was a war in Europe – it expected Britain to remain stalwartly opposed to concessions to Japan.

The incompatibility of interests revealed during the period of the 'Phoney War' not only rendered any Anglo-Japanese reconciliation impossible, it also demonstrated how conflict could arise in the future. The Japanese obsession with ending the war in China led in June 1940 to its demand that Britain close the Burma Road. Japan's 'arrogant' behaviour over this issue and its subsequent failure to honour the terms of the Burma Road Agreement alienated Britain and convinced Churchill and the Foreign Office that Japan could not be appeased. The transformation of Anglo-Japanese relations from acrimony to confrontation was not, however, simply the result of regional tensions, it was due also to the fact that with the signing of the Tripartite Pact in September 1940 Britain could no longer afford to treat Japan as a neutral. In fact it could be said that Britain was in a state of hostility, if not hostilities, towards Japan from October 1940 onwards. Faced with increasing evidence of Japanese collaboration with the Axis Powers in the economic, diplomatic and military fields, Britain had no choice but to pursue a policy of containment which would limit the assistance Japan could give to its partners and also reduce its ability to go to war.

From this point on the prospect of war between Britain and Japan became far more serious. The two countries were locked in a battle for influence in South-East Asia and as a result Britain, realizing that it could not contain Japan single-handed, began to encourage the development of a multilateral barrier to Japanese expansionism with the Dutch, the Americans and to a degree the Chinese. This ABCD encirclement, as the Japanese described it, did not simply entail military planning as a deterrent to expansion, the facet which historians have tended to focus on, it also included the co-ordination of sanctions against Japan. This policy, which was directed by the FEC and the MEW, did not involve a sweeping indiscriminate attack on Japan's exports, it was rather a policy designed to weaken without provoking, a kind of 'death by a thousand cuts'. However, as the United States became more dominant the initiative shifted to Washington, and in July 1941 the Roosevelt administration raised the ante in the economic war by freezing Japan's assets and prohibiting the export of oil.

This approach to the policy of sanctions was a drastic change to that previously pursued by Britain and was a key element in leading to the outbreak of hostilities four and a half months later. This raises the question of whether it would have been wiser to have continued to follow the more cautious British line. Certainly there were some doubts in Whitehall about the possible consequences of the American policy and about the State Department's wish not to provide Japan with any prior warning, and in addition it is important to note that historians such as W.N. Medlicott and Michael Barnhart have demonstrated the relative moderation of the pre-July restrictions.[1] It is important, however, to put the American decision in context, for as Waldo Heinrichs has noted in *Threshold of War*, the complete embargo introduced in July 1941 was designed to stop Japanese expansion not just to the south but also to the north, and the only way to take away Japan's freedom of movement was to prohibit its imports of oil.[2] One must also note that although the MEW expressed its satisfaction with the results of its sanctions policy in June 1941, it was this very policy, and specifically the co-ordination of exports of rubber and tin with the Dutch East Indies and the collapse of the Dutch–Japanese talks in Batavia, which led to the Japanese decision to occupy south Indo-China. It must also be noted too that in the background such measures as the Anglo-American pre-emptive buying in Latin America, the increasingly strict controls over shipping and the fact that most of the goods Japan imported from the West had been brought under licence demonstrated to the government in Tokyo that, if Japan did not safeguard its position by increasing its control over South-East Asia, Britain and the United States had the potential to cause much greater damage. It is therefore a mistake to dismiss the effect of the British-led sanctions policy and to concentrate exclusively on those introduced after the United States had taken the lead. One must realize that from the very date when restrictions were first introduced there was a danger, as the Board of Trade noted in August 1940, that they could have the opposite effect to that intended.

It is also important not to underestimate the significance of Britain's role from July 1941 until the outbreak of war. British policy towards Japan was still primarily based on the need to avoid war and it was assumed that this could only be achieved by a rigid policy of deterrence. However, there was a problem in that it was now Washington rather than London that took the lead in policy towards

Japan. This led to two potential dangers. The first was that if the Roosevelt administration pursued a tough policy this might lead Japan to renew its advance into South-East Asia, which could involve a clash with Britain when the latter still had no guarantee of American armed support. The second fear was that an American–Japanese settlement might be bought at Britain's and China's expense and that this too might endanger British possessions. This led to two trends in British policy in late 1941, first its constant reiteration to Washington of the need for warnings to Japan, which was a round-about way of forcing Roosevelt to define what would constitute a Japanese act of war, and second, its efforts to scotch the Hull–Nomura talks by, when invited, casting doubt on the wisdom of making concessions to Japan. Britain achieved some success in these policies; in both October and November it was able to persuade the State Department that concessions would be unwise and in December it finally received an American guarantee.

These are, however, only the public manifestations of success and influence; it is also possible that Britain tried to manipulate the situation by the judicious passing on of intelligence information to the Americans. The daily collations of intelligence material sent by 'C' to Churchill from August 1941 show a number of occasions when Churchill asked for information to be forwarded to the Americans, and it is important to note that the US Army's wartime board of inquiry into Pearl Harbor was told that on 26 November 1941 the United States had received from a British source 'specific evidence of the Japanese intention to wage offensive war against Great Britain and the United States'. It is by no means clear what information was passed on, but it is pertinent that it arrived while the Roosevelt administration was still in two minds about whether to proceed with the *modus vivendi*, and apparently had the desired effect.[3] This is an interesting and vital avenue to pursue but it is one that due to British government secrecy remains largely closed.

The failure of the preferred policy of deterrence and the disaster in Singapore in February 1942 obviously raises the question of whether the Churchill government would have been wise to have pursued a more moderate line towards Japan. This was certainly the view of Sir Robert Craigie, who after his return from internment in Tokyo wrote a final report in which he launched a blistering attack on the British and American governments for not having taken the opportunity to avoid war in November 1941. Historians critical of Churchill have made much of this paper's conclusions.[4] The possibility that war could have been postponed or permanently averted if Britain had encouraged Hull to make a moderate reply to the Japanese proposals of 21 November is an interesting idea which raises a bewildering number of questions. Would the Japanese military have accepted Hull's original *modus vivendi* proposal with its demand for a retreat from south Indo-China? If so, would the American and British military position have been so impregnable after the three months of the *modus vivendi* had elapsed as to make any chance of a successful Japanese assault impossible? The answer is that we do not know; but that in itself leads to the question of why, if circumstances were so uncertain, did leaders in London and Washington not take the risk of making one last diplomatic overture? What would they have lost if it had been rejected?

One can discuss such questions *ad infinitum* but in doing so it is worth considering two points that arise from Craigie's final report. The first is that Craigie notes that the course of the war in November 1941 appeared from Tokyo to be running away from Germany with Britain on the advance in north Africa and the Soviet Union stemming the German tide on the Eastern Front, and that in this situation the Japanese might have been nervous enough to grasp any olive branch proffered by the West. This is a peculiar statement which can only be seen as the result of hindsight; such a rose-tinted picture bears little resemblance to the air of 'pervasive and deadly threat' which Waldo Heinrichs has identified as characterizing the last week of November, with Britain's Operation Crusader stalling in the Libyan desert and the Germans poised to take Moscow, and it seems difficult to believe that this was how events were perceived in Japanese circles.[5] The second point is the curious omission from the report of any mention of the possible effect of the *modus vivendi* on China, the very issue which Churchill mentioned in his famous telegram of 26 November to Roosevelt. As noted in the previous chapter this was not a frivolous concern but a real fear; if Chinese resistance had collapsed, the military pressure Japan could have brought to bear on South-East Asia would have rendered any level of British reinforcements ineffective.

There are also other factors to bear in mind when studying late November 1941. One has to take note of the constant stream of intelligence reports filtering into the policy-making process, virtually all of which showed Japan as a potential aggressor, and in the background the shadow of appeasement hovering over those like Eden and Cadogan who had been closer to that phenomenon in the late 1930s than they would care to admit. One must also bear in mind the legacy of all the previous failures to reach an understanding with Japan; the

Leith-Ross mission, the Craigie–Ugaki talks, the Tientsin negotiations, the war-trade talks, the Burma Road Agreement, which all shared two things in common – they had failed and they had made Britain look foolish. After October 1940 the British government had sworn to itself 'never again' and this was the lesson that still registered in November 1941. One also has to admit that Churchill's reluctance to seek peace at any price was due to a dangerous underestimation of Japan's military capability and overestimation of the deterrent value of British and American forces in the region, which proved to be a costly error.

If one comes to the conclusion that the *modus vivendi* was unlikely to have worked and that it is understandable why the United States with Britain's prompting gave it a premature burial, this does beg the question of whether a diplomatic solution to the problems between the West and Japan might have worked at an earlier date. This study has shown that on a number of occasions thought was diverted within Whitehall to the task of trying to frame an understanding with Japan. The most notable exercise after the start of the war in Europe was the draft produced at Butler's request in July 1940. This document was, however, then torn to shreds by other government ministries and it is important to note that the criticisms made were not simply because some terms of the draft were impossible to achieve in wartime, but that it was contended that even after the war it would be unthinkable to introduce such measures as the lowering of colonial tariffs and quotas or Japanese immigration into the dominions or the colonies.

This adverse reaction reflected an in-built dislike within the corridors of power of concessions to Japan which can be seen in place even before the outbreak of the Sino-Japanese war. The history of Anglo-Japanese commercial relations in the 1930s was one on Britain's part of ingrained resistance to change. In the summer of 1936 Leith-Ross's desire for an initiative over textile quotas in the colonies was watered down by the Board of Trade, throughout 1936–7 there was opposition to the idea of allowing Japan to benefit in any way from measures to expand the 'open door' in tropical Africa, and in June 1937 the Interdepartmental Committee on Trade Policy's conclusions that Lancashire would have to make sacrifices for the sake of Anglo-Japanese relations were challenged within the Cabinet's Foreign Policy Committee. Thus even in the period when it was recognized that a real chance of *rapprochement* existed, there was still no desire to make concessions which would have eased Japan's economic burden and sense of discrimination.

It would be satisfying to say that one could see an alternative path to that taken by Britain in the 1930s, but if anything the clash between Britain and Japan was, as Ismay noted in 1935, frighteningly inevitable. It is very hard to see how any satisfactory compromise could have been achieved. Over China the two countries were diametrically opposed; for Britain the aim was to maximize its influence and to re-establish the dominance of British capital; for Japan the aim was to expel British political influence from the region and to minimize its economic power. For a settlement to be reached it would have been necessary for one side to change fundamentally its policy towards East Asia: for Britain to have accepted Japanese predominance rather than simply treating her as a junior partner or for Japan to have given up the gains it had gathered from the decline of the Washington system.

This question of whether Japan could have sacrificed its position in China leads on to the problem that behind the regional disagreements lay an even more fundamental divide. This was the question of how to deal with the fact that the Japanese felt their rapidly expanding economy was stultified by the obstacles inherent in the Anglo-American *status quo*, namely the lack of free access to raw materials and markets. As noted above, the problem here was that Britain was resolutely opposed to any revision of tariffs, preferences and quotas. This to some degree was understandable, Britain was after all suffering an economic slump and concessions to Japan would have had a negative effect on its exports, and certainly it would have been a brave or even foolhardy politician who suggested that British workers should in effect sacrifice their jobs for the sake of better relations with Japan. The long-term result, however, was that the inability to address the issues that provoked Japan's quest for autarky doomed Britain to a war which fatally undermined its prosperity and its rank.

Another problem, and one that still afflicts *status quo* powers today, is the arrogant assumption on Britain's part that the system which gave it prosperity was the natural, moral order of things. The British seem at times in the 1930s to have believed that their Empire was God-given, forgetting that it had been forged over generations by conquest, cruelty and treachery. The British therefore looked askance at Japan's efforts at empire-building, regarding them as out of place in the modern world, a world which Britain had helped to shape and from which it benefited as much as and probably more than any other state. As well as this misplaced moralism there was an unfortunate tendency to live under the delusion that time could be made to stand still, that Britain's wealth could be held for perpetuity. There seemed to be little realization that a frozen *status quo* was one that would inevitably break down and that the only way to maintain peace was to interest oneself in positive reforms, nor was there any real effort to try to see the world as the Japanese did. These conservative attitudes had the unfortunate effect of strengthening the opposition within Whitehall to change – the Japanese were all too easily dismissed as unwelcome parvenues who did not know their proper place.

This does not, however, mean that this book is designed as a vehicle to shift the blame for the Pacific War from Japan to Britain, it is rather an effort to understand the motivations that lay behind the Anglo-Japanese confrontation and to rise above the issue of blame. The sheer complexity of the events outlined above shows that the idea of Japanese guilt is hard to apply to the Pacific War – it was rather the result of the never-ending struggle between those who 'have' and those who 'have not'. This does, however, raise the issue of how far *status quo* powers should be responsible for the maintenance of peace. While recognizing the problems that hindered Britain at the time, there is surely a lesson to be drawn about the dangers of refusing to countenance managed change. This was realized at the time; individuals such as Craigie, Sir George Mounsey and Sir Alexander Cadogan did on occasion recognize that the inequalities within the international system could lead to conflagration, they were, however, fighting a losing battle against circumstance and entrenched attitudes.

It is sad, however, to report that in the end this study must remain tentative. While a great number of sources are available on British policy, a full assessment of British perceptions is still hampered by the holding back of much of the British intelligence material, both diplomatic and military, for this period. To give an example of the scale of the problem one needs to realize that on 8 November 1935 the serial number for the BJ diplomatic intercepts stood at 062694 by 8 December 1941 this number had risen to 098694, in other words in a period of six years and one month 36,000 BJs had passed through GCCS.[6] By no means were all of these intercepts of Japanese documents, they also included French, Italian, Spanish, Turkish, Irish, Chinese, Thai and even American telegrams, but certainly without seeing this material and its military and naval equivalents, and noting how it was assessed, any history of the road to the events at Kota Bharu on 8 December 1941 remains incomplete.

Notes

ADDITIONAL ABBREVIATIONS USED IN THE NOTES

BAD	British Admiralty Delegation
BNLO	British Naval Liaison Officer
BOT	Board of Trade
C Dept	Central Department (FO)
C in C	Commander-in-Chief
CO	Colonial Office
COIS	Chief of Intelligence Staff (FECB)
COS	Chiefs of Staff
C/S	Captain on Staff (see also COIS)
DBFP	*Documents on British Foreign Policy*
DDMI	Deputy Director of Military Intelligence
DO	Dominions Office
FE Dept	Far Eastern Department (FO)
FO	Foreign Office
N Dept	Northern Department (FO)
no.	Denotes correspondence sent to the FO by bag rather than cable
PRO	Public Record Office, Kew
T	Treasury
tel.	Telegram (the suffixes Tour, Saving and Arfar denote that such telegrams are in a different series from the usual FO series)
WO	War Office

1 INTRODUCTION

1 PRO FO371/27893 F13424/17/23 FO minute 8 December 1941.
2 I. Nish, 'Japan and the Outbreak of War in 1941', in A. Sked and C. Cook (eds), *Crisis and Controversy: Essays in Honour of A.J.P. Taylor*, London, Macmillan, 1976, pp. 130–47, and C. Hosoya, 'Britain and the US in Japan's View of the International System, 1937–1941,'in I. Nish (ed.), *Anglo-Japanese Alienation 1919–1952*, Cambridge, Cambridge University Press, 1982, pp. 57–75.
3 PRO WO106/5392 'Order of Priority of MI2 Countries From S.S. Point of View' SIS report undated (1933?).
4 On Craigie, see P. Lowe, 'The Dilemmas of an Ambassador: Sir Robert

Craigie in Tokyo, 1937–41', *Proceedings of the British Association for Japanese Studies*, 1977, vol. 2, pp. 34–56, S.O., Agbi, 'The Pacific War Controversy in Britain: Sir Robert Craigie versus the Foreign Office', *Modern Asian Studies*, 1983, vol. 17, pp. 489–517, and A.M. Best, 'Sir Robert Craigie as Ambassador to Japan, 1937–41', in I. Nish (ed.), *Britain and Japan: Biographical Portraits*, Folkestone, Japan Library, 1994, pp. 238–51.
5 For the argument that Britain knew beforehand about the plan to attack Pearl Harbor see J. Rusbridger and E. Nave, *Betrayal at Pearl Harbor: How Churchill Lured Roosevelt into War*, London, Michael O'Mara, 1991.

2 HALTING A POLICY OF DRIFT

1 *DBFP* Second Series Vol.XX doc.450 CP12(36) 'The Importance of Anglo-Japanese Friendship' Duff Cooper memorandum 17 January 1936 pp. 752–6.
2 Ibid p. 755.
3 On the British stake in China see P.J. Cain & A.G. Hopkins, *British Imperialism: Crisis and Deconstruction, 1914–1990*, London, Longman, 1993, pp. 251–9.
4 On the origins of the Amō Statement see T. Shimada, 'Designs on North China, 1933–1937', in J.W. Morley (ed.), *The China Quagmire: Japan's Expansion on the Asian Continent, 1933–1941*, New York, Columbia University Press, 1983, pp. 79–91.
5 PRO WO106/5604 BJ.956489 Tokyo to Peking 13 April 1934, decrypted 20 April 1934, and BJ.956937 Tokyo to Washington 22 May 1934, decrypted 29 May 1934.
6 PRO WO106/5604 BJ.956489 Tokyo to Peking 13 April 1934, decrypted 20 April 1934.
7 PRO WO106/5597 BJ.960814 Tokyo to London 31 May 1935, decrypted 5 June 1935.
8 On American policy see R. Dallek, *Franklin Roosevelt and American Foreign Policy, 1932–1945*, New York, Oxford University Press, 1979, pp. 75–7.
9 PRO FO371/18176 F823/316/23 Randall (FE Dept) memorandum 9 February 1934.
10 On naval issues see C. Hall, *Britain, America and Arms Control, 1921–1937*, London, Macmillan, 1987, pp. 180–6, and S. Pelz, *Race to Pearl Harbour: The Failure of the Second London Naval Conference and the Onset of World War II*, Cambridge, Harvard University Press, 1974, pp. 159–64.
11 *DBFP* 2/XX doc.174 F6577/591/23 Sansom (Tokyo) to Crowe (Department of Overseas Trade) 12 October 1934 pp. 319–21, and doc.188 F7162/591/23 Sansom memorandum 29 October 1934 pp. 337–340.
12 See for example PRO FO371/19343 F6416/717/61 Vansittart minute 12 October 1935.
13 PRO FO371/19343 F1737/717/61 'Memorandum Respecting the Situation in the Far East' Orde (FE Dept) memorandum 16 March 1935.
14 On Edwardes and Gwynne, see I. Nish, 'Anglo-Japanese Alienation

Revisited', in S. Dockrill (ed.), *From Pearl Harbor to Hiroshima: The Second World War in Asia and the Pacific, 1941–45*, London, Macmillan, 1994, pp. 19–22.

15 *DBFP* Series 2 Vol.XIII doc.14 F6189/591/23 'The Naval Conference and Relations with Japan' Chamberlain memorandum 1 September 1934 pp. 24–31.

16 On the silver crisis see Wang Xi, 'A Test of the Open Door Policy: America's Silver Policy and Its Effect on East Asia, 1934–1937', in A. Iriye & W. Cohen (eds), *American, Chinese, and Japanese Perspectives on Wartime Asia 1931–1949*, Wilmington, Scholarly Resources, 1990, pp. 30–47, and S. Endicott, *Diplomacy and Enterprise. British China Policy 1933–1937*, Manchester, Manchester University Press, 1975, pp. 82–101.

17 On the Leith-Ross mission and conditions in north China see A. Trotter, *Britain and East Asia 1933–1937*, Cambridge, Cambridge University Press, 1975, pp. 143–67, and Endicott, op. cit., pp. 102–29.

18 PRO CAB53/25 COS 405 'Strategical Situation in the Far East, with Particular Reference to Hong Kong' Chiefs of Staff memorandum 10 October 1935.

19 PRO WO106/5499 Ismay (MI2) minute 22 August 1935.

20 On north China see Shimada, op. cit., pp. 136–61. For the British knowledge of IJN movements see PRO WO106/5597 C/S Hong Kong to DNI (Admiralty) 7 December 1935 tel.1225/7.

21 PRO WO106/5530 'German–Japanese Relations' MI2c memorandum 19 August 1935.

22 *DBFP* 2/XIII doc.584 A10617/22/45 Clive (Tokyo) to Eden 17 December 1935 pp. 737–8 and doc.593 A10893/22/45 Clive to Eden 27 December 1935 p. 748

23 PRO WO106/5509 Ismay minute 1 January 1936 and Anderson (DDMI) minute 3 January 1936.

24 See K. Usui, 'Japanese Approaches to China in the 1930s: Two Alternatives' in Iriye and Cohen (eds), op. cit., pp. 93–116.

25 PRO FO371/19692 W7711/7711/98 Mounsey (Western Dept FO) minute 4 September 1935.

26 *DBFP* Series 2 Volume XIV appendix IV J4729/1/1 Hoare speech 11 September 1935 pp. 784–90.

27 PRO FO371/19692 W9558/7711/98 Wigram (C Dept) minute 8 November 1935 and W10033/7711/98 Collier (N Dept) minute 27 November 1935.

28 PRO CAB24/259 CP15(36) 'Freedom of Access to Raw Materials' Eden memorandum 17 January 1936.

29 PRO FO371/19692 W9558/7711/98 Vansittart minute 31 December 1935.

30 PRO CAB23/83 2(36) Cabinet conclusions 29 January 1936.

31 *DBFP* 2/XX doc.454 F701/89/23 Orde memorandum 22 January 1936 pp. 761–4.

32 *DBFP* 2/XIII doc.598 A126/4/45 Clive to Eden 6 January 1936 p. 753, and doc.615 A126/4/45 Phillips/Eden conversation 8 January 1936 pp. 768–70.

33 *DBFP* 2/XX doc.454 F701/89/23 Orde memorandum 22 January and

footnote 7 Vansittart minute 25 January 1936 p. 763 and p. 764 respectively.
34 Ibid., doc.457 Cabinet conclusions No.3(36) 29 January 1936 pp. 768–9.
35 See Endicott, op. cit., pp. 125–8.
36 PRO T160/850/F14375/1 Overton (BOT) to Orde 5 May 1936.
37 PRO FO371/20290 F3348/1391/23 Clive to Eden 10 June 1936 tel.168.
38 *DBFP* 2/XX appendix 1 F4498/1/10 'The Leith-Ross Mission' Leith-Ross note 23 July 1936 pp. 1003–30.
39 Chamberlain diary entry 25 October 1936, N. Chamberlain Papers, Birmingham University Library, NC2/23a Political Diary 1933–1936.
40 *DBFP* 2/XX doc.590 F6511/89/23 Eden to Clive 31 October 1936 pp. 988–90.
41 For FO criticisms of Yoshida's terms see FO371/20279 F6511/89/23 Pratt (FE Dept) minute 28 October 1936, and Cadogan minute 29 October 1936.
42 *DBFP* Series 2 Volume XXI doc.10 F7427/553/23 Drummond (Rome) to Eden 23 November 1936 pp. 19–21, and PRO FO371/20279 F6724/89/23 Clive to Eden 3 November 1936 tel.318.
43 PRO FO371/21029 F214/28/23 Cadogan minute 7 January 1937, and F290/28/23 Chamberlain to Eden 13 January 1937.
44 *DBFP* 2/XXI doc.46 F357/28/23 Eden to Clive 18 January 1937 pp. 60–7.
45 PRO FO371/21029 F570/22/23 Vansittart minute 28 January 1937.
46 PRO WO106/5279 Hankey (Cabinet Office) to Dill (DMI) 21 April 1936, FO371/20278 F3395/2258/61 Hankey to Vansittart 18 June 1936, and FO371/20249 F1648/166/10 Intelligence Shanghai to WO 21 March 1936 tel.3395.
47 PRO FO371/20273 F2153/2153/10 Clive to Eden 27 March 1936 tel.158, and F2925/2153/10 Mackillop (Moscow) to Eden 19 May 1936 tel.295.
48 PRO FO371/20251 F5612/166/10 Howe (Nanking) to Eden 31 July 1936 tel.860.
49 PRO FO371/20250 F3715/166/10 Henderson (FE Dept) minute 30 June 1936.
50 PRO FO371/20243 F5643/96/10 COIS Hong Kong to C in C China 14 September 1936 tel.1601/14.
51 PRO FO371/20244 F5897/96/10 GOC Hong Kong to WO 28 September 1936 tel.3150, F5830/96/10 Eden to Clive 29 September 1936 tel.191, and Eden to Knatchbull-Hugessen (Nanking) 29 September 1936 tel.86 (Tour).
52 PRO AIR2/1728 'Chinese Defensive Measures' SIS report 22 October 1936, and 'Sino-Japanese Relations: Stiffening of Chiang Kai-shek's Attitude' SIS report 28 October 1936.
53 PRO FO371/20252 F7807/166/10 Chilston (Moscow) to Eden 15 December 1936 tel.712, and F7811/166/10 COIS Hong Kong to C in C China 17 December 1936 tel.1057/17.
54 See Endicott, op. cit., pp. 156–9.
55 *DBFP* 2/XXI doc.11 F7223/303/23 Clive to Eden 25 November 1936 pp. 21–3.
56 PRO FO371/20286 F7448/303/23 Clive to Eden 2 December 1936 tel.357, and F7504/303/23 Ronald (FE Dept) memorandum 4 December 1936. The BJs that revealed the terms of the secret protocol were

BJ.067109 25 November 1936 and BJ.067161 4 December 1936, see WO208/859.

57 On Japan and the South Seas see PRO FO371/20285 F2032/273/23 Clive to Eden 11 March 1936 tel.114. For the defence appreciation see PRO CAB55/2 JP 101st meeting 16 June 1936, and CAB56/2 JIC13 'Far Eastern Appreciation' JIC report 7 October 1936.

58 *DBFP* Series 2 volume XVII appendix II C8998/8998/18 'The World Situation and British Rearmament' Vansittart memorandum 16 December 1936 p. 776.

59 Chatfield notes on Vansittart memorandum 5 January 1937, Chatfield Papers, National Maritime Museum, Greenwich, CHT3/1.

60 PRO CAB24/268 CP73(37) 'Imperial Conference 1937. Review of Imperial Defence' Inskip memorandum 26 February 1937. For the army's approval of Chatfield's initiative in this field see W106/130 Deverell note 2 February 1937.

61 See *DBFP* 2/XXI doc.64 F1366/28/23 Clive to Eden 6 March 1937 p. 99, and PRO FO371/20948 F1486/5/10 Clive to Eden 12 March 1937 tel.98. On Satō, see Usui, op. cit., pp. 103–7.

62 On the change in American policy see R.A. Harrison, 'A Presidential Demarché: Franklin D. Roosevelt's Personal Diplomacy and Great Britain, 1936–37', *Diplomatic History*, 1981, vol. 5, pp. 245–72.

63 PRO AIR2/1728 'Chiang Kai-shek's Policy, etc.' SIS report 22 February 1937 and Endicott, op. cit., pp. 159–60.

64 See *The Times* 13 March 1937.

65 PRO FO371/19910 C5313/4/18 Craigie memorandum 8 July 1936.

66 PRO FO371/19787 A9996/9996/51 Craigie minute 22 December 1936.

67 *DBFP* 2/XXI doc.63 F1325/597/61 Knatchbull-Hugessen to Cadogan 2 March 1937 pp. 96–9.

68 *DBFP* 2/XXI doc.70 F2214/597/61 Davis/Eden conversation 9 April 1937 p. 107.

69 *DBFP* 2/XXI doc.86 T9200/226/384 Imperial Conference 4th meeting 22 May 1937 pp. 126–31.

70 PRO FO371/21025 F3281/597/61 Craigie minute 3 June 1937.

71 PRO T188/162 Ashton-Gwatkin (FO Economic Section) memorandum 20 February 1937.

72 PRO T188/162 Leith-Ross memorandum 22 February 1937.

73 PRO CAB16/182 DP(P)3 'New Standard of Naval Strength' Hoare memorandum 29 April 1937, and CAB16/181 DP(P) 2nd meeting 11 May 1937.

74 *DBFP* 2/XXI doc.88 F3416/28/23 Yoshida/Craigie conversation 2 June 1937 pp. 134–8. On the evidence that the BJ source was assisting British evaluations of Japanese foreign policy at this point, see PRO FO371/21028 F10334/26/23 Thomas (FE Dept) minute 2 November 1937.

75 PRO FO371/21024 F2638/597/61 'British Policy in the Far East' FO memorandum undated [June 1937] and FE Dept note 5 July 1937.

76 PRO CAB27/622 FP(36) 3rd meeting 21 July 1936. See also Usui, op. cit., pp. 105–6.

77 PRO T160/859 F14848/2 Interdepartmental meeting 26 February 1937, and FO371/21246 W5122/393/98 Leith-Ross to Eden 9 March 1937.

78 PRO CAB27/622 FP(36) 7th meeting 18 March 1937.

79 PRO FO371/21215 W6363/5/50 Eden to Chamberlain 24 March 1937.
80 PRO CAB27/626 FP(36)34 'The "Open Door" in the Colonies' Inter-departmental Committee on Trade Policy report 7 June 1937.
81 PRO CAB27/622 FP(36) 12th meeting 11 June 1937, and 13th meeting 16 June 1937.
82 PRO FO371/21247 W12639/393/98 Leith-Ross note 29 June 1937.
83 PRO FO371/21248 W16996/393/98 League of Nations report E/MP/27(2) 7 September 1937.
84 PRO WO106/5371 CX28059/29 'The Government and the Chinese Reds' SIS report 26 April 1937, and CX28059/39 'The Government and the Chinese Reds' SIS report 18 June 1937.
85 PRO FO371/20970 F4531/35/10 Knatchbull-Hugessen to Eden 7 June 1937 tel.604.
86 Endicott, op. cit., pp. 166–70. For the Cabinet discussion on extraterri-toriality see PRO CAB23/88 24(37) Cabinet conclusions 17 June 1937.

3 NEW CIRCUMSTANCES, NEW PROBLEMS

1 PRO WO106/5307 'Sino-Japanese Clash Near Peking' MI2c apprecia-tion 12 July 1937.
2 *DBFP* Second Series Volume XXI doc.105 F4071/9/10 Eden to Dodds (Tokyo) 12 July 1937 pp. 154–5, and doc.107 F4806/9/10 Eden to Lindsay (Washington) 13 July 1937 pp. 155–6.
3 See Y-L. Sun, *China and the Origins of the Pacific War, 1931–1941*, New York, St Martin's Press, 1993, pp. 87–9.
4 *DBFP* 2/XXI doc.188 F5292/9/10 Knatchbull-Hugessen (Nanking) to Eden 16 August 1937 pp. 247–8.
5 PRO FO371/20954 F5552/9/10 Dodds (Tokyo) to Eden 21 August 1937 tel.304, and F5603/9/10 Knatchbull-Hugessen to Eden 23 August 1937 tel.377.
6 On the details of the attack and the subsequent diplomacy, see P. Lowe, *Great Britain and the Origins of the Pacific War: A Study of British Policy in East Asia, 1937–1941*, Oxford, Clarendon, 1977, pp. 21–2, and B.A. Lee, *Britain and the Sino-Japanese War, 1937–1939: A Study in the Dilemmas of British Decline*, Stanford, Stanford University Press, 1974, pp. 40–1.
7 Kennedy diary entry 30 August 1937, in Captain Malcolm Kennedy papers, Sheffield University Library, Diary 4/31.
8 Kennedy diary entries 27 and 28 August 1937, Kennedy papers, Diary 4/31.
9 See for example PRO FO371/21020 F10443/28/23 Craigie to Cadogan 4 November 1937, and F9575/28/23 Craigie (Tokyo) to Eden 15 November 1937 tel.680.
10 PRO FO371/20956 F7318/9/10 Craigie to Eden 3 October 1937 tel.479. Craigie's protest failed to have any effect and the Archbishop spoke at the meeting on 5 October, leading to criticism in the Japanese press.
11 *DBFP* 2/XXI doc.246 F6634/9/10 Edmonds (Geneva) to Foreign Office 17 September 1937 pp. 327–8.
12 For the peace terms see *DBFP* 2/XXI doc.245 F6619/9/10 Craigie to Eden 17 September 1937 pp. 325–6, and PRO FO371/20956 F6973/9/10

Craigie to Eden 25 September 1937, tel.440. For Craigie's espousal of peace talks see *DBFP* 2/XXI doc.258 F6972/9/10 Craigie to Eden 25 September 1937 p. 340.

13 For the Chamberlain/Eden talk, see *DBFP* 2/XXI doc.263 F6972/9/10 Eden to Craigie 27 September 1937 p. 344 footnote 3. On Chiang Kai-shek's reaction to the proposals, see doc.285 F7479/9/10 Howe (Nanking) to Eden 5 October 1937 pp. 368–9.

14 See H. Stimson, *The Far Eastern Crisis*, New York, Harper, 1936.

15 For Eden's concern to keep in line with the United States see his comments in *DBFP* 2/XXI doc.269 Cabinet conclusions 29 September 1938 pp. 348–50, and doc.272 F7240/7240/10 Eden to Mallet (Washington) 30 September 1937 p. 355

16 Halifax to Eden 27 September 1937, Avon Papers, Birmingham University Library, AP20 38/46.

17 On the 'Quarantine Speech', see R. Dallek, *Franklin D. Roosevelt and American Foreign Policy*, 1932–1945, New York, Oxford University Press, 1979, pp. 149–52.

18 PRO FO371/20969 F9511/31/10 Eden minute undated [November 1937].

19 *DBFP* 2/XXI doc.326 F8982/9/10 Eden minute 7 November 1937 p. 418 footnote 3.

20 *DBFP* 2/XXI doc.291 Cabinet conclusions 6 October 1937 p. 317.

21 PRO CAB27/634 FES(37)4 'Reinforcement of British Naval Forces in the Far East', Chatfield memorandum 23 September 1937.

22 *DBFP* 2/XXI doc.283 F7372/6799/10 Phillips to Cranborne 4 October 1937 pp. 364–7.

23 PRO FO371/21015 F8143/6799/10 Interdepartmental meeting 13 October 1937.

24 On the Brussels Conference, see Lowe, op. cit., pp. 29–31 and Lee, op. cit., pp. 71–4.

25 *DBFP* 2/XXI doc.369 Cabinet conclusions 17 November 1937 pp. 500–3.

26 *DBFP* 2/XXI doc.334 'Economic Sanctions Against Japan', ATB Committee report 5 November 1937 pp. 432–46.

27 *DBFP* 2/XXI doc.345 British Shipping in the Far East Cabinet Committee, 2nd meeting, 9 November 1937 pp. 460–4.

28 PRO FO371/21028 F10334/26/23 Thomas minute 2 November 1937.

29 PRO FO371/20959 F9536/9/10 Craigie to Eden 13 November 1937 tel.669. On the German mediation see J.P. Fox, *Germany and the Far Eastern Crisis 1931–1938: A Study in Diplomacy and Ideology*, Oxford, Oxford University Press, 1982, pp. 260–90.

30 *DBFP* 2/XXI doc.369 Cabinet conclusions 17 November 1937 pp. 500–3.

31 PRO CAB2/7 CID 303rd meeting 2 December 1937, and CAB23/90 46(37) Cabinet conclusions 8 December 1937.

32 PRO FO371/21005 F11070/2595/10 Craigie to Eden 14 December 1937 tel.812.

33 DBFP 2/XXI doc.433 F11201/9/10 Lindsay to Eden 17 December 1937 pp. 589–91.

34 For the British reaction to Roosevelt's initiative, see R.J. Pritchard, *Far Eastern Influences Upon British Strategy Towards the Great Powers, 1937-1939*, New York, Garland, 1987, pp. 81–85.

35 FO837/527 Ryan (CID) to Morton (IIC) 28 December 1937.

36 *DBFP* 2/XXI doc.438 F11749/4880/10 FE Dept memorandum 18 December 1937 pp. 598–603.

37 *DBFP* 2/XXI doc.450 F11749/4880/10 Cadogan minute 28 December 1937 p. 616.

38 See for example PRO ADM116/3916 Staff Officer (Intelligence) Shanghai to DNI (Admiralty) 22 December 1937 tel.1216/22. This document reported that between 13–15 December 6,000 troops left Shanghai on ships bound for south China.

39 *DBFP* 2/XXI doc.471 FO to Lindsay 7 January 1938 pp. 635–7, and doc.478 F407/84/10 Lindsay to FO 10 January 1938 p. 645.

40 *DBFP* 2/XXI doc.478 F407/84/10 Cadogan to Chamberlain 11 January 1938 p. 647 footnote 1.

41 On Roosevelt's plan for a World Conference and the British response see Pritchard, op. cit., pp. 87–9 and Lee, op. cit., pp. 102–5.

42 PRO FO371/22054 F4463/16/10 Hornbeck (State Dept) to Cadogan 13 April 1938.

43 *DBFP* 2/XXI doc.497 F1023/78/10 'British Policy in the Far East', Pratt memorandum 24 January 1938 p. 668.

44 On the League of Nations, see *DBFP* 2/XXI doc.507 F1397/78/10 Edmonds to Eden 2 February 1938 pp. 680–2.

45 PRO FO371/22107 F1679/84/10 Craigie to Eden 9 February 1938 tel.179.

46 For Piggott's background see F.S.G. Piggott, *Broken Thread: An Autobiography*, Aldershot, Gale & Polden, 1950, chapters I–IX.

47 PRO FO262/2016 153/70/38 Piggott minute 23 March 1938.

48 A good illustration of the generation gap is that Piggott was an old acquaintance of General Ōshima's Anglophile father and refused to believe that the younger Ōshima could possibly be anti-British as 'filial piety' was too strong in Japan for such a contradiction to take place, see PRO WO208/4703 Piggott report 17 October 1938.

49 Hall-Patch to Clark Kerr 18 November 1938, in Inverchapel Papers, Bodleian Library, Oxford, General Correspondence 1937–8.

50 PRO T160/1134 F15194/07/5 Fisher (T) minute 8 July 1938.

51 PRO PREM1/308 Ministerial conference 14 February 1938.

52 DBFP 2/XXI doc.517 F1788/78/10 Interdepartmental meeting 11 February 1938 pp. 695–7.

53 For Kung's revival of the loan proposal, see *DBFP* 2/XXI doc.491 F787/78/10 Mackillop to Eden 19 January 1938 pp. 659–60.

54 For the obstacles facing a loan, see PRO T160/1134 F15194/07/1 Leith-Ross (T) to Phillips (T) 2 February 1938, and Fisher note to Simon 3 February 1938.

55 PRO FO371/22102 F1788/78/10 Interdepartmental meeting 11 February 1938.

56 PRO T160/1134 F15194/07/3 Simon to Chamberlain 5 April 1938.

57 PRO FO371/22108 F4582/84/10 Halifax to Simon 9 May 1938.

58 *DBFP* 2/XXI doc.570 F5039/15/10 Craigie to Halifax 10 May 1938 p. 766.

59 PRO T188/224 Leith-Ross to Young (T) 12 May 1938.

60 *DBFP* 2/XXI doc.584 CAB27/623 FP(36) Cabinet Foreign Policy Committee 30th meeting 1 June 1938 pp. 785–94. Craigie's telegram

was circulated at the meeting as an enclosure to a Foreign Office memorandum.

61 See PRO PREM 1/315 Phillips to Leith-Ross 17 June 1938.

62 PRO PREM1/303 Fisher to Simon and Chamberlain 18 June 1938.

63 PRO T160/1134 F15194/07/5 J. Fisher (Bank of England) to Waley (T) 8 July 1938, see also Addis (China Consortium) memorandum 6 July 1938.

64 *DBFP* 2/XXI doc.591 F6449/25/10 Craigie to Halifax 14 June 1938 p. 800.

65 PRO PREM 1/315 Wilson (T) minute 28 June 1938.

66 *DBFP* 2/XXI doc.595 CP152(38) 'Assistance to China', Halifax memorandum 1 July 1938 p. 807.

67 *DBFP* 2/XXI doc.597 Cabinet conclusions 6 July 1938 p. 815.

68 *DBFP* 2/XXI doc.599 Cabinet conclusions 13 July 1938 pp. 819–22.

69 *DBFP* 2/XXI doc.592 F7001/62/10 Clark Kerr (Shanghai) to Halifax 27 June 1938 pp. 801–2, and doc.594 F7031/62/10 Craigie to Halifax 29 June 1938 p. 804.

70 For Craigie's initial judgment of Ugaki, see PRO FO371/22181 F7605/71/23 Craigie to Howe 7 June 1938. For the currency issue see PRO FO371/22091 F7418/62/10 Craigie to Halifax 18 June 1938 no.409E.

71 For the text of the Customs Agreement, see *DBFP* 2/XXI doc.565 F6072/15/10 Craigie to Halifax 4 May 1938 pp. 757–9.

72 *DBFP* 2/XXI doc.599 Cabinet conclusions 13 July 1938 p. 820.

73 *DBFP* 2/XXI doc.600 F8491/12/10 Craigie to Halifax 14 July 1938 p. 826. For the Foreign Office's telegram see PRO T160/1134 F15194/07/5 [F7273/25/10] Halifax to Craigie 13 July 1938 tel.472.

74 *DBFP* 2/XXI doc.598 F7991/62/10 Interdepartmental meeting 12 July 1938 pp. 817–9.

75 PRO FO371/22092 F7944/62/10 Craigie to Halifax 26 July 1938 tel.894, and F8151/62/10 Craigie to Halifax 26 July 1938 tel.902.

76 *DBFP* 2/XXI doc.603 F8129/16/10 Craigie to Halifax 26 July 1938 pp. 831–3.

77 *DBFP* Series 3 Volume VIII doc.5 F8378/16/10 Halifax to Clark Kerr 4 August 1938 p. 4–5

78 PRO WO208/243 CX28037/30 'Reported Approach by General Hata to Chiang Kai-shek' SIS report 14 March 1938.

79 *DBFP* 3/VIII doc.12 F8751/16/10 Craigie to Halifax 12 August 1938 pp. 13–14.

80 *DBFP* 3/VIII doc.107 F10125/62/10 Craigie to Halifax 22 September 1938 pp. 96–7.

81 R. Craigie, *Behind the Japanese Mask*, London, Hutchinson, 1946, p. 62.

82 On Britain and the Changkufeng incident, see P.W. Doerr, 'The Changkufeng/Lake Khasan Incident of 1938: British Intelligence on Soviet and Japanese Military Performance', *Intelligence and National Security*, 1990, vol. 5, pp. 184–99.

83. PRO WO208/847 Ronald minute 23 August 1938 on BJ.072044 Tokyo to Paris undated [August 1938].

4 GROWING TENSIONS

1 PRO FO371/22110 F10949/84/10 Howe (FE Dept) minute 10 October 1938, and Halifax minute 14 October 1938.
2 PRO T160/1134 F15194/07/5 Clark Kerr (Chungking) to Halifax 24 October 1938 tel.7(Tour).
3 *DBFP* Third Series Volume VIII doc.233 F11989/84/10 Clark Kerr to Halifax 7 November 1938 pp. 216–18, and doc.234 F11991/84/10 Clark Kerr to Halifax 11 November 1938 pp. 218–19.
4 PRO FO371/21001 F5690/1098/10 Ronald (FE Dept) minute 25 August 1937.
5 PRO AIR40/1357 'Soviet Help to China' Air Intelligence report 12 April 1938 no.6232.
6 PRO WO106/5365 Shanghai Intelligence Report No.42 Part 1 30 September 1938.
7 PRO T160/1322 F13468/3 Ronald to Somerville Smith (Export Credits Guarantee Department) 1 September 1938.
8 On Japan's policy towards China in autumn 1938 and the Western reaction, see K. Usui, 'The Politics of War, 1937–1941' in J.W. Morley (ed.), *The China Quagmire: Japan's Expansion on the Asian Continent, 1933–1941*, New York, Columbia University Press, 1983, pp. 348–54, P. Lowe, *Great Britain and the Origins of the Pacific War: A Study of British Policy in East Asia, 1937–1941*, Oxford, Clarendon, 1977, pp. 50–3, and B.A. Lee, *Britain and the Sino-Japanese War, 1937–1939: A Study in the Dilemmas of British Decline*, Stanford, Stanford University Press, 1973, pp. 149–65.
9 *DBFP* 3/VIII doc.249 F12133/11783/10 Craigie (Tokyo) to Halifax 17 November 1938 pp. 234–6.
10 PRO FO371/22164 F13875/11783/10 Craigie to Halifax 30 November 1938 no.958.
11 *DBFP* 3/VIII doc.323 F13739/11783/10 Craigie to Halifax 12 December 1938 pp. 304–6.
12 PRO WO208/859 BJ.070829 Tokyo to Berlin (undated) decrypted 19 March 1938, and WO106/5606 BJ.072208 Berlin to Tokyo 31 August 1938 decrypted 14 September 1938.
13 For the tripartite negotiations in the autumn of 1938, see T. Ōhata, 'The Anti-Comintern Pact, 1935–1939' in J.W. Morley (ed.), *Deterrent Diplomacy: Japan, Germany, and the USSR 1935–1940*, New York, Columbia University Press, 1976, pp. 65–77, M. Toscano, *The Origins of the Pact of Steel*, Baltimore, John Hopkins Press, 1967, pp. 3–85, and D.C. Watt, *How War Came: The Immediate Origins of the Second World War, 1938–1939*, London, Heinemann, 1989, pp. 46–55.
14 PRO T160/1134 F15194/07/5 Leith-Ross (T) minute 11 November 1938.
15 PRO CAB24/280 CP266(38) 'Assistance to China' Halifax memorandum 25 November 1938, and CP268(38) 'Assistance to China' Simon memorandum 25 November 1938, and CAB23/96 57(38) Cabinet conclusions 30 November 1938.
16 *DBFP* 3/VIII doc.298 F12771/62/10 Lindsay (Washington) to Halifax 1 December 1938 pp. 278–9. See also W. Heinrichs, *American Ambassador: Joseph C. Grew and the Development of the United States Diplomatic Tradition*, New York, Oxford University Press, 1966, pp. 262–4.

17 *DBFP* 3/VIII doc.311 F12819/25/10 Craigie to Halifax 4 December 1938 pp. 295–6.

18 *DBFP* 3/VIII doc.382 F44/44/10 Craigie to Halifax 1 January 1939 pp. 359–60.

19 PRO FO371/22183 F10997/103/23 Craigie to Halifax 19 October 1938 tel.1213.

20 *DBFP* 3/VIII doc.440 F418/44/10 Halifax to Mallet (Washington) 23 January 1939 pp. 411–14.

21 *DBFP* 3/VIII doc.465 F1172/44/10 Mallet to Halifax 3 February 1939 pp. 435–6.

22 PRO CAB23/97 1(39) Cabinet conclusions 18 January 1939, and T160/1135 F15194/07/8 Chamberlain/Simon meeting 23 February 1939.

23 PRO WO208/859 BJ.073458 Tokyo to Berlin 9 January 1939 decrypted 26 January 1939, and *DBFP* 3/VIII doc.467 C1500/421/62 Halifax to Mallet 4 February 1939 pp. 437–9. For more on the talks see Ōhata, op. cit., pp. 76–7, and Watt, op. cit., pp. 54–5.

24 PRO WO208/859 BJ.073480 Tokyo to Berlin 24 January 1939 decrypted 27 January 1939, and BJ.O73533 Tokyo to Rome 27 January 1939 decrypted 1 February 1939.

25 For Shiratori's and Ōshima's objections to Tokyo's stance, see PRO WO208/859 MI2a to AHQ India 9 February 1939.

26 For French policy see J. Dreifort, *Myopic Grandeur: The Ambivalence of French Foreign Policy Toward the Far East, 1919–1945*, Kent, Kent State University Press, 1991, pp. 148–69.

27 *DBFP* 3/VIII doc.338 F471/471/61 Craigie to Halifax 14 December 1938 p. 320. On the controversy over naval policy in the winter of 1938/9 see R.J. Pritchard, *Far Eastern Influences Upon British Strategy Towards the Great Powers, 1937–1939*, New York, Garland, 1987, pp. 131–49.

28 *DBFP* 3/VIII appendix 1 enclosure in doc.(ii) F3147/471/61 Phillips (Admiralty) to Howe 29 March 1939 pp. 549–50.

29 PRO FO371/23560 F3478/456/23 Ronald minute 28 February 1939.

30 PRO CAB24/284 CP76(39) 'Situation in the Far East' Halifax memorandum 30 March 1939.

31 PRO FO371/23560 F3696/456/23 Wills (BOT) to Ronald 14 April 1939, and Ronald to Wills 26 April 1939.

32 PRO FO371/23567 F3732/982/23 Cambon/Ronald conversation 17 April 1939, and F4827/982/23 Howe to Corbin 2 June 1939.

33 PRO FO371/23549 F2742/2742/61 Lambert (WO) to Butler (FO) 18 March 1939.

34 PRO FO371/23517 F2882/2882/10 Quo/Butler conversation 22 March 1939, and F3024/2882/10 Mounsey minute 30 March 1939.

35 PRO FO371/23697 N1459/1459/38 Collier (N Dept) minute 25 February 1939, and Howe minute 28 February 1939.

36 PRO FO371/23697 N1459/1459/38 Oliphant minute 28 February 1939. See also WO106/5606 Colonel Dennys (MI2) to DDMI 15 May 1939.

37 *DBFP* Series 3 Volume IX doc.62 F4527/456/23 Craigie to Halifax 13 May 1939 p. 65.

38 PRO FO371/23555 F4419/176/23 Shigemitsu/Butler conversation 9 May 1939. On Shigemitsu's thoughts on the tripartite talks see FO371/22994 C1895/421/62 Collier minute 28 February 1939.

39 For the introduction of the new cypher machines at the Japanese embassies, see E.T. Layton, R. Pineau and J. Costello, *'And I Was There' Pearl Harbor and Midway: Breaking the Secrets*, New York, William Morrow, 1985, p. 80.

40 *DBFP* 3/VIII appendix II doc.(i) F10469/717/10 Craigie to Halifax 4 October 1939 p. 551, doc.(xi) F11145/717/10 Clark Kerr to Halifax 23 October 1938 pp. 556–7, and doc.277 F12167/717/10 Halifax to Clark Kerr and Craigie 24 November 1938 p. 259.

41 For the imposition of the blockade, see *DBFP* 3/VIII doc.336 Jamieson (Tientsin) to British Embassy, Shanghai 14 December 1938 p. 315.

42 *DBFP* 3/VIII doc.554 F2430/1/10 Jamieson to British Embassy, Shanghai 19 March 1939 p. 509.

43 PRO FO371/23396 F2960/1/10 Jamieson to Homma 24 March 1939, enclosure in Jamieson to Clark Kerr 24 March 1939 tel.142.

44 PRO FO371/23396 F2867/1/10 Craigie to Halifax 22 March 1939 tel.271, and F2986/1/10 Craigie to Halifax 27 March 1939 tel.292.

45 *DBFP* 3/IX doc.1 F3484/1/10 Jamieson to Clark Kerr 10 April 1939 p. 1, and doc.64 F4531/1/10 Jamieson to Halifax 13 May 1939 pp. 66–7. For events up until the Japanese introduced the blockade on 14 June, see Lowe, op. cit., pp. 74–7, Watt, op. cit., pp. 350–4, and Lee, op. cit., pp. 183–5.

46 *DBFP* 3/IX doc.64 F4531/1/10 Jamieson to Halifax 13 May 1939 pp. 66–7.

47 PRO FO371/23397 F4808/1/10 Clark Kerr to Halifax 17 May 1939 tel.45 (Tour), and *DBFP* 3/IX doc.130 F5053/1/10 Halifax to Clark Kerr 30 May 1939 p. 117.

48 PRO FO371/23399 F5871/1/10 Brenan (FE Dept) minute 16 June 1939, on Jamieson to Halifax 14 June 1939 tel.226.

49 PRO FO371/23397 F4781/1/10 Craigie to Halifax 19 May 1939 tel.451, and FO371/23398 F5168/1/10 Grasset (Hong Kong) to Pownall (DMI) 29 May 1939 tel.5122.

50 PRO CAB23/99 31(39) Cabinet conclusions 7 June 1939.

51 Sir A. Cadogan diary entry for 20 June 1939, in D. Dilks (ed.), *The Diaries of Sir Alexander Cadogan, 1938–1945*, London, Cassell, 1971, p. 189.

52 PRO WO106/125 J.N.G. undated minute (June 1939).

53 For the European background to the Tientsin Crisis, see Watt, op. cit., pp. 188–338.

54 *DBFP* 3/IX doc.196 F5784/1/10 Clark Kerr to Halifax 14 June 1939 p. 168.

55 *DBFP* 3/IX doc.227 F6017/1/10 Craigie to Halifax 18 June 1939 p. 196.

56 PRO FO371/23999 F5883/1/10 Craigie to Halifax 15 June 1939 tel.566.

57 PRO FO371/23400 F6036/1/10 Craigie to Halifax 19 June 1939 tel.608.

58 PRO CAB27/627 FP(36)95 'Retaliation for the Tientsin Blockade' Halifax memorandum 16 June 1939, FP(36)94 'Economic Retaliation Against Japan' Halifax/Stanley memorandum 16 June 1939, and FP(36)96 'The Situation in the Far East' COS report 18 June 1939.

59 PRO CAB27/625 FP(36) Cabinet Foreign Policy Committee 52nd meeting 19 June 1939.

60 PRO PREM1/316 Runciman to Chamberlain 19 June 1939.

61 PRO CAB104/70 Chamberlain/Chatfield conversation 20 June 1939.

62 PRO CAB27/625 FP(36) Cabinet Foreign Policy Committee 53rd meeting 20 June 1939.

63 *DBFP* 3/IX doc.228 F6029/1/10 Craigie to Halifax 18 June 1939 pp. 198–9.

64 *DBFP* 3/IX doc.268 F6431/1/10 Craigie to Halifax 27 June 1939 pp. 231–2.

65 N. Chamberlain to Ida, 25 June 1939, N. Chamberlain papers, Birmingham University Library, NC18/1/1104.

66 PRO CAB47/12 ATB(EPG) 13th meeting 22 June 1939.

67 PRO CAB47/6 ATB201 'Economic Measures to Restrain Japan From Further Action Inimical to British Interests in the Far East' Elliot memorandum 20 July 1939.

68 PRO FO371/23489 F7338/44/10 Morton (IIC) to Ryan (CID) 14 July 1939.

69 PRO FO371/23489 F7014/44/10 Halifax to Stanley 13 July 1939.

70 *DBFP* 3/IX doc.322 F7340/44/10 Craigie to Halifax 14 July 1939 p. 227. For Sansom's views see PRO CAB47/12 ATB(EPG) 13th meeting 22 June 1939.

71 N. Chamberlain to Hilda 15 July 1939, N. Chamberlain papers, NC18/1/1107.

72 *DBFP* 3/IX doc.325 F7347/6457/10 Craigie to Halifax 15 July 1939 p. 279.

73 *DBFP* 3/IX doc.327 F7348/6457/10 Craigie to Halifax 15 July 1939 pp. 281–2.

74 *DBFP* 3/IX doc.337 Halifax to Craigie 17 July 1939 p. 290.

75 *DBFP* 3/IX doc.353 F7645/6457/10 Craigie to Halifax 21 July 1939 pp. 304–5.

76 N. Chamberlain to Ida 23 July 1939, N. Chamberlain papers, NC18/1/1109.

77 PRO CAB23/100 39(39) Cabinet conclusions 26 July 1939.

78 *DBFP* 3/IX doc.593 F7899/44/10 Craigie to Halifax 26 July 1939 pp. 338–9, doc.423 F8103/11/10 Craigie to Halifax 28 July 1939 p. 354, and PRO BT11/694 Interdepartmental meeting of Ministers 31 July 1939. The Export Credit Guarantee Agreement was finally signed on 18 August 1939 when it was clear that the Tientsin talks were on the point of collapse.

79 PRO FO371/23528 F8244/6457/10 Craigie to Halifax 31 July 1939 tel.902. For the Tientsin negotiations, see Usui, op. cit., pp. 362–4, and Lowe, op. cit., pp. 90–3.

80 *DBFP* 3/IX doc.403 F8071/6457/10 Craigie to Halifax 27 July 1939 pp. 346–7.

81 *DBFP* 3/IX doc.442 F8303/6457/10 Craigie to Halifax 1 August 1939 p. 380.

82 PRO CAB23/100 40(39) Cabinet conclusions 2 August 1939.

83 For the American motives behind this decision, see M. Barnhart, *Japan Prepares For Total War: The Search For Economic Security, 1919–1941*, Ithaca, Cornell University Press, 1987, pp. 133–5, and Heinrichs, op. cit. pp. 289–90.

84 PRO CAB23/100 40(39) Cabinet conclusions 2 August 1939.

85 *DBFP* 3/IX doc.444 F8245/6457/10 Craigie to Halifax 1 August 1939 p. 382

86 *DBFP* 3/IX appendix 1 F8502/6457/10 'Memorandum on British Policy in the Far East' Sansom memorandum 3 August 1939 pp. 528–32.

87 *DBFP* 3/IX doc.516 F8792/6457/10 Campbell (Paris) to Halifax 11 August 1939 pp. 446–50, and doc.511 F8981/6457/10 Lindsay to Halifax 11 August 1939 pp. 443–4.

88 PRO PREM1/316 Halifax to Chamberlain 16 August 1939.

89 PRO PREM1/316 Chamberlain to Halifax 17 August 1939.

90 PRO FO371/23404 F9379/1/10 Craigie to Jamieson 21 August 1939 tel.29.

91 *DBFP* 3/IX doc.651 F9159/1/10 Jamieson to Halifax 20 August 1939 p. 479.

92 For the turmoil in Japan caused by the Nazi–Soviet Pact see K. Sato, *Japan and Britain at the Crossroads, 1939–1941: A Study in the Dilemmas of Japanese Policy*, Tokyo, Senshu University Press, 1986, pp. 14–16, and Watt, op. cit., pp. 473–7.

93 *DBFP* 3/IX doc.584 F9421/87/10 Craigie to Halifax 24 August 1939 p. 496.

94 PRO FO371/23532 F9583/6457/23 Edwardes/Butler conversation 26 August 1939, and *DBFP* 3/IX doc.598 F9601/176/23 Halifax to Craigie 26 August 1939 pp. 507–8.

5 A FALSE DAWN

1 PRO FO371/23444 F10415/69/10 Craigie to Halifax 23 September 1939. See also P. Lowe, *Great Britain and the Origins of the Pacific War: A Study of British Policy in East Asia, 1937–1941*, Oxford, Clarendon, 1977, pp. 108–9.

2 See PRO CAB65/1 WM26(39) War Cabinet conclusions 25 September 1939 and WM28(39) War Cabinet conclusions 26 September 1939, and FO371/23444 F10597/69/10 Craigie to Halifax 1 October 1939 tel.1319, and F10691/69/10 Craigie to Halifax 11 October 1939 tel.1366.

3 PRO CAB66/2 WP(39)56 'Sino-Japanese Hostilities' COS report 28 September 1939.

4 PRO FO371/23556 F10710/176/23 Butler minute 22 September 1939.

5 PRO FO371/23533 F10278/6457/10 Craigie to Halifax 18 September 1939 tel.1242, and CAB65/1 WM24(39) War Cabinet conclusions 23 September 1939.

6 PRO FO371/23534 F10971/6457/10 Craigie to Halifax 12 October 1939 tel.1371. On Grew's speech see W.H. Heinrichs, *American Ambassador: Joseph C. Grew and the American Diplomatic Tradition*, New York, Oxford University Press, 1966, pp. 294–5, and J. Utley, *Going to War With Japan, 1937–1941*, Knoxville, Tennessee University Press, 1985, pp. 67–9.

7 PRO FO371/23534 F11946/6457/10 Craigie to Halifax 16 November 1939 tel.1515, and CAB65/2 WM96(39) War Cabinet conclusions 27 November 1939.

8 PRO FO371/23462 F11233/105/10 Clark Kerr to Halifax 24 October 1939 tel.71 (Tour).

9 PRO FO371/23462 F11981/87/10 Clark Kerr to Halifax 17 November 1939 tel.1267.

10 On the build-up of Soviet troops in Sinkiang see PRO FO371/23451 F10758/77/10 Seeds (Moscow) to Halifax 4 October 1939 tel.360, and WO208/293 Shanghai Intelligence Monthly Report no.54 28 October 1939. For a more general study of Soviet influence in Sinkiang see J. Garver, *Chinese–Soviet Relations 1937–1945: The Diplomacy of Chinese Nationalism*, New York, Oxford University Press, 1988, pp. 153–61.

11 PRO FO371/23558 F9456/347/23 Craigie to Halifax 25 August 1939 tel.1099, and F10218/347/23 Craigie to Halifax 16 September 1939 tel.1228.

12 PRO FO371/23559 F12088/347/23 Craigie to Halifax 22 November 1939 tel.1532. For the pressures on Japan to seek an understanding with Russia, see C. Hosoya,'The Tripartite Pact, 1939–1940,' in J.W. Morley (ed.), *Deterrent Diplomacy: Japan, Germany and the USSR, 1935–1940*, New York, Columbia University Press, 1976, pp. 196–9.

13 PRO FO371/23559 F12108/347/23 Seeds to Halifax 25 November 1939 tel.471, and F12189/347/23 Roché (French Embassy)/Dening (FE Dept) conversation 24 November 1939.

14 PRO FO371/23678 N6423/57/38 Collier minute 25 November 1939, FO371/23559 F12088/347/23 Howe minute 27 November 1939, and FO371/23551 F12090/4027/61 Lothian (Washington) to Halifax 22 November 1939 tel.801.

15 PRO FO371/23698 N6442/1459/38 Lascelles (N. Dept) minute 8 December 1939. The Chiefs of Staff held a similar view, see CAB80/15 COS(39)158 'The present Sino-Japanese Military Situation, December 1939' COS report 9 December 1939.

16 PRO FO837/519 vol. 1 COIS Singapore to DNI (Admiralty) 19 September 1939 tel.1901/1.

17 PRO FO371/23567 F10500/1054/23 Edwardes (Japanese Embassy) to Harrison (FO) enclosing memorandum from Y. Shudo 23 September 1939. See also W.N. Medlicott, *The Economic Blockade*, vol. 1, London, HMSO, 1952, p. 389, and Lowe, op. cit., pp. 106–10. For the general effect of the start of the European war on Japan's access to raw materials see M. Barnhart, *Japan Prepares For Total War: The Search for Economic Security, 1919–1941*, Ithaca, Cornell University Press, 1987, pp. 148–52.

18 PRO T160/1094 F16244/1 Hall-Patch (T) minute 6 October 1939.

19 PRO FO371/23568 F10898/1054/23 Shigemitsu/Sansom conversation 6 October 1939.

20 PRO FO837/519 vol. 1 Wellesley (MEW) minute 28 September 1939.

21 PRO FO371/23568 F11195/1094/23 Craigie to Halifax 20 October 1939 tel.1404.

22 PRO FO837/519 vol. 1 Wellesley minute 6 November 1939 and undated MEW memorandum. The FO's draft memorandum, also undated, is in FO371/23568 F11899/1054/23.

23 For the sterling issue see PRO T160/1094 F16244/1 Waley (T) to Stephens (T) 20 November 1939. For the Board of Trade, see T160/1094 F16244/1 Owen (T) to Waley 25 November 1939.

24 PRO FO371/23568 F12160/1054/23 Sansom minute 27 November 1939.

25 PRO CAB67/2 WP(G)(39)90 'Seizure of Exports From Germany' Cross memorandum 15 November 1939.

26 See Medlicott, op. cit., pp. 393–5.

27 PRO CAB65/2 WM 96(39) War Cabinet conclusions 27 November 1939.

28 PRO CAB65/2 WM 104(39) War Cabinet conclusions 4 December 1939. For the new Japanese proposal over Tientsin see FO371/23534 F12288/6457/10 Craigie to Halifax 2 December 1939 tel.1581. On the American–Japanese talks about the reopening of Yangtse see Heinrichs, op. cit., pp. 295–7.

29 PRO FO371/23534 F12359/6457/10 Craigie to Halifax 4 December 1939 tel.1588.

30 PRO FO371/23535 F12663/6457/10 Clark Kerr to Halifax 13 December 1939 tel.1364.

31 PRO FO371/23535 F12663/6457/10 Halifax to Clark Kerr 17 December 1939 tel.1227.

32 PRO FO371/23535 F12939/6457/10 Craigie to Halifax 21 December 1939 tel.1667, and F12973/6457/23 Craigie to Halifax 23 December 1939 tel.1687.

33 PRO FO371/23953 W18091/16015/49 Shigemitsu/Howe conversation 5 December 1939. It appears that the information about the 'secret cargo' came from a decrypted telegram, presumably from consular sources, see PRO CAB67/3 WP(G)(39)92 'The Seizure of Enemy Exports. The Case of the Japanese Ship the "Sanyo Maru"' Halifax memorandum 10 December 1939. The 'secret cargo' according to the records of a War Cabinet meeting consisted of magnetic mines, see CAB65/2 WM111(39) War Cabinet conclusions 11 December 1939.

34 PRO FO371/23954 W18720/16015/49 Shigemitsu/Halifax conversation 15 December 1939.

35 PRO FO371/23551 F12625/4027/61 Lothian to Halifax 9 December 1939 tel.883. On the general issue of Anglo-American relations see D. Reynolds, *The Creation of the Anglo-American Alliance 1937–1941: A Study in Competitive Co-operation*, London, Europa, 1981, pp. 73–83.

36 For the ferro-alloy proposal see PRO FO371/22836 A8712/6041/45 Lothian to Halifax 12 December 1939 tel.894, and Barnhart, op. cit., pp. 178–81, Medlicott, op. cit., pp. 367–71, and Utley, op. cit., pp. 77–9. On the failure of the Grew-Nomura talks, see Heinrichs, op. cit., pp. 297–301.

37 PRO CAB67/4 WP(G)(40)14 'Possibility of United States Cooperation in Preventing Certain Vital Commodities From Reaching Germany, Russia and Japan.' Halifax/Cross memorandum 19 January 1940.

38 PRO CAB65/5 WM21(40) War Cabinet conclusions 23 January 1940.

39 PRO FO371/24731 F330/103/23 Craigie to Halifax 13 January 1940 tel.39. On Japan's economic difficulties, see Barnhart, op. cit., pp. 154–7.

40 PRO ADM116/4157 Admiralty to C in C China 9 January 1940 tel.1900/10.

41 PRO FO371/25108 W1205/31/49 Craigie to Halifax 22 January 1940 tel.97. On the *Asama Maru* crisis, see K. Sato, *Japan and Britain at the Crossroads, 1939–1941: A Study in the Dilemmas of Japanese Diplomacy*, Tokyo, Senshu University Press, 1986, pp. 44–9, and Lowe, op. cit., pp. 119–20.

42 PRO FO371/25108 W1281/31/49 Craigie to Halifax 23 January 1940 tel.110.

43 For Craigie's favourable assessment of the Yonai government see R. Craigie, *Behind the Japanese Mask*, London, Hutchinson, 1946, pp. 81–2.

44 PRO FO371/25108 W1397/31/49 Shigemitsu/Halifax conversation 24 January 1940, and FO371/25109 W1468/31/49 Butler (San Francisco) to Halifax 25 January 1940.

45 PRO FO371/25109 W1547/31/49 Craigie to Halifax 27 January 1940 tel.154, and FO371/25110 W2061/31/49 Craigie to Halifax 5 February 1940 tel.247.

46 PRO FO371/24708 F297/193/61 Craigie to Halifax 1 January 1940 no.1 (Saving).

47 PRO FO371/23698 N7134/57/38 Sargent to Ismay (COS Secretariat) 22 December 1939.

48 PRO WO193/646 COS(40)252 'Military Implications of Hostilities with Russia in 1940' COS memorandum 8 March 1940.

49 PRO FO371/23556 F13005/176/23 Shigemitsu/Butler conversation 21 December 1939, FO371/24724 F2072/23/23 Shigemitsu/Butler conversation 18 March 1940, and FO371/24724 F3017/22/23 Shigemitsu/Halifax conversation 26 April 1940.

50 PRO FO371/24708 F1429/193/61 Craigie to Halifax 26 February 1940 tel.354. For the expectation that Japan would make an anti-Soviet overture to France, see FO371/24672 F1442/51/10 Campbell (Paris) to Halifax 27 February 1940 tel.160 (Saving).

51 PRO FO371/24708 F1462/193/61 Craigie to Halifax 29 February 1940 tel.366.

52 For those who favoured an overture to Japan see PRO FO371/24843 N3363/30/38 Sargent minute 24 March 1940 and Seymour minute 25 March 1940. For those opposed see ibid Cadogan minute 25 March 1940 and Halifax minute 27 March 1940, and FO371/24846 N3485/40/38 Butler minute 29 March 1940. See also S. Miner, *Between Churchill and Stalin: The Soviet Union, Great Britain and the Origins of the Grand Alliance*, Chapel Hill, University of North Carolina Press, 1988, p. 25.

53 PRO WO106/2436 'Japan as an Ally' MO2 memorandum 31 March 1940, MI2c minute 4 April 1940, and van Curtsem (DDMI) minute 4 April 1940.

54 PRO FO371/24724 F2169/23/23 Craigie to Halifax 31 March 1940 tel.517, Butler minute 1 April 1940, and Seymour minute 6 April 1940.

55 PRO WO106/5134 Hammond (MI2) minute 28 March 1940, and DMI minute 29 March 1940, and FO371/24724 F2942/23/23 Lambert (WO) to Butler 24 April 1940.

56 PRO FO371/25084 W610/14/49 Craigie to Halifax 11 January 1940 tel.30.

57 PRO FO837/520 vol. 3 FO/MEW meeting 7 February 1940.

58 PRO FO371/25086 W3054/14/49 Shigemitsu/Halifax/Ronald conversation 20 February 1940.

59 PRO FO371/25139 W4640/79/49 Lothian to Halifax 16 March 1940 tel.373.

60 PRO FO371/25085 W2283/14/49 MEW Intelligence Report I.613/1 5 February 1940. See also Medlicott, op. cit., pp. 405–6.

61 PRO CAB67/5 WP(G)(40)72 'Soviet–German Trade' Cross memorandum 11 March 1940, and CAB65/6 WM68(40) War Cabinet conclusions 14 March 1940.
62 PRO CAB65/6 WM76(40) War Cabinet conclusions 27 March 1940.
63 PRO FO371/25075 W5015/8/49 Craigie to Halifax 26 March 1940 tel. 496, and Halifax to Craigie 29 March 1940 tel.237. See also Medlicott, op. cit., p. 324 and p. 405.
64 PRO FO371/25075 W5253/8/49 Supreme War Council meeting 28 March 1940.
65 PRO FO371/24732 F2162/103/23 Waley (T) to Howe 29 March 1940, and F2336/103/23 Waley to Leith-Ross (MEW) 29 March 1940.
66 PRO FO371/25088 W5547/14/49 Shigemitsu/Halifax conversation 3 April 1940.
67 Edwardes to Butler 27 March 1940, in Butler Papers, Trinity College, Cambridge, RAB E3/5.
68 PRO FO371/25077 W6205/8/49 Butler to Cross 5 April 1940.
69 PRO FO371/25077 W6205/8/49 Halifax to Craigie 14 April 1940 tel.296.
70 PRO FO371/25077 W6383/8/49 Craigie to Halifax 16 April 1940 tel.605.
71 For the record of the inter-departmental meeting, see PRO FO837/524 vol. 2. FO/MEW meeting 24 April 1940. The telegrams from Australia were circulated by Eden as annexes to his memorandum on the subject, see CAB67/6 WP(G)(40)108 'Soviet–German Trade' Eden memorandum 17 April 1940. See also Medlicott, op. cit., pp. 406–7.
72 PRO FO371/25077 W6638/8/49 Lothian to Halifax 18 April 1940 tel.563, and FO371/25078 W7617/8/49 Lothian to Halifax 4 May 1940.
73 PRO FO371/24725 F3255/23/23 Shigemitsu/Butler conversation 7 May 1940, and PRO FO371/25078 W7794/8/49 Shigemitsu/Cross/Leith-Ross conversation 10 May 1940. For the economic talks in May/June 1940 see Medlicott, op. cit., pp. 409–11.
74 See Barnhart, op. cit., p. 183.
75 PRO FO371/25078 W7794/8/49 Okamoto/Leith-Ross conversation 14 May 1940 and FO371/24725 F3275/23/23 Shigemitsu/Butler conversation 13 May 1940.
76 PRO FO371/25090 W7849/14/49 Butler to Shigemitsu 15 May 1940.
77 For the records of these two meetings, see PRO FO837/524 vol. 3 Okamoto/Leith-Ross conversations 23 May and 4 June 1940.
78 PRO FO371/24725 F3284/23/23 Shigemitsu/Butler conversation 11 June 1940, and FO837/524 vol. 4 Okamoto/Keswick (MEW) conversation 12 June 1940.
79 For the record of the last meeting, see PRO FO837/524 vol. 4 Okamoto/Leith-Ross conversation 28 June 1940.
80 PRO FO371/24650 F1978/5/10 Clark Kerr to Halifax 19 March 1940 tel.110 (Tour).
81 PRO FO371/24651 F2731/5/10 Craigie to Halifax 13 April 1940 tel.583.
82 PRO FO371/24652 F3889/5/10 Craigie to Halifax 24 June 1940 no.327A

6 THE BURMA ROAD CRISIS

1 PRO FO371/24655 F3392/16/10 Craigie to Halifax 11 June 1940 tel.792.
2 PRO FO371/24725 F3432/23/23 Craigie to Halifax 19 June 1940 tel.

1032. On the Burma Road crisis see K. Sato, *Japan and Britain at the Crossroads, 1939–1941: A Study in the Dilemmas of Japanese Diplomacy*, Tokyo, Senshu University Press, 1986, pp. 61–6, D. Reynolds, *The Creation of the Anglo-American Alliance, 1937–1941: A Study in Co-operative Competition*, London, Europa, 1981, pp. 132–5 and P. Lowe, *Great Britain and the Origins of the Pacific War: A Study in British Policy in East Asia, 1937–1941*, Oxford, Clarendon, 1977 pp. 140–53.

3 For the background to these decisions see I. Hata, 'The Army's Move into Northern Indochina' in J.W. Morley (ed.), *The Fateful Choice: Japan's Advance into Southeast Asia, 1939–1941*, New York, Columbia University Press, 1980, pp. 158–9.

4 PRO FO371/24725 F3432/23/23 Halifax to Craigie 21 June 1940 tel.598, and Shigemitsu/Halifax conversation 21 June 1940.

5 PRO FO371/24725 F3465/23/23 Craigie to Halifax 22 June 1940 tel.1068.

6 Ibid.

7 PRO FO371/24666 F3479/43/10 Craigie to Halifax 25 June 1940 tel.1087.

8 PRO FO371/24725 F3465/23/23 Halifax to Lothian 25 June 1940 tel. 1262, and Lothian to Halifax 28 June 1940 tel.1163. For the American refusal to sanction a British concession over the Burma Road, see R. Dallek, *Franklin D. Roosevelt and American Foreign Policy, 1932–1945*, New York, Oxford University Press, 1979, pp. 238–9, and A. Iriye, *The Origins of the Second World War in Asia and the Pacific*, London, Longman, 1987, p. 100.

9 PRO FO371/24847 N5648/40/38 Howe minute 22 May 1940. See also S. Miner, *Between Churchill and Stalin: The Soviet Union, Great Britain and the Origins of the Grand Alliance*, Chapel Hill, University of North Carolina Press, 1988, p. 37.

10 PRO FO371/24844 N5863/30/38 Ashley Clarke (FE Dept) minute 24 June 1940. See also Miner, op. cit., pp. 67–8.

11 PRO FO371/24725 F3450/23/23 Clark Kerr to Halifax 24 June 1940 tel.499, and FO371/24666 F3528/43/10 Quo/Halifax conversation 28 June 1940.

12 PRO CAB66/9 WP(40)234 'Policy in the Far East' Halifax memorandum 29 June 1940.

13 PRO CAB65/8 WM189(40) War Cabinet conclusions 1 July 1940.

14 PRO FO371/24666 F3544/43/10 Craigie to Halifax 3 July 1940 tel.1149, and Craigie to Halifax 4 July 1940, tels. 1154, 1156 and 1158.

15 PRO ADM116/5757 Admiral Godfrey minute 25 July 1940.

16 PRO CAB79/5 COS(40) 207th meeting 4 July 1940. The risk of France entering the conflict was so high that on 5 July the War Cabinet were told that Charles Corbin, the long-standing French Ambassador in London, had resigned rather than face the task of handing over a declaration of war, see CAB65/8 WM194(40) War Cabinet conclusions 5 July 1940. For further details on Anglo-French tensions see CAB69/1 DO(40) Defence Committee (Operations) 19th Meeting 3 July 1940. See also Lowe, op. cit., pp. 143–4.

17 PRO CAB79/5 COS(40) 209th meeting 5 July 1940 Annex 2 Ismay to Bruce 4 July 1940.

18 PRO CAB 66/9 WP(40)249 'Policy in the Far East' COS report 4 July 1940.

19 PRO FO371/24725 F3565/23/23 Dening minute 4 July 1940.

20 PRO CAB65/8 WM194(40) War Cabinet conclusions 5 July 1940.

21 PRO FO371/24666 F3544/43/10 Halifax to Craigie 6 July 1940 tel.657, and FO371/24667 F3568/43/10 Craigie to Halifax 8 July 1940 tel.1187.

22 PRO FO371/24667 F3568/43/10 Craigie to Halifax 9 July 1940 tel.1196.

23 PRO CAB65/8 WM199(40) War Cabinet conclusions 10 July 1940, and FO371/24667 F3606/43/10 Craigie to Halifax 17 July 1940 tel.1277. On the collapse of the Yonai Cabinet, see Sato, op. cit., pp. 65–6.

24 PRO FO371/24667 F3606/43/10 Sterndale Bennett minute 20 July 1940.

25 PRO FO371/24667 F3606/43/10 Lothian to Halifax 16 July 1940 tel.1402, and Gage (FE Dept) minute 20 July 1940.

26 PRO FO371/24667 F3606/43/10 Lothian to Halifax 15 July 1940 tel.1356, Butler/Maisky conversation 16 July 1940, and Dening minute 18 July 1940.

27 PRO FO371/24741 F3634/677/23 Lothian to Halifax 19 July 1940 tel.1425.

28 PRO FO371/24741 F3634/677/23 Ashley Clarke (FE Dept) minute, and Churchill minute to Ismay 21 July 1940. For American policy, see J.G. Utley, *Going To War With Japan, 1937–1941*, Knoxville, University of Tennessee Press, 1985, pp. 97–100, I. Anderson, *The Standard Vacuum Oil Company and United States East Asian Policy, 1933–1941*, Princeton, Princeton University Press, 1975, pp. 131–46, and M. Barnhart, *Japan Prepares For Total War: The Search For Economic Security, 1919–1941*, Ithaca, Cornell University Press, 1987, pp. 187–91.

29 PRO CAB66/10 WP(40)302 'Far Eastern Appreciation' COS report 5 August 1940.

30 PRO CAB66/10 WP(40)289 'Far Eastern Policy' COS report 27 July 1940. On the suspicion of the Dutch forces, see CAB81/97 JIC(40)105 'Relationship with the Dutch East Indies' DMI memorandum 5 June 1940.

31 PRO FO371/24725 F3465/23/23 Lothian to Halifax 25 June 1940 tel.1117, and Clark Kerr to Halifax 5 July 1940 tel.558.

32 PRO FO371/24725 F3465/23/23 Craigie to Halifax 14 July 1940 tel.1241.

33 Churchill to Halifax 20 July 1940, in Winston Churchill papers, Churchill College, Cambridge, CHAR20/13.

34 PRO FO371/24708 F3633/193/61 Butler minute 25 July 1940. On the discussion of a general settlement, see Lowe, op. cit., pp. 154–60, and Reynolds, op. cit., p. 135.

35 PRO FO371/24708 F3633/193/61 Butler to Drogheda etc 10 August 1940.

36 PRO FO371/24709 F3859/193/61 Archer (DO) to Butler 27 August 1940, and Calder (CO) to Butler 17 August 1940.

37 PRO FO371/24709 F4108/193/61 Shackle (BOT) to Butler and Keswick (MEW) to Butler 2 September 1940.

38 PRO FO371/24667 F3590/43/10 Shigemitsu/Butler conversation 19 July 1940. On Matsuoka's appointment see Iriye, op. cit., pp. 106–7.

39 For Japanese policy towards South-East Asia in summer 1940 see C.

Hosoya, 'Miscalculations in Deterrent Policy: Japanese–U.S. Relations, 1938–1941', *Journal of Peace Research* 1968, no. 2, pp. 108–9, Sato, op. cit., pp. 70–5, and Barnhart, op. cit., pp. 162–5.

40 For the history of this crisis see the file PRO FO371/24738, and also Sato, op. cit., pp. 76–7. For the British 'harbour-watchers' see J.W.M. Chapman, 'Japanese Intelligence, 1919–1945: A Suitable Case For Treatment', in C. Andrew and J. Noakes (eds), *Intelligence and International Relations 1900–1945*, Exeter, Exeter University Publications, 1987, p. 151.

41 Kennedy diary entry 29 July 1940, in Captain Malcolm Kennedy Papers, Sheffield University Library, Diary 4/35.

42 PRO FO371/24738 F3685/653/23 Craigie to Halifax 31 July 1940 tel.1407.

43 PRO FO371/24738 F3680/653/23 Craigie to Halifax 30 July 1940 tel.1373, and CAB65/8 WM217(40) War Cabinet conclusions 1 August 1940.

44 PRO CAB65/8 WM220(40) War Cabinet conclusions 6 August 1940.

45 PRO FO371/24733 F3900/103/23 Interdepartmental meeting 14 August 1940.

46 PRO FO371/24735 F3267/205/23 Halifax to Craigie 14 August 1940 tel.837.

47 PRO FO371/24739 F3944/653/23 Craigie to Halifax 18 August 1940 tel.1606, and FO371/24730 F4030/66/23 Craigie to Halifax 26 August 1940 tel.1688.

48 PRO FO371/25090 W1014014/49 Keswick to Sterndale Bennett 4 September 1940.

49 PRO FO371/24669 F4074/43/10 Craigie to Halifax 30 August 1940 tel.1716, CAB66/11 WP(40)348 'Reopening of the Burma Road' Halifax memorandum 2 September 1940, and CAB65/9 WM239(40) War Cabinet conclusions 2 September 1940.

50 PRO CAB81/98 JIC(40)263 'Exchange of Information with the United States Authorities' Edwards (JIC Secretary) note 1 September 1940.

51 PRO FO371/24709 F4290/193/61 Lothian to Halifax 16 September 1940 tel.2027. On the growing Anglo-American co-operation, see Reynolds, op. cit., pp. 121–44, and Dallek, op. cit., pp. 241–8.

52 PRO FO371/24729 F4634/60/23 Churchill to Halifax 4 October 1940 M.161. For the earlier doubts see FO371/24670 F4328/43/10 Craigie to Halifax 19 September 1940 tel.1834, and FO371/24709 F4290/193/61 Vansittart minute on Lothian to Halifax 16 September 1940 tel.2027.

53 For the Dutch–Japanese economic talks see Barnhart, op. cit., pp. 165–7, and Anderson, op. cit., pp. 146–55. For the background to the Japanese occupation of north Indo-China see Hata, op. cit., pp. 172–93, and Iriye, op. cit., pp. 117–18.

54 On the United States decision to implement further sanctions see Hosoya, op. cit., p. 110, Barnhart, op. cit., pp. 193–4, and Utley, op. cit., pp. 106–7.

55 PRO FO371/24710 F4770/193/61 Butler minute 18 September 1940, and F4772/193/61 'The possibility of a general Far Eastern settlement' Sterndale Bennett memorandum 25 September 1940.

56 On the making of the Tripartite Pact see C. Hosoya, 'The Tripartite Pact,

1939–1940', in J.W. Morley (ed.), *Deterrent Diplomacy: Japan, Germany and the USSR, 1935–1940*, New York, Columbia University Press, 1976, pp. 214–57, Sato, op. cit., pp. 81–3, and Iriye, op. cit., pp. 113–16.

57 See Sato, op. cit., pp. 85–6.

58 PRO FO371/24736 F4495/626/23 Lothian to Halifax 30 September 1940 tel.2146.

59 PRO CAB96/1 FE(40)3 MEW to Butler 5 September 1940.

60 PRO FO371/24734 F4432/103/23 Bewley (T) to Sterndale Bennett 25 September 1940.

61 PRO BT11/1009 Pares (BOT) minute 15 August 1940.

62 PRO BT11/1009 Shackle (BOT) minute 22 August 1940.

63 PRO FO371/24734 F4432/103/23 Cadogan minute, and FO371/24670 F4489/43/10 Sterndale Bennett Memorandum 1 October 1940.

64 PRO CAB65/9 WM264(40) War Cabinet conclusions 2 October 1940.

65 PRO CAB66/14 WP(40)484 FEC report 17 December 1940. For the work of the FEC see Lowe, op. cit. pp. 292–4, and Medlicott, op. cit. p. 68.

66 PRO FO371/24737 F5295/626/23 Craigie to Halifax 11 October 1940 no.470.

7 CONFRONTATION

1 PRO CAB96/1 FE(40)4 'Restrictions on Japanese Imports' MEW memorandum 8 October 1940, CAB96/7 FE(E)40 Economic Sub-Committee 1st meeting 11 October 1940, CAB96/1 FE(40) 4th meeting 18 October 1940, and FO371/24709 F4462/193/61 Halifax to N. Butler (Washington) 19 October 1940 tel.2719. On British sanctions policy, see W.N. Medlicott, *The Economic Blockade*, vol. II, London, HMSO, 1959, pp. 65–76, and P. Lowe, *Great Britain and the Origins of the Pacific War: A Study of British Policy in East Asia, 1937–1941*, Oxford, Clarendon, 1977, p. 236 & pp. 292–4.

2 PRO FO371/24710 F4888/193/61 N. Butler to Halifax 23 October 1940 tel.2389. On American policy over sanctions, see M. Barnhart, *Japan Prepares For Total War: The Search For Economic Security, 1919–1941*, Ithaca, Cornell University Press, 1987, pp. 192–7.

3 PRO FO371/24722 F4627/4605/61 Lothian (Washington) to Halifax 9 October 1940 tel.2241, and FO371/24709 F4556/193/61 Lothian to Halifax 4 October 1940 tel.2197.

4 PRO CAB96/1 FE(40) 10th meeting 28 November 1940.

5 PRO CAB96/1 FE(40)44 'Restriction of Exports to Japan' FEC memorandum 8 November 1940, and FO837/558 Economic Questions Affecting the Netherlands meeting 27 November 1940.

6 For the evidence of the increasing Japanese and German interest in Latin America, see PRO FO837/174 MEW to N. Butler 28 October 1940 tel.2259 (Arfar), and FO837/439 German Economic Developments report L.1/3/6/Z no.62 25 November 1940.

7 For the case of the Chilean iodine, see PRO FO371/24734 F5407/103/23 Leith-Ross (MEW) to Waley (T) 30 November 1940 and MEW/Ministry of Supply meeting 18 December 1940.

8 PRO FO371/25081 W12417/8/49 Ovey (Buenos Aires) to MEW 25

November 1940 tel.462 (Arfar), and W12790/8/49 Knox (Rio de Janeiro) to MEW 18 December 1940 tel.374 (Arfar).

9 PRO CAB66/14 WP(40)484 FEC report 18 December 1940.

10 PRO FO371/24711 F5359/193/61 Halifax to Alexander 26 November 1940, and Alexander to Halifax 29 November 1940.

11 Churchill to Alexander and Pound 22 November 1940 M.333, Winston Churchill papers, Churchill College, Cambridge, CHAR20/13.

12 PRO FO371/24709 F4554/193/61 Cripps to Halifax 4 October 1940 tel.826, and FO371/24845 N6875/30/38 Cripps to Halifax 13 October 1940 tel.865.

13 PRO FO371/24845 N6875/30/38 Cripps to Halifax 22 October 1940 tel.911. See also S. Miner, *Between Churchill and Stalin: The Soviet Union, Great Britain, and the Origins of the Grand Alliance*, Chapel Hill, University of North Carolina Press, 1988, pp. 83–94.

14 PRO FO371/24674 F4817/57/10 Clark Kerr to Halifax 19 October 1940 tel.141, and F4999/57/10 Clark Kerr to Halifax 4 November 1940 tel.165.

15 PRO FO371/24674 F5210/57/10 Clark Kerr to Halifax 19 November 1940 tel.202. See also WO208/242 CX28037/125 'China, Germany and Japan' SIS report 6 November 1940.

16 See Lowe, op. cit., pp. 208–16.

17 PRO FO371/24692 F5415/230/10 Halifax to Clark Kerr 9 December 1940 tel.294.

18 On the Thai–French dispute, see S. Nagaoka, 'The Drive into Southern Indochina and Thailand', in J.W. Morley (ed.), *The Fateful Choice: Japan's Advance into Southeast Asia, 1939–1941*, New York, Columbia University Press, 1980, pp. 209–21, and R. Aldrich, *The Key to the South: Britain, the United States, and Thailand during the Approach of the Pacific War, 1929–1942*, Kuala Lumpur, Oxford University Press, 1993, pp. 257–84.

19 A list of disturbing developments in German–Japanese relations is included in PRO FO371/24737 F5696/626/23 Craigie to Halifax 21 December 1940 tel.2515. For the Japanese collaboration with the German raiders see the files FO371/25162, FO371/28814 and ADM1/10294, and J.W.M. Chapman (ed.), *The Price of Admiralty: The War Diary of the German Naval Attaché in Japan, 1939–1943*, vol. 2 (4 vols), Lewes, University of Sussex Press, 1984, pp. 343–4. On British knowledge of German–Japanese intelligence collaboration see ADM223/321 OIC Special Intelligence Summary no.85 25 October 1940, no.103 19 November 1940, and no.111 29 November 1940.

20 For details on the tide of events in January 1941 see S. Hatano and S. Asada, 'The Japanese Decision to Move South 1939–1941' in R. Boyce and E.M. Robertson (eds), *Paths to War: New Essays on the Origins of the Second World War*, London, Macmillan, 1989, pp. 392–4, Nagaoka, op. cit., pp. 222–31, and Aldrich, op. cit., pp. 284–9.

21 PRO WO208/892 COIS Singapore to DNI (Admiralty) 24 January 1941 tel.0953Z/24, and COIS to DNI 25 January 1941 tel.0532Z/25. For general accounts of these events, see A.M. Best, ' "Straws in the Wind": Britain and the February 1941 War Scare in East Asia', in *Diplomacy and Statecraft*, 1994, vol. 5 pp. 642–65, C. Hosoya, 'Britain and the US in Japan's View of the International System, 1937–1941', in

I.H. Nish (ed.), *Anglo-Japanese Alienation 1919–1952*, Cambridge, Cambridge University Press, 1982, pp. 66–70, and Lowe, op. cit., pp. 220–5.

22 PRO WO208/892 COIS Singapore to DNI 23 January 1941 tel.0826Z/23.

23 PRO WO208/892 BJ.087213 Japanese Minister (Bangkok) to Tokyo undated decrypted 28 January 1941. For the Dutch information, which talked of an attack to be launched on 10 February, see PRO FO371/27962 F523/523/23 Meiklereid (Sourabaya) to COIS Singapore 1 February 1941 tel.2100/1. For Matsuoka's speech see FO371/27878 F298/12/23 Craigie to Eden 20 January 1941 tel.103.

24 PRO CAB81/100 JIC(41)55 'Japanese Intentions' JIC report 5 February 1941.

25 PRO CAB80/25 COS(41)73 Annex 1 'Measures to Avert War With Japan' COS report 6 February 1941.

26 PRO WO208/855 Summary of Intelligence 5 February to 25 February 1941, entries for 5 and 6 February, MI2c undated report. For the effect of the embassy source, see Cadogan diary entry for 6 February 1941 in D. Dilks (ed.), *The Diaries of Sir Alexander Cadogan, 1938–1945*, London, Cassell, 1971 p. 353, Dalton diary entry for 7 February 1941 in B. Pimlott (ed.), *The Second World War Diary of Hugh Dalton 1940–45*, London, Jonathan Cape, 1986, p. 154, and Major-General Davidson diary entry for 5 February 1941, Davidson papers, Liddell Hart Centre for Military Archives, Kings College, London, Item O.

27 PRO CAB66/15 WP(41)28 'The Asaka Maru' Eden memorandum 8 February 1941.

28 PRO CAB96/2 FE(41) 6th meeting 6 February 1941 and CAB79/9 COS(41) 46th meeting 8 February 1941.

29 For propaganda policy, see PRO CAB81/100 JIC(41)61 'Possible Action Against Japan' JIC report 7 February 1941, and CAB96/3 FE(41)38 Ad-hoc Sub-Committee report 11 February 1941. On the fleet to Singapore rumour, see HS1/344 Cadogan (FO) to Jebb (SOE) 11 February 1941. For a Japanese perspective on the British propaganda see K. Sato, *Japan and Britain at the Crossroads, 1939–1941: A Study in the Dilemmas of Japanese Diplomacy*, Tokyo, Senshu University Press, 1986, p. 101, and Hosoya, op. cit., p. 70.

30 See PRO CAB80/25 COS(41)73 Annex 1 'Measures to Avert War With Japan' COS report 6 February 1941, and CAB79/9 Eden/COS meeting 7 February 1941. For the overtures to the US, see Hopkins/Butler conversation 6 February 1941 in Butler Papers, Trinity College, Cambridge, RAB G/12, and PRO FO371/27886 F677/17/23 Eden to Halifax 11 February 1941, tel.693.

31 PRO FO371/27886 F648/17/23 Shigemitsu/Eden conversation 7 February 1941.

32 PRO WO208/855 Chapman and Mackenzie (MI2c) minutes 16 May 1941.

33 PRO FO371/27887 F1173/17/23 DNI to Sterndale Bennett 12 February 1941.

34 PRO FO371/27878 F1009/12/23 Craigie to Eden 15 February 1941 tel.252, and WO208/855 Summary of Intelligence 5 February to 25 February 1941, entry for 15 February, MI2c undated report.

35 For the US transfer of Purple material to Britain, see PRO WO208/1220A Military Attaché (Washington) to DMI (WO) 29 January 1941 tel.3729. The visit of the US intelligence mission is confirmed by HW1/2 'C' to Churchill 26 February 1941 C/5906, but see also B. Smith, *The Ultra-Magic Deals and the Most Secret Special Relationship, 1940–1946*, Shrewsbury, Airlife, 1993, pp. 55–63. On the information regarding Matsuoka's visit to Europe see WO208/855 Ridsdale (MI2c) note 15 February 1941, which stated 'It has been reported that Mr. Matsuoka is to visit Europe. . .', it then listed what was believed to be his intended itinerary, see also PREM3/252/6A Churchill to Cadogan 16 February 1941.

36 PRO WO208/892 COIS Singapore to DNI 1 March 1941 tel.0249Z/1, but see also WO208/896 'Short Summary of Recent BJ's on Japan' Chapman (MI2c) report 26 February 1941.

37 For the signs of British optimism see PRO FO371/27887 F1159/17/23 Craigie to FO 20 February 1941 tel.279, and PREM4 27/9 Halifax to Churchill 21 February 1941. For Japan's hesitation in February 1941 see J. Tsunoda, 'The Navy's Role in the Southern Strategy', in Morley (ed.), op. cit., pp. 283–95, and Nagaoka, op. cit., pp. 232–4.

38 See R.J. Leutze, *Bargaining for Supremacy: Anglo-American Naval Relations, 1937–1941*, Chapel Hill, University of North Carolina Press, 1977, pp. 234–66, and Reynolds, *The Creation of the Anglo-American Alliance, 1937–1941: A Study in Competitive Co-operation*, London, Europa, 1981, pp. 225–9.

39 PRO PREM3/326 Amery to Churchill 6 February 1941, and Churchill to FO and Ismay 17 February 1941, Winston Churchill papers, CHAR20/36.

40 PRO FO371/27888 F1627/17/23 Halifax to FO 5 March 1941 tel.984, FO371/27891 F3612/17/23 Halifax to Eden 4 May 1941 tel.1976. For Matsuoka's fears see WO208/892 BJ.089788 Tokyo to London 11 April 1941, decrypted 14 April 1941..

41 PRO CAB69/2 DO(41) 12th meeting 9 April 1941.

42 PRO CAB69/2 DO(41) 21st Meeting 30 April 1941 and 22nd Meeting 1 May 1941.

43 On the transfer of Enigma, see HW1/2 'C' to Churchill 26 February 1941 and Churchill minute 27 February 1941. For the Thai-Japanese telephone conversations, see Churchill to Cadogan 21 February 1941, Winston Churchill papers, CHAR20/36.

44 PRO ADM199/1477 C/S Singapore to DNI 14 March 1941 tel.0828Z/14, and C/S Singapore to DNI 23 March 1941 tel.0416Z/23. For the collaboration over JN–25 see ADM223/297 NID Vol.42 Far East and Pacific III Special: Collaboration of British and U.S. Radio Intelligence (undated internal history).

45 PRO HS1/340 'C' to Broad (FO) 1 March 1941 C/5933.

46 PRO CAB81/102 JIC(41)241 'Co-operation with the USA in Intelligence Matters in the Far East' Capel-Dunn note 2 June 1941 and WO193/927 WO to C in C FE and C in C China 11 June 1941 tel.71536.

47 PRO HS1/202 'SOE Far Eastern Organization' SOE report 5 February 1941. On Thailand, see WO193/911 C in C FE to WO 15 July 1941 tel.27496, on Indo-China, see HS1/340 GJ to CD 23 June 1941. On

co-ordination with the US see CAB122/8 Eden to Halifax 18 May 1941 tel.2659.

48 PRO CAB81/98 JIC(40)316 'Rumours of a Military Nature Intended to Mystify and Mislead the Enemy' Secretary's note 12 October 1940.

49 On the civil propaganda programme see CAB96/10 FEC Propaganda Sub-Committee meetings and memoranda. On the 'rumours', see CAB81/102 JIC(41)207 'Rumours of a Military Nature Intended to Mystify and Mislead the Enemy' Secretary's note 12 May 1941.

50 PRO HS1/333 D/Q9 to A.D/A1 3 June 1941. For the German 'fifth column' article see HS1/340 SOE to Craigie 23 July 1941 tel.723.

51 For this complaint see PRO FO371/27894 F1221/18/23 MEW to Halifax 20 February 1941 tel.847 (Arfar).

52 See Medlicott, op. cit. pp. 87–90. For the report on large sales of rubber to Germany and Japan see PRO CAB96/2 FE(41) 15 May 1941.

53 PRO FO837/559 Anglo-Netherlands Committee on Economic Affairs 2nd meeting 14 January 1941, and Lincoln (MEW) to Peekema (Dutch CO) 10 February 1941.

54 PRO FO837/562 CO to Thomas (Straits Settlement) 2 May 1941 tel.560, and Walsh (Batavia) to Eden 20 May 1941 tel.89.

55 See Medlicott, op. cit. pp. 80–2. On the British intelligence role, see PRO ADM199/1477 C/S Singapore to DNI 20 March 1941 tel.0348Z/20, and DNI to C/S Singapore 13 April 1941 tel.1744Z/13.

56 On the rubber issue, see PRO FO837/440 Summary of German Economic Developments L.1/3/6/Z No.71 27 January 1941. For copper, see Churchill to Dalton 1 February 1941 M.115/1, Winston Churchill papers, CHAR20/36.

57 PRO FO371/28868 W197/197/49 N. Butler to Eden 18 January 1941, and FO837/1086 Dalton to Hopkins 6 February 1941.

58 PRO FO371/28868 W1070/197/49 Halifax to Eden 30 January 1941 tel.463, and Eden to Halifax 7 February 1941 tel.730.

59 PRO FO371/28868 W1925/197/49 Halifax to Eden 20 February 1941 tel.812.

60 PRO FO837/186 Stirling (MEW) minute 24 February 1941.

61 PRO FO371/25987 A3292/1116/51 Halifax to MEW 30 April 1941 tel.2281 (Arfar), A3576/1116/51 Knox (Rio) to MEW 16 May 1941 tel.289 (Arfar), and Medlicott, op. cit. pp. 127–31.

62 On the American expansion of economic restrictions, see J. Utley, *Going to War with Japan, 1937–1941*, Knoxville, University of Tennessee Press, 1985, pp. 121–2, Barnhart, op. cit., pp. 221–2, and Medlicott, op. cit., pp. 96–9 and 129–31.

63 PRO FO371/25214 W11699/9160/49 Halifax to N. Butler 15 November 1940 tel.3057, FO837/539 MEW to Halifax 21 March 1941 tel.1403 (Arfar), and Barnhart, op. cit., p. 222.

64 PRO FO837/539 MEW to Halifax 8 March 1941 tel.1126 (Arfar), and FO837/1096 Halifax to MEW 13 May 1941 tel.2502 (Arfar)

65 PRO CAB96/3 FE(41)113 MEW report 18 June 1941.

66 PRO FO371/27918 F1836/122/23 Craigie to FO 11 March 1941 tel.415.

67 PRO FO371/27894 F3593/18/23 Craigie to Eden 30 April 1941 tel.712, and FO371/27895 F3647/18/23 Craigie to Eden 30 April 1941 tel.713.

228 *Notes*

68 PRO FO837/533 T33/65/Z Vol.3 Troutbeck (MEW) minute 10 June 1941.
69 PRO FO371/27895 F3647/18/23 Eden to R. Craigie 21 May 1941 tel.596.
70 On German imports of cooking oil, see FO837/440 Summary of German Economic Developments L.1/3/6/Z No.83 21 April 1941. For Craigie's concern, see PRO FO371/27895 F4694/18/23 Craigie to Eden 30 May 1941 tel.896.
71 PRO FO371/27895 F4810/18/23 Craigie to Eden 3 June 1941 tel.913.
72 PRO CAB96/2 FE(41) 21st meeting 12 June 1941.
73 See for example PRO FO371/24726 F4992/23/23 Shigemitsu/Butler conversation 1 November 1940, and Dening minute 11 November 1940, and F5077/23/23 Shigemitsu/Butler conversation 8 November 1940, and Cadogan minute 9 November 1940.
74 Hankey affidavit for Shigemitsu, Defence Exhibit 3547, in R.J. Pritchard and S.M. Zaide (eds), *The Tokyo War Crimes Trial,* Vol. XIV (22 vols), New York, Garland, 1981, p. 34512–3.
75 Ibid., pp. 34513–4.
76 PRO FO371/27901 F234/27/23 Halifax to Lloyd 17 December 1940.
77 PRO FO371/27787 F1069/17/23 Matsuoka memorandum 16 February 1941, and F1239/17/23 Churchill memorandum 24 February 1941. On this correspondence, see Lowe, op. cit., pp. 225–30, and Sato, op. cit., pp. 100–3.
78 PRO CAB63/177 Hankey papers, Piggott to Hankey 30 March 1941, and FO371/27889 F2541/17/23 Shigemitsu/Butler conversation 31 March 1941.
79 PRO PREM3/252/6A Butler to Churchill 28 March 1941, CAB63/177 Hankey Papers, Hankey to Churchill 31 March 1941, and CAB65/18 WM33(41) War Cabinet conclusions 31 March 1941.
80 PRO BT11/1278A Okamoto/Waley/Hall-Patch meeting 11 June 1940.
81 PRO FO371/24733 F4013/103/23 Waley to Okamoto 26 August 1940, and CAB96/1 FE(40) 6th meeting 31 October 1940.
82 PRO FO371/24734 F5433/103/23 Kamimura to Waley 16 December 1940.
83 PRO CAB96/2 FE(41) 16th meeting 8 May 1941.
84 PRO FO371/27907 F4156/69/23 Shigemitsu/Butler conversation 16 May 1941.
85 PRO FO371/28020 F4737/4564/23 Shigemitsu/Butler conversation 30 May 1941.
86 For Shigemitsu's recall, see *The "Magic" Background to Pearl Harbor* vol.III. doc.491 Tokyo to London 22 May 1941, Washington DC, Department of Defense, 1977, p. 243, which contrasts with Shigemitsu's claim at the time and in his memoirs that it was his decision to return home, see PRO FO371/27907 F4658/4564/23 Shigemitsu/Butler conversation 24 May 1941. For the feting of Shigemitsu, see PREM4 20/1 Eden to Churchill 27 May 1941, and FO371/27892 F5019/17/23 Shigemitsu/Eden/Moyne/Butler meeting 9 June 1941. After his departure Churchill paid tribute to Shigemitsu in a speech to the House of Commons referring to him in passing as 'a man most friendly to peace between our countries', see W. Churchill, *War Speeches 1939–1945*, vol. 2, London, Cassell, 1952, p. 15.

87 For the evidence from Vichy telegrams, see PRO WO208/1899 BJ.089056 Hanoi to Tokyo 18 March 1941 decrypted 25 March 1941, and BJ.089091 Hanoi to Tokyo 15 March 1941 decrypted 26 March 1941. On Japanese interest in Thai rubber, see WO208/859 BJ.091033 no details decrypted 16 May 1941.

88 PRO CAB96/2 FE(41) 18th meeting 22 May 1941. See also Aldrich, op. cit., pp. 319–28.

89 On the pact, see J. Haslam, *The Soviet Union and the Threat From the East, 1933–41*, London, Macmillan, 1992, pp. 145–50, and C. Hosoya, 'The Japanese-Soviet Neutrality Pact' in Morley (ed.), op. cit., pp. 51–85.

90 See, for example, PRO FO371/27956 F3114/421/23 Craigie to Eden 16 April 1941 tel.618, and WO193/913 COIS Singapore to DNI 21 May 1941 tel.0242Z/21.

91 PRO FO371/27833 F4345/1732/61 Craigie to Eden 22 May 1941 tel.842. For details on the talks in Batavia see S. Nagaoka, 'Economic Demands on Dutch East Indies', in Morley (ed.), op. cit., pp. 146–53, and Medlicott, op. cit., pp. 79–86.

92 PRO FO371/27833 F4376/1732/61 Ashley Clarke (FE Dept) minute 31 May 1941.

93 PRO CAB81/103 JIC(41)246 'Possible Effect of Japanese-Dutch Economic Negotiations' JIC report 6 June 1941, and CAB79/12 COS(41) 206th meeting 9 June 1941. For Churchill, see CAB69/2 DO(41) 30th meeting 15 May 1941.

94 N. Ike (ed.), *Japan's Decision For War. Records of the 1941 Policy Conferences*, Stanford, Stanford University Press, 1967, pp. 53–6. See also Nagaoka, 'The Drive into Southern Indochina and Thailand,' p. 234–5, Barnhart, op. cit., p. 208, and Hatano and Asada, op. cit., p. 396–8.

8 CONFLICT

1 For the conferences held in Tokyo see N. Ike (ed.), *Japan's Decision For War: Records of the 1941 Policy Conferences*, Stanford, Stanford University Press, 1967, pp. 56–90.

2 PRO FO371/27881 F5593/12/23 Craigie to Eden 25 June 1941 tel.1603, and CAB96/2 FE(41) 23rd meeting 26 June 1941.

3 PRO ADM199/1474 DNI to C/S Singapore 21 June 1941 tel.2313B/21.

4 PRO WO193/866 DMI to CIGS 25 June 1941, and CAB79/12 COS(41) 224th meeting 25 June 1941.

5 PRO ADM199/1474 DNI to C/S Singapore 4 July 1941 tel.2222B/4.

6 PRO CAB65/19 WM66(41) War Cabinet conclusions 7 July 1941. The memorandum drawn up by the FEC was CAB66/17 WP(41)154 'Japanese Intentions in Indo-China' Eden memorandum 6 July 1941.

7 PRO FO371/27763 F6022/9/61 Halifax (Washington) to Eden 9 July 1941 tel.3190. On the American motivation for such an extreme response see W.H. Heinrichs, *Threshold of War: Franklin D. Roosevelt and American Entry into World War II*, New York, Oxford University Press, 1988, pp. 133–45.

8 PRO FO371/27881 F6101/12/23 Eden to Halifax 13 July 1941 tel.4016.

9 PRO FO371/27882 F6272/12/23 Halifax to Eden 14 July 1941 tel.3304.

10 PRO FO837/534 Vol.4 Leith-Ross (MEW) minute 14 July 1941.

11 PRO CAB79/12 COS(41) 246th meeting 15 July 1941, and FO371/27764 F6606/9/61 Churchill to Eden and Ismay 16 July 1941 M.745/1.

12 PRO FO371/27972 F6408/1299/23 Halifax to Eden 17 July 1941 tel.3371, and F6588/1299/23 Halifax to Eden 21 July 1941 tel.3409.

13 PRO FO371/27972 F6489/1299/23 Waley (T) to Sterndale Bennett (FE Dept) 18 July 1941

14 PRO FO371/28846 W4956/54/49 Heppel (FE Dept) minute 12 May 1941.

15 PRO CAB66/17 WP(41)172 'Japanese Plans in Indo-China' Eden memorandum 20 July 1941.

16 PRO CAB65/19 WM72(41) War Cabinet conclusions 21 July 1941, and CAB65/23 WM72(41) Secretary's Standard File 21 July 1941.

17 PRO FO371/27765 F6811/9/61 Craigie to Eden 26 July 1941 tel.1281.

18 PRO FO371/27974 F7170/1299/23 Menzies (Canberra) to Cranborne (DO) 30 July 1941 tel.486, and CAB65/19 WM76(41) War Cabinet conclusions 31 July 1941.

19 PRO FO371/27974 F7169/1299/23 Eden to Halifax 1 August 1941 tel.4357.

20 PRO WO208/895 CX37065/102 'The Japanese and Thailand. American Information' SIS report 2 August 1941, and CAB81/103 JIC(41)309 'Japan's Next Move' JIC report 2 August 1941.

21 PRO CAB69/2 54th, 55th, 56th meetings 5, 7 and 8 August respectively, CAB120/25 Attlee to Churchill 9 August 1941 tel.23 (Abbey), and Menzies to Churchill 12 August 1941 tel.34 (Abbey).

22 See T.A. Wilson, *The First Summit: Roosevelt and Churchill in Placentia Bay*, Lawrence, University of Kansas Press, 1991.

23 See Heinrichs, op. cit., pp. 161–3.

24 PRO FO371/27977 F8195/1299/23 'Freezing of Japanese Assets' Ashley Clarke (FE Dept.) minute 18 August 1941.

25 PRO FO371/27977 F8195/1299/23 Eden minute 20 August 1941.

26 PRO FO371/27909 F7883/86/23 Halifax to Eden 17 August 1941 tel.3823.

27 PRO FO371/27880 F4187/12/23 Halifax to Eden 17 May 1941 tel.2221, Eden to Halifax 21 May 1941 tel.2727, and FO371/27909 F4430/86/23 Halifax to Eden 24 May 1941 tel.2343.

28 PRO FO371/27616 F9109/60/10 Clark Kerr to Eden 8 September 1941 tel.454, and Churchill to Eden 10 September 1941 M885/1, W. Churchill papers, Churchill College, Cambridge, CHAR20/36.

29 PRO FO371/27910 F9321/86/23 Campbell (Washington) to Eden 14 September 1941 tel.4227.

30 PRO FO371/27882 F7088/12/23 Craigie to Eden 29 July 1941 tel.1304, FO371/27892 F7724/17/23 Craigie to Eden 12 August 1941 tel.1423 and F8410/17/23 Craigie to Eden 25 August 1941 tel.1534.

31 For Roosevelt's and the State Department's reactions to the Konoe proposal see Heinrichs, op. cit., pp. 161–3.

32 For the record of the 6 September Imperial Conference see Ike, op. cit., pp. 133–51.

33 PRO FO371/27883 F9164/12/23 Craigie to Eden 8 September 1941. For Grew's opinions at this point see W.H. Heinrichs, *American Ambassador*.

Joseph C. Grew and the Development of the United States Diplomatic Tradition, New York, Oxford University Press, 1966, pp. 345–50.

34 PRO FO371/27883 F9172/12/23 Craigie to Eden 9 September 1941 tel.1655.

35 PRO HW1/32 BJ 094947 Berlin to Tokyo 20 August 1941 decrypted 29 August 1941, and HW1/52 BJ 095229 Rome to Washington 2 September 1941 decrypted 7 September 1941.

36 PRO HW1/64 BJ 095427 Tokyo to Berlin 10 September 1941 decrypted 13 September 1941. Churchill was moved to add an exclamation mark by this passage.

37 PRO HW1/62 BJ 095379 Tokyo (Indelli) to Rome (Ciano) 8 September 1941 decrypted 12 September 1941.

38 PRO CAB66/18 WP(41)223 Weekly Resumé 18 September 1941.

39 For a discussion of the possibility of a Japanese attack on Russia see PRO WO193/864 MO1 memorandum 19 August 1941 and MO10 minute 24 August 1941. For the effect of the European situation on Japan see FO371/27781 F10223/54/61 Eden minute undated.

40 PRO FO371/27981 F9615/1299/23 Eden to Churchill 12 September 1941.

41 PRO FO371/27980 F9322/1299/23 Halifax to Eden 13 September 1941 tel.4231, and FO371/27883 F9172/12/23 Eden to Craigie 18 September 1941 tel.1187.

42 PRO FO371/27910 F9987/86/23 Craigie to Eden 27 September 1941 tel.1834, and FO371/27910 F10116/86/23 Craigie to Eden 30 September 1941 tel.1854.

43 PRO FO371/27883 F10117/12/23 Craigie to Eden 30 September 1941 tel.1853A.

44 PRO FO371/27883 F10117/12/23 Sterndale Bennett minute 1 October 1941.

45 PRO FO371/27883 F9403/12/23 Craigie to Eden 15 September 1941 tel.1717, and F9164/12/23 Craigie to Eden 8 September 1941 tel.1637. See also A. Iriye, *The Origins of the Second World War in Asia and the Pacific*, London, Longman, 1987, pp. 153–7.

46 K. Usui, 'A Consideration of Anglo-Japanese Relations: Japanese Views of Britain, 1937–1941.' in I. Nish (ed.), *Anglo-Japanese Alienation 1919–1952*, Cambridge, Cambridge University Press, 1982, p. 95.

47 PRO CAB122/577 Turner/Danckwerts conversation 19 August 1941, and PREM4/27/9 Halifax to Churchill 11 October 1941.

48 PRO AIR20/2112 DWO to VCAS 18 July 1941, AIR20/289 C in C FE to WO 24 July 1941 tel.447/5, and AIR20/290 Air Ministry to AHQ FE 24 August tel.WX706.

49 PRO WO193/865 C in C FE & C in C China to WO 1 October 1941 tel.47875. For the propaganda issue see PRO WO208/644 C in C FE to WO 14 August 1941 tel.295/4, and AIR20/291 C in C FE to WO 5 September 1941 tel.12/5.

50 PRO AIR20/291 WO to C in C FE 10 October tel.FE35.

51 For the contrasting views see PREM 3/163/3 Pound to Churchill 28 August 1941, and Churchill to Pound 29 August 1941 M845/1. For Eden's views see his record of a conversation with Churchill, in Eden

diary entry 12 September 1941, Avon Papers, Birmingham University Library, AP20 1/21.

52 PRO FO371/27906 F10942/33/23 Eden to Churchill 16 October 1941 PM/41/142.

53 PRO CAB69/8 DO(41) 65th meeting 17 October 1941, CAB69/8 DO(41) 66th meeting 20 October 1941, and Churchill to Roosevelt 20 October 1941, W. Churchill papers, CHAR20/20.

54 On the concern for Russia see PRO WO193/928 MI2 minute 17 October 1941, and FO371/27958 F10947/421/23 Maisky/Eden conversation 17 October 1941. For the message to Washington see FO371/27910 F10885/86/23 Eden to Halifax 17 October 1941 tel.5623.

55 PRO FO371/27911 F10960/86/23 Halifax to Eden 17 October 1941 tel.4570, Churchill minute 19 October 1941, and Eden to Halifax 21 October 1941 tel.5704. See also CAB65/23 WM(41)104 Secretary's Standard File 20 October 1941.

56 PRO CAB66/19 WP(41)252 Weekly Resumé 30 October 1941, and WO208/654 Halifax to Eden 31 October 1941 tel.4928.

57 PRO FO371/27664 F11714/145/10 Clark Kerr to Eden 1 November 1941 tel.550, F11868/145/10 Churchill to Roosevelt 5 November 1941 T.780, and F12144/145/10 Roosevelt to Churchill 9 November 1941 T.795.

58 PRO WO208/654 'Short brief for COS meeting' MI2c minute 6 November 1941.

59 PRO CAB65/24 WM(41)112 Secretary's Standard File 12 November 1941.

60 PRO ADM199/1474 C/S Singapore to DNI 9 November 1941 tel.0431Z/9.

61 PRO FO371/27911 F11672/86/23 Craigie to Eden 1 November 1941 tel.2186.

62 Ibid.

63 PRO FO371/27884 F11947/12/23 Craigie to Eden 6 November 1941 tel.2233.

64 PRO FO371/27911 F11809/86/23 Craigie to Eden 5 November 1941 tel.2226.

65 PRO HW1/211 BJ.097639 Rome to Washington 10 November 1941 decrypted 13 November 1941, and HW1/197 BJ.097420 Tokyo to Berlin 6 November 1941 decrypted 8 November 1941.

66 PRO FO371/27911 F11672/86/23 Eden to Craigie 15 November 1941 tel.1523.

67 PRO WO208/874 DDMI Singapore to WO 14 November 1941 tel.25774, WO193/869 DDMI Singapore to WO 15 November 1941 tel.25853, ADM223/321 OIC Special Intelligence Summary no.404 16 November 1941, and CAB81/105 JIC(41)439 'Japanese Intentions' JIC report 18 November 1941.

68 PRO HW1/240 BJ.097993 Tokyo to Hong Kong 14 November 1941 decrypted 21 November 1941.

69 PRO FO371/27912 F12475/86/23 Campbell to Eden 18 November 1941 tel.5233, and Eden to Halifax 21 November 1941 tel.6355.

70 PRO FO371/27912 F12655/86/23 Halifax to Eden 22 November 1941 tel.5353.

71 PRO FO371/27912 F12654/86/23 Halifax to Eden 22 November 1941 tel.5352.

72 PRO FO371/27912 F12813/86/23 Churchill to Eden 23 November 1941, F12655/86/23 Eden to Halifax 24 November 1941 tel.6424, and F12766/86/23 Halifax to Eden 25 November 1941 tel.5380.

73 Eden diary entry 25 November 1941, Avon Papers, BUL, AP20 1/21. See also PRO FO371/27912 F12675/86/23 Halifax to Eden 24 November 1941 tel.5378.

74 PRO FO371/29713 F12818/86/23 Churchill to Roosevelt 26 November 1941 T.871.

75 For critical assessments of the British response to the *modus vivendi* see D. Klein and H. Conroy, 'Churchill, Roosevelt and the China Question in Pre-Pearl Harbor Diplomacy.' in H. Conroy and H. Wray (eds), *Pearl Harbor Reexamined: Prologue to the Pacific War*, Honolulu, University of Hawaii Press, 1990, pp. 133–8, and R.J. Grace, 'Whitehall and the Ghost of Appeasement, November 1941', *Diplomatic History*, 1979, Vol.3, pp. 173–91.

76 See Heinrichs, *Threshold of War*, p. 213, and PRO ADM223/321 OIC Special Intelligence Summary no.426 24 November 1941.

77 PRO HW1/264 BJ.098159 Kuibyshev to Chungking 17 November 1941 decrypted 26 November 1941. On Anglo-Chinese relations in autumn 1941 see Iriye, op. cit., p. 179.

78 PRO ADM223/494 NID Vol. 40 Far East and Pacific 1, History, Pearl Harbour and the Loss of Prince of Wales and Repulse (undated 1945?), and CAB122/70 C/S Singapore to DNI 25 November 1941 tel.1007Z/25.

79 PRO HW1/259 BJ.098151 Tokyo to European capitals 20 November 1941 decrypted 25 November 1941.

80 PRO ADM223/231 OIC Special Intelligence Summary no.429 25 November 1941.

81 PRO ADM199/1477 C in C China to BNLO Batavia 28 November 1941 tel.0843Z/28.

82 PRO FO371/27767 F12823/9/61 Meiklereid (Saigon) to Eden 26 November 1941 tel.226.

83 PRO ADM223/494 NID vol. 40 Far East and Pacific 1, History, Pearl Harbour and the Loss of Prince of Wales and Repulse (undated 1945?), FO371/27694 F13068/523/23 C/S Singapore to DNI 27 November 1941 tel.0532Z/27, ADM199/1477 Admiralty to Senior Officer Force G 28 November 1941 tel.2355A/28, and WO193/869 DDMI Singapore to WO 29 November 1941 tel.26338.

84 PRO CAB81/105 JIC(41)449 'Possible Japanese Action' JIC report 28 November 1941.

85 PRO HW1/264 BJ.098178 Bangkok to Rome 24 November 1941 decrypted 26 November 1941, HW1/272 BJ.098255 Bangkok to Rome 24 November 1941 decrypted 28 November 1941, and BJ.098276 Bangkok to Tokyo 21 November 1941 decrypted 28 November 1941.

86 PRO ADM199/1477 Thomas (Straits Governor) to C in C China 29 November 1941 tel.1140/29, and CAB107/3 Ad-hoc meeting 30 November 1941.

87 PRO AIR20/291 WO to C in C FE 25 November 1941 tel.FE43.

88 PRO FO371/27913 F13053/86/23 Churchill to Roosevelt 30 November 1941 T.902, and F13144/86/23 Halifax to Eden 1 December 1941 tel.5519.

89 PRO FO371/27913 F13144/86/23 Churchill to Eden 2 December 1941 M.1072/1.

90 PRO FO371/27914 F13219/86/23 Halifax to Eden 3 December 1941 tel.5577, HW1/290 BJ.098509 Tokyo to London 1 December 1941 decrypted 3 December 1941, HW1/294 'C' to Churchill 4 December 1941 C/8238, and HW1/288 BJ.098452 Tokyo to Berlin 30 November 1941 decrypted 2 December 1941.

91 PRO CAB65/24 WM(41)124 Secretary's Standard File 4 December 1941.

92 This sighting is mentioned in a number of telegrams and discussions but it is very difficult to trace a copy of the actual document, it appears to be C in C China to Admiralty 6 December 1941 tel.0745Z/6.

93 PRO AIR20/291 Directors of Plans/Joint Intelligence Staff meeting 6 December 1941.

94 PRO ADM199/1475 DNI to COIS Singapore 2 December 1941 tel.0024A/3, HW1/303 BJ.098583 Bangkok to Tokyo 25 November 1941 decrypted 6 December 1941, BJ.098606 Bangkok to Tokyo 28 November 1941 decrypted 6 December 1941, and PREM3/158/6 COS to Churchill 6 December 1941. See also R. Aldrich, *The Key to the South: Britain, the United States, and Thailand during the Approach of the Pacific War, 1929–1942*, Kuala Lumpar, Oxford University Press, 1993, pp. 345–9.

95 PRO ADM205/9 Pound to Little (BAD Washington) 6 December 1941.

96 PRO AIR20/291 C in C FE to WO 7 December 1941 tel.1605Z/7. For the latest reports on the convoy see PREM3/158/6 COIS Singapore to DNI 7 December 1941 tel.0611Z/7.

97 PRO PREM3/158/6 Churchill to COS and Eden 7 December 1941 D311/1.

98 PRO FO371/12789 F13503/1299/23 C in C FE to WO 7 December 1941 tel.2300/7, and WO106/2514 C in C FE to WO 8 December 1941 tel.0412Z/8.

99 A Brooke diary entry 6 and 7 December 1941, Alanbrooke Papers, Liddell Hart Centre for Military Archives, Kings College, London 5/5. See J. Rusbridger and E. Nave, *Betrayal at Pearl Harbor: How Churchill Lured Roosevelt Into War*, London, Michael O'Mara, 1991. For reviews refuting the case made by the latter see R. Aldrich, 'Conspiracy or Confusion? Churchill, Roosevelt and Pearl Harbor,' *Intelligence and National Security*, 1992, vol. 7, pp. 335–46, and D. Kaiser, 'Conspiracy or Cock-up? Pearl Harbor Revisited,' and D.C.S. Sissons, 'More on Pearl Harbor,' *Intelligence and National Security*, 1994, vol. 9, pp. 354–72 and pp. 373–9 respectively.

100 PRO ADM223/494 NID vol. 40 Far East and Pacific 1, History, Pearl Harbour and the Loss of Prince of Wales and Repulse (undated 1945?)

101 PRO ADM199/1477 BNLO Batavia to C in C China 27 November 1941 tel.1004Z/27, CAB81/105 JIC(41)449 'Possible Japanese Action' JIC report 28 November 1941, and WO193/322 BAD Washington to Admiralty 3 December 1941 tel.1753R/2.

102 PRO WO193/322 NID comment on BAD Washington to Admiralty 3 December 1941 tel.1753R/2.

9 CONCLUSIONS

1 See W.N. Medlicott, *The Economic Blockade*, vol. 2, London, HMSO, 1959, pp. 101–3, and Michael Barnhart, *Japan Prepares For Total War: The Search For Economic Security, 1919–41*, Ithaca, Cornell University Press, 1987, pp. 223–7.

2 W.H. Heinrichs, *The Threshold of War: Franklin D. Roosevelt and the American Entry Into World War II*, New York, Oxford University Press, 1988, pp. 121–136.

3 E.T. Layton, R. Pineau and J. Costello, *' And I Was There' : Pearl Harbor and Midway: Breaking the Secrets*, New York, William Morrow, 1985, p. 202. For Churchill's interest in passing on intelligence to the United States see PRO HW1/25 Churchill note to 'C' on BJ.094723 24 August 1941, and HW1/297 Churchill minute on BJ.098541 4 December 1941.

4 PRO FO371/35957 F821/821/23 Craigie report 4 February 1943. See also J. Rusbridger and E. Nave, *Betrayal at Pearl Harbor: How Churchill Lured Roosevelt Into War*, London, Michael O'Mara, 1991, p. 140.

5 Heinrichs, op. cit., p. 213.

6 PRO WO106/5140 BJ.062694 Rome to Peking (undated) decrypted 8 November 1935, and HW1/307 BJ.098694 Tokyo to London 7 December 1941 decrypted 8 December 1941.

Bibliography

PRIMARY SOURCES

Public Record Office, Kew (PRO)

ADM 1   Admiralty and Secretariat Papers.
ADM 116   Admiralty and Secretariat Papers.
ADM 199   War of 1939–45, War History Cases.
ADM 205   First Sea Lord Papers.
ADM 223   Naval Intelligence Division.
AIR 2   Air Ministry Registered Papers.
AIR 20   Air Ministry Unregistered Papers.
AIR 23   Air Ministry Overseas Commands.
AIR 40   Directorate of Air Intelligence.
BT 11   Board of Trade Commercial Relations and Treaty Department.
CAB 2   Committee of Imperial Defence (CID) Minutes.
CAB 4   CID Memoranda.
CAB 16   CID Sub-Committees Minutes and Memoranda.
CAB 21   Cabinet Secretariat Registered Files.
CAB 23   Cabinet Minutes.
CAB 24   Cabinet Memoranda.
CAB 27   Cabinet Committees Minutes and Memoranda.
CAB 47   Advisory Committee on Trade Questions in Time of War Minutes and Memoranda.
CAB 53   Chiefs of Staff Committee Minutes and Memoranda.
CAB 55   Joint Planning Sub-Committee Minutes and Memoranda.
CAB 56   Joint Intelligence Sub-Committee Minutes and Memoranda.
CAB 65   War Cabinet Minutes.
CAB 66   War Cabinet Memoranda (WP Series).
CAB 67   War Cabinet Memoranda (WP(G) Series).
CAB 69   War Cabinet Defence Committee (Operations) Minutes and Memoranda.
CAB 79   Chiefs of Staff Committee (Wartime) Minutes.
CAB 80   Chiefs of Staff Committee (Wartime) Memoranda.
CAB 81   Joint Intelligence Sub-Committee (Wartime) Minutes and Memoranda.
CAB 84   Joint Planning Sub-Committee Minutes and Memoranda.

CAB 96   Far Eastern Committee Minutes and Memoranda.
CAB 99   Commonwealth and International Conferences.
CAB 104   Supplementary Registered Papers.
CAB 107   Co-ordination of Departmental Action in the Event of War with Japan.
CAB 120   Ministry of Defence Papers.
CAB 122   Joint Staff Mission Washington.
FO 115   Papers of the British Embassy Washington.
FO 262   Papers of the British Embassy Tokyo.
FO 371   FO General Correspondence.
FO 837   Industrial Intelligence Centre and Ministry of Economic Warfare.
HS 1   Special Operations Executive (Far East).
HW 1   Intelligence for the Prime Minister.
INF 1   Ministry of Information.
PREM 1   Correspondence and Papers of the Prime Minister's Office.
PREM 3   Operational Papers of the Prime Minister's Office.
PREM 4   Confidential Papers of the Prime Minister's Office.
T 160   Finance Papers.
T 172   Chancellor of the Exchequer's Papers.
WO 116   Directorate of Military Operations and Intelligence Papers.
WO 193   Directorate of Military Operations Papers.
WO 208   Directorate of Military Intelligence Papers.

Private papers

Lord Alanbrooke Papers, LHCMA, Kings College, London.
Lord Avon Papers, PRO and Birmingham University Library.
Lord Butler Papers, Trinity College Library, Cambridge.
Sir Alexander Cadogan Papers, PRO and Churchill College, Cambridge.
Neville Chamberlain Papers, Birmingham University Library.
Admiral Lord Chatfield Papers, National Maritime Museum Library, Greenwich.
Winston Churchill Papers, Churchill College, Cambridge.
General Sir Francis Davidson, LHCMA, Kings College, London.
Admiral Sir John Godfrey Papers, Churchill College, Cambridge.
Joseph Grew Papers, Houghton Library, Harvard.
H.A. Gwynne Papers, Bodleian Library, Oxford.
Lord Halifax Papers, PRO and Churchill College, Cambridge.
Lord Hankey Papers, PRO and Churchill College, Cambridge.
Lord Inverchapel Papers, PRO and Bodleian Library, Oxford.
Captain Malcolm Kennedy Papers, Sheffield University.
Sir Hughe Knatchbull-Hugessen Papers, PRO and Churchill College, Cambridge.
Sir Frederick Leith-Ross Papers, PRO.
Lord Norwich Papers, Churchill College, Cambridge
Sir Horace Seymour Papers, Churchill College, Cambridge.
Viscount Simon Papers, Bodleian Library, Oxford.

PUBLISHED DOCUMENTS

Churchill, W., *War Speeches 1939–1945*, vol. 2, London, Cassell, 1952.
Documents on British Foreign Policy 1919–1939, 2nd and 3rd series, London, HMSO, 1955–84.
Foreign Relations of the United States, Washington DC, Government Printing Office, 1943–64.
Ike, N. (ed.), *Japan's Decision For War: Records of the 1941 Policy Conferences*, Stanford, Stanford University Press, 1967.
Kimball, W. (ed.), *Churchill and Roosevelt: The Complete Correspondence*, vols I–III, Princeton, Princeton University Press, 1984.
The 'Magic' Background to Pearl Harbor, vols 1–8, Washington DC, Department of Defense, 1977.
Pritchard, R.J. and Zaide, S.M. (ed), *The Tokyo War Crimes Trial*, New York, Garland, 1981–7.

SECONDARY SOURCES

Published diaries and memoirs

Avon, Lord, *Memoirs: Facing The Dictators*, London, Cassell, 1962.
———, *Memoirs: The Reckoning*, London, Cassell, 1965.
Bond, B. (ed.), *Chief of Staff: The Diaries of Lt. General Sir Henry Pownall*, vols 1–2, London, Leo Cooper, 1972 and 1974.
Butler, R.A., *The Art of the Possible*, London, Hamish Hamilton, 1971
Chapman, J.W.M. (ed.), *The Price of Admiralty: The War Diary of the German Naval Attache in Japan 1939–1943*, vols 1–3, Lewes, University of Sussex Press, 1982–8.
Chatfield, Lord, *It Might Happen Again*, London, Heinemann, 1948.
Churchill, W.S.,*The Second World War*, vols 1–3, London, Cassell, 1948–50.
Cooper, Duff, *Old Men Forget: the Autobiography of Duff Cooper*, London, Hart Davis, 1953.
Craigie, R., *Behind the Japanese Mask*, London, Hutchinson, 1946.
Dilks, D. (ed.), *The Diaries of Sir Alexander Cadogan, 1938–1945*, London, Cassell, 1971.
Gore-Booth, P. *With Great Truth and Respect*, London, Constable, 1974.
Grew, J.C. *Ten Years in Japan*, New York, Simon & Schuster, 1944.
———, *Turbulent Era: A Record of Forty Years in the U.S. Diplomatic Service*, vol. 2, Boston, Houghton Mifflin, 1952.
Harvey, J. (ed.), *The Diplomatic Diaries of Oliver Harvey 1937–1940*, London, Collins, 1970.
———, *The War Diaries of Oliver Harvey 1941–1945*, London, Collins, 1978.
Kase, T., *Eclipse of the Rising Sun*, London, Jonathan Cape, 1951.
Knatchbull-Hugessen, K., *Diplomat in Peace and War*, London, John Murray, 1949.
Layton, E.T., Pineau, R. and Costello, J., *'And I Was There' Pearl Harbor and Midway: Breaking the Secrets*, New York, William Morrow, 1985.
Leith-Ross, F., *Money Talks: Fifty Years of International Finance*, London, Hutchinson, 1968.

Piggott, F.S.G., *Broken Thread: An Autobiography*, Aldershot, Gale & Polden, 1950.

Pimlott, B. (ed.), *The Second World War Diary of Hugh Dalton, 1940–45*, London, Jonathan Cape, 1986.

Rhodes James, R. (ed.), *Chips: The Diaries of Sir Henry Channon*, London, Weidenfeld & Nicolson, 1967.

Sansom, K. (ed.), *Sir George Sansom and Japan: A Memoir*, Tallahassee, Diplomatic Press, 1972.

Shigemitsu, M., *Japan and her Destiny: My Struggle for Peace*, London, Hutchinson, 1958.

SECONDARY SOURCES

Agbi, S.O., 'The Foreign Office and Yoshida's Bid for Rapprochement with Britain in 1936–1937: A Critical Reappraisal of the Anglo-Japanese Conversations', *Historical Journal*, 1978, vol. 21, pp. 173–9.

———, 'The British Foreign Office and the Roosevelt-Huggessen Bid to Stabilize Asia and the Pacific in 1937', *Australian Journal of Politics and History*, 1980, vol. 26, pp. 85–95.

———, 'The Pacific War Controversy in Britain: Sir Robert Craigie versus the Foreign Office', *Modern Asian Studies*, 1983, vol. 17, pp. 489–517.

Aldrich, R., 'Conspiracy or Confusion? Churchill, Roosevelt and Pearl Harbor', *Intelligence and National Security*, 1993, vol. 7, pp. 335–46.

———, *The Key to the South: Britain, the United States and Thailand During the Approach of the Pacific War, 1929–1942*, Kuala Lumpar, Oxford University Press, 1993.

Anderson, I., *The Standard Vacuum Oil Company and United States East Asian Policy, 1933–1941*, Princeton, Princeton University Press, 1975.

———, 'The 1941 De Facto Embargo On Oil to Japan: A Bureaucratic Reflex', *Pacific Historical Review*, 1975, vol. 44, pp. 201–31.

Barnhart, M., *Japan Prepares For Total War: The Search for Economic Security 1919–1941*, Ithaca, Cornell University Press, 1987.

Beasley, W.G., *Japanese Imperialism 1894–1945*, Oxford, Clarendon Press, 1987.

Bennett, G., 'British Policy in the Far East 1933–1936: Treasury and Foreign Office', *Modern Asian Studies*, 1992, vol. 26, pp. 545–68.

Ben-Zvi, A., *The Illusion of Deterrence: The Roosevelt Presidency and the Origins of the Pacific War*, Boulder, Westview Press, 1987.

Best, A.M., 'Shigemitsu Mamoru as Ambassador to Great Britain 1938–1941', in Nish, I.H. (ed.), *Shigemitsu Studies*, LSE STICERD, International Studies Series, 1990, pp. 1–44.

———, 'Sir Robert Craigie as Ambassador to Japan, 1937–41', in Nish, I. (ed.), *Britain and Japan: Biographical Portaits*, Folkestone, Japan Library, 1994.

———, ' "Straws in the Wind": Britain and the February 1941 War Scare in East Asia', *Diplomacy and Statecraft*, 1994, vol. 5 pp. 642–65.

Borg, D., *The United States and the Far Eastern Crisis of 1933–1938*, Cambridge, Harvard University Press, 1964.

Borg, D. and Okamoto, S. (eds), *Pearl Harbor as History: Japanese-*

American Relations 1931–1941, New York, Columbia University Press, 1973.

Boyce, R. and Robertson, E.M. (eds), *Paths to War: New Essays on the Origins of the Second World War*, London, Macmillan, 1989.

Boyd, C., *The Extraordinary Envoy: General Hiroshi Ōshima and Diplomacy in the Third Reich 1934–1939*, Washington DC, University Press of America, 1980.

———, 'Significance of MAGIC and the Japanese Ambassador to Berlin: The Formative Months Before Pearl Harbor', *Intelligence and National Security*, 1987, vol. 2, pp. 150–69.

Boyle, J.H., *China and Japan at War 1937–1945: The Politics of Collaboration*, Stanford, Stanford University Press, 1972.

Brailey, N.J., *Thailand and the Fall of Singapore: A Frustrated Asian Revolution*, Boulder, Westview Press, 1986.

———, 'Southeast Asia and Japan's Road to War', *Historical Journal*, 1987, vol. 30, pp. 995–1011.

Brune, L.H., 'Considerations of Force in Cordell Hull's Diplomacy, July 26 to November 26 1941', *Diplomatic History*, 1978, vol. 2, pp. 389–407.

Bunker, G.E., *The Peace Conspiracy: Wang Ching-wei and the China War 1937–1941*, Cambridge, Harvard University Press, 1972.

Burns, R.D. and Bennett, E.M. (eds), *Diplomats in Crisis: United States–Chinese–Japanese Relations 1918–1941*, Santa Barbara, American Bibliographical Centre, 1974.

Butow, R.J.C., 'Backdoor Diplomacy in the Pacific: The Proposal for a Konoye–Roosevelt Meeting', *Journal of American History*, 1972, vol. 59, pp. 48–72.

———, *The John Doe Associates: Backdoor Diplomacy For Peace, 1941*, Stanford, Stanford University Press, 1974.

———, 'Marching Off to War on the Wrong Foot: The Final Note Tokyo Did *Not* Send to Washington', *Pacific Historical Review*, 1993, vol. 63, pp. 67–79.

Cain, P.J. and Hopkins, A.G., *British Imperialism: Crisis and Deconstruction, 1914–1990*, London, Longman, 1993.

Calvocoressi, P., Wint, G. & Pritchard, J., *Total War: The Cause and Courses of the Second World War*, vols 1–2, London, Penguin, 1989.

Carr, W., *Poland to Pearl Harbor: The Making of the Second World War*, London, Edward Arnold, 1985.

Cave Brown, A., *The Secret Servant: The Life of Sir Stewart Menzies, Churchill's Spymaster*, London, Michael Joseph, 1987.

Chapman, J.W.M., 'Forty Years On: The Imperial Japanese Navy, the European War and the Tripartite Pact', *Proceedings of the British Association of Japanese Studies*, 1980, vol. 5, no.1, pp. 69–86.

———, 'The "Have-Nots" Go to War: The Economic and Technological Basis of the German Alliance With Japan', in Nish, I.H. (ed.), *The Tripartite Pact of 1940*, LSE STICERD International Studies Series, 1984, pp. 25–73.

———, 'Commander Ross R.N. and the Ending of Anglo-Japanese Friendship, 1933–1936', in Nish, I.H. (ed.), *Anglo-Japanese Naval Relations*, LSE STICERD, International Studies Series, 1985, pp. 33–56.

———, 'Japanese Intelligence, 1919–1945: A Suitable Case For Treatment', in Andrew, C. and Noakes, J. (eds), *Intelligence and International Relations 1900–1945*, Exeter, Exeter University Publications, 1987.

———, 'Pearl Harbor: the Anglo-Australian Dimension', *Intelligence and National Security*, 1989, vol. 4, pp. 451–60.

———, 'Signals Intelligence Collaboration Among the Tripartite Pact States on the Eve of Pearl Harbor', *Japan Forum*, 1991, vol. 3, pp. 231–56.

———, 'Tricyle Recycled: Collaboration Among the Secret Intelligence Services of the Axis States, 1940–41', *Intelligence and National Security*, 1992, vol. 7, pp. 268–99.

Chi, H.S., *Nationalist China at War: Military Defeats and Political Collapse 1937–1945*, Ann Arbor, Michigan University Press, 1982.

Clifford, N., *Retreat from China: British Policy in the Far East 1937–41*, London, Longman, 1967.

Coble, P.M., *Facing Japan: Chinese Politics and Japanese Imperialism, 1931–1937*, Cambridge, Harvard University Press, 1991.

Conroy, H. and Wray H. (eds), *Pearl Harbor Reexamined: Prologue to the Pacific War*, Honolulu, University of Hawaii Press, 1990.

Coox, A.D. *The Anatomy of a Small War: The Soviet-Japanese Struggle for Changkufeng/Khasan 1938*, London, Greenwood Press, 1977.

———, *Nomonhan: Japan Against Russia, 1939*, 2 Vols, Stanford, Stanford University Press, 1985.

Crowley, J.B., *Japan's Quest for Autonomy: National Security and Foreign Policy 1930–1938*, Princeton, Princeton University Press, 1966.

——— (ed.), *Modern East Asia: Essays in Interpretation*, New York, Harcourt, Brace & World Inc., 1970.

Dallek, R., *Franklin D. Roosevelt and American Foreign Policy, 1932–1945*, New York, Oxford University Press, 1979.

Day, D., *Menzies and Churchill at War*, Sydney, Angus & Robertson, 1986.

———, *The Great Betrayal: Britain, Australia and the Onset of the Pacific War*, Sydney, Angus & Robertson, 1988.

Dayer, R., *Finance and Empire: Sir Charles Addis, 1861–1945*, London, Macmillan, 1988.

Dingman, R., 'Farewell to Friendship: The USS Astoria's Visit to Japan, April 1939', *Diplomatic History*, 1986, vol. 10, pp. 121–40.

Dockrill, S. (ed.), *From Pearl Harbor to Hiroshima: The Second World War in Asia and the Pacific, 1941–45*, London, Macmillan, 1994.

Doerr, P.W., 'The Changkufeng/Lake Khasan Incident of 1938: British Intelligence on Soviet and Japanese Military Performance', *Intelligence and National Security*, 1990, vol. 5, pp. 184–99.

R. Dore and R. Sinha (eds), *Japan and World Depression*, London, Macmillan, 1987.

Dower, J.W., *Empire and Aftermath: Yoshida Shigeru and the Japanese Experience 1878–1954*, Cambridge, Harvard University Press, 1979.

———, *War Without Mercy: Race and Power in the Pacific War*, London, Faber & Faber, 1986.

Dreifort, J., *Myopic Grandeur: The Ambivalence of French Foreign Policy Toward the Far East, 1919–1945*, Ohio, Kent State University Press, 1991.

Düffler, J., 'The Tripartite Pact of 27th September 1940: Fascist Alliance or

Propaganda Trick?', in I. Nish, *The Tripartite Pact of 1940*, LSE STICERD International Studies series, 1984, pp. 1–24.

Eastman, L.E., *The Abortive Revolution: China Under Nationalist Rule 1927–1937*, Cambridge, Harvard University Press, 1974.

———, *Seeds of Destruction: Nationalist China in War and Revolution 1937–1949*, Stanford, Stanford University Press, 1984.

Endicott, S., *Diplomacy and Enterprise: British China Policy 1933–1937*, Manchester, Manchester University Press, 1975.

Ferretti, V., 'Captain Fujii Shigeru and the Decision for War in 1941' *Japan Forum*, 1991, vol. 3, pp. 221–30

Ferris, J., 'From Broadway House to Bletchley Park: The Diary of Captain Malcolm Kennedy 1934–1946', *Intelligence and National Security*, 1989, vol. 4, pp. 421–50.

———, ' "Worthy of Some Better Enemy?": The British Estimate of the Imperial Japanese Army 1919–41, and the Fall of Singapore', *Canadian Journal of History*, 1993, vol. 28, pp. 223–56.

Flood, E.T., 'The 1940 Franco-Thai Border Dispute and Phibuun Sonkhraam's Commitment to Japan', *Journal of Southeast Asian History*, 1969, vol. 10, pp. 304–25.

Fox, J.P., *Germany and the Far Eastern Crisis 1931–1938: A Study in Diplomacy and Ideology*, Oxford, Clarendon Press, 1982.

Garver, J.W., *Chinese–Soviet Relations 1937–1945: The Diplomacy of Chinese Nationalism*, New York, Oxford University Press, 1988.

———, 'The Origins of the Second United Front: The Comintern and the Chinese Communist Party', *China Quarterly*, 1988, no. 113, pp. 29–59.

———, 'The Soviet Union and the X'ian Incident', *Australian Journal of Chinese Affairs*, 1991, no. 26, pp. 145–75.

Gilchrist, A., *Malaya 1941: The Fall of a Fighting Empire*, London, Robert Hale, 1992.

Gordon, G.A.H., *British Seapower and Procurement Between the Wars: A Reappraisal of Rearmament*, London, Macmillan, 1988.

Grace, R.J. *Anglo-American Relations Regarding the Far East 1937–1941*, vols 1–2, Ann Arbor, University Microfilms, 1974.

———, 'Whitehall and the Ghost of Appeasement, November 1941', *Diplomatic History*, 1979, vol. 3, pp. 173–91.

Haggie, P., *Britannia at Bay: The Defence of the British Empire Against Japan 1931–1941*, Oxford, Clarendon Press, 1981.

Haight, J.M., 'Franklin D. Roosevelt and a Naval Quarantine of Japan', *Pacific Historical Review*, 1971, vol. 40, pp. 203–26.

Hall, C., *Britain, America and Arms Control 1921–1937*, London, Macmillan, 1987.

Hamill, I., *The Strategic Illusion: The Singapore Strategy and the Defence of Australia and New Zealand*, Singapore, Singapore University Press, 1981.

Harris, R.R., 'The "Magic" Leak of 1941 and Japanese–American Relations', *Pacific Historical Review*, 1981, vol. 50, pp. 76–95.

Harrison, R.A., 'A Presidential Demarché: Franklin D. Roosevelt's Personal Diplomacy and Great Britain, 1936–37', *Diplomatic History*, 1981, vol. 5, pp. 245–72.

———, 'A Neutralization Plan for the Pacific: Roosevelt and

Anglo-American Cooperation, 1934–1937', *Pacific Historical Review*, 1988, vol. 50, pp. 47–72.

Haslam, J., *The Soviet Union and the Threat From the East, 1933–41*, London, Macmillan, 1992.

Hata, I. 'The Army's move into Northern Indochina', in Morley, J.W. (ed.), *The Fateful Choice: Japan's Advance into Southeast Asia, 1939–1941*, New York, Columbia University Press, 1980.

Hatano, S. and Asada S., 'The Japanese Decision to Move South (1939–1941)', in Boyce, R. and Robertson, E.M. (eds), *Paths to War: New Essays on the Origins of the Second World War*, London, Macmillan, 1989.

Heinrichs, W.H., *American Ambassador: Joseph C. Grew and the Development of the American Diplomatic Tradition*, Oxford, Oxford University Press, 1966.

————, *Threshold of War. Franklin D. Roosevelt and American Entry into World War II*, New York, Oxford University Press, 1988.

Herzog, J., *Closing the Open Door: American–Japanese Diplomatic Negotiations 1936–1941*, Annapolis, Naval Institute Press, 1973.

Hosoya, C., 'Miscalculations in Deterrent Policy: Japanese-US Relations 1938–1941', *Journal of Peace Research*, 1968, no. 2, 97–115.

————,'The Tripartite Pact, 1939–1940', in Morley, J.W. (ed.) *Deterrent Diplomacy: Japan, Germany and the USSR, 1935–1940*, New York, Columbia University Press, 1976.

————, 'The Japanese–Soviet Neutrality Pact', in Morley, J.W. (ed.), *The Fateful Choice: Japan's Advance into Southeast Asia, 1939–1941* New York, Columbia University Press, 1980.

————, 'Britain and the US in Japan's view of the International System, 1937–1941', in Nish, I.H. (ed.), *Anglo-Japanese Alienation 1919–1952*, Cambridge, Cambridge University Press, 1982.

Howard, M., *The Continental Commitment: the Dilemma of British Defence Policy in the Era of the Two World Wars*, London, Temple Smith, 1972.

Inoue, Y., 'Arita's Conversations With Ambassador Craigie on the Creation of a Japanese Economic Bloc', *Proceedings of the British Association of Japanese Studies*, 1978, vol. 3 pp. 126–137.

Iriye, A., *After Imperialism: The Search for a New Order in the Far East 1921–1931*, Cambridge, Harvard University Press, 1965.

————, *Power and Culture: The Japanese–American War 1941–1945*, Cambridge, Harvard University Press, 1981.

————, *The Origins of the Second World War in Asia and the Pacific*, London, Longman, 1987.

Iriye, A. and Cohen, W. (eds), *American, Chinese, and Japanese Perspectives on Wartime Asia 1931–1949*, Wilmington, Scholarly Resources, 1990.

Johnson, C., *MITI and the Japanese Miracle: The Growth of Industrial Policy 1925–1976*, Stanford, Stanford University Press, 1982.

————, *An Instance of Treason: Ozaki Hotsumi and the Sorge Spy Ring*, Stanford, Stanford University Press, 1990.

Jones, F.C., *Japan's New Order In East Asia: Its Rise and Fall 1937–1945*, Oxford, Oxford University Press, 1954.

Jordan, D.A., *Chinese Boycotts Versus Japanese Bombs: The Failure of China's " Revolutionary Diplomacy" 1931–1932*, Ann Arbor, University of Michigan Press, 1991.

Kahn, D., 'The Intelligence Failure of Pearl Harbor', *Foreign Affairs*, 1991–2, vol. 70, pp. 138–52.

Kaiser, D., 'Conspiracy or Cock-up? Pearl Harbor Revisited', *Intelligence and National Security*, 1994, vol. 9, pp. 354–72.

Kennedy, M.D., *The Estrangement of Great Britain and Japan, 1917–1935*, Manchester, Manchester University Press, 1969.

Kennedy, P., *The Rise and Fall of British Naval Mastery*, London, Macmillan, 1976.

———, *The Realities Behind Diplomacy: Background Influences on British External Policy, 1865–1980*, London, Allen and Unwin, 1981.

———, *The Rise and Fall of the Great Powers: Economic Change and Miltary Conflict 1500–2000*, London, Unwin Hyman, 1988.

King, E., *The Hongkong Bank Between the Wars and the Bank Interned, 1919–1945*, Cambridge, Cambridge University Press, 1988.

Klein, D. and Conroy, H. 'Churchill, Roosevelt and the China Question in Pre-Pearl Harbor Diplomacy', in Conroy, H. and Wray, H. (eds.), *Pearl Harbor re-examined: Prologue to the Pacific War*, Honolulu, University of Hawaii Press, 1990.

Laffey, J., 'French Far Eastern Policy in the 1930s', *Modern Asian Studies*, vol. 23, pp. 117–49.

Lee, B.A., *Britain and the Sino-Japanese War, 1937–1939: A Study in the Dilemmas of British Decline*, Stanford, Stanford University Press, 1973.

Leutze, J.R., *Bargaining for Supremacy: Anglo-American Naval Cooperation 1937–1941*, Chapel Hill, North Carolina University Press, 1977.

Louis, W.R., *British Strategy in the Far East, 1919–1939*, Oxford, Oxford University Press, 1971.

Lowe, P., *Great Britain and the Origins of the Pacific War: A Study of British Policy in East Asia, 1937–1941*, Oxford, Clarendon, 1977.

———, 'The Dilemmas of an Ambassador: Sir Robert Craigie in Tokyo 1937–41', *Proceedings of the British Association for Japanese Studies*, 1977, vol. 2, pp. 34–56.

———, 'The Soviet Union in Britain's Far Eastern Policy, 1941', in Nish, I.H. (ed.), *The Russian Problem in East Asia*, LSE STICERD, International Studies series, 1981, pp. 27–46.

———, *Britain in the Far East: a Survey From 1819 to the Present*, London, Longmans, 1981.

Lowe, P. and Moeshart, H. (eds), *Western Interactions With Japan: Expansion, the Armed Forces and Readjustment 1859–1956*, Folkestone, Paul Norbury, 1990.

Lu, D.J., *From the Marco Polo Bridge to Pearl Harbor: Japan's Entry into World War II*, Washington DC, Public Affairs Press, 1961.

Marder, A.J., *Old Friends, New Enemies: The Royal Navy and the Imperial Japanese Navy, Strategic Missions 1936–1941*, Oxford, Clarendon Press, 1981.

May, E.R. (ed.), *Knowing One's Enemy: Intelligence Assessment Before the Two World Wars*, Princeton, Princeton University Press, 1984.

Medlicott, W.N., *The Economic Blockade*, 2 vols, London, HMSO, 1952 and 1959.

Millman, B., 'Toward War with Russia: British Naval and Air Planning for

Conflict in the Near East, 1939–40', *Journal of Contemporary History*, 1994, vol. 29, pp. 259–83.

Miner, S., *Between Churchill and Stalin: The Soviet Union, Great Britain, and the Origins of the Grand Alliance*, Chapel Hill, University of North Carolina Press, 1988.

Mommsen, W.J. and Kettenacker L. (eds), *The Fascist Challenge and the Policy of Appeasement*, London, Allen & Unwin, 1983.

Mommsen, W.J. and Osterhammel, J. (eds), *Imperialism and After: Continuities and Discontinuities*, London, Allen & Unwin, 1986.

Morley, J.W. (ed.), *Dilemmas of Growth in Prewar Japan*, Princeton, Princeton University Press, 1971.

—— (ed.), *Japan's Foreign Policy 1868–1941; A Research Guide*, New York, Columbia University Press, 1974.

—— (ed.), *Deterrent Diplomacy: Japan, Germany and the U.S.S.R, 1935–1940*, New York, Columbia University Press, 1976.

—— (ed.), *The Fateful Choice: Japan's Advance into Southeast Asia, 1939–1941*, New York, Columbia University Press, 1980.

—— (ed.), *The China Quagmire: Japan's Expansion on the Asian Continent, 1933–1941*, New York, Columbia University Press, 1983.

—— (ed.), *Japan Erupts: The London Naval Conference and the Manchurian Incident, 1928–1932*, New York, Columbia University Press, 1984.

Myers, R. and Peattie, M. (eds), *The Japanese Colonial Empire, 1895–1945*, Princeton, Princeton University Press, 1984.

Nagaoka, S., 'The Drive into Southern Indochina and Thailand', in Morley, J.W. (ed.) *The Fateful Choice: Japan's Advance into Southeast Asia, 1939–1941*, New York, Columbia University Press, 1980.

——, 'Economic demands on Dutch East Indies', in Morley, J.W. (ed.), *The Fateful Choice: Japan's Advance into Southeast Asia, 1939–1941* New York, Columbia University Press, 1980.

Nish, I.H., 'Japan and the Outbreak of War in 1941', in Sked, A. and Cook, C. (eds), *Crisis and Controversy: Essays in Honour of A.J.P. Taylor*, London, Macmillan, 1976.

——, *Japanese Foreign Policy 1869–1942: Kasumigaseki to Miyakezaka*, London, Routledge & Kegan Paul, 1977.

——, 'Mr. Yoshida at the London Embassy 1936–38', *Bulletin of the Japan Society of London*, 1979, vol. 87, pp. 1–7.

—— (ed.), *Anglo-Japanese Alienation 1919–1952*, Cambridge, Cambridge University Press, 1982.

——, 'Ambassador at Large: Yoshida and His Mission to Britain 1932–7', in Henny, S. and Lehmann, J.P. (eds), *Themes and Theories in Modern Japanese History: Essays in Honour of Richard Storry*, London, Faber & Faber, 1988.

——, (ed.), *Contemporary European Writings on Japan*, Ashford, Paul Norbury, 1988.

——, *Japan's Struggle With Internationalism: Japan, China and the League of Nations, 1931–3*, London, Kegan Paul, 1993.

Nish, I. and Dunn C. (eds), *European Studies on Japan*, Tenterden, Paul Norbury, 1979.

Ōhata, T., 'The Anti-Comintern Pact, 1935–1939', in Morley, J.W. (ed.),

Deterrent Diplomacy: Japan, Germany and the USSR 1935–1940, New York, Columbia University Press, 1976.

Oka, K., *Konoe Fumimaro: A Political Biography*, Tokyo, University of Tokyo Press, 1983.

O'Neill, P.G (ed.), *Tradition and Modern Japan*. Tenterden, Paul Norbury, 1981.

Ong, C.-C., 'Churchill, Japan and Singapore Defence, 1940–1941' in Nish, I.H. (ed.), *Anglo-Japanese Naval Relations*, LSE STICERD, International Studies series, 1985, pp. 57–72.

Osterhammel, J., 'Imperialism in Transition: British Business and the Chinese Authorities, 1931–37', *China Quarterly*, 1984, vol. 98, p. 260–86.

Ovendale, R., ' *Appeasement' and the English Speaking World: Britain, The United States, The Dominions and the Policy of ' Appeasement', 1937–1939*, Cardiff, University of Wales Press, Cardiff, 1975.

Parker, R.A.C., *Chamberlain and Appeasement: British Policy and the Coming of the Second World War*, London, Macmillan, 1993.

Peattie, M., *Ishiwara Kanji and Japan's Confrontation with the West*, Princeton, Princeton University Press, 1975.

Peden, G.C., *British Rearmament and the Treasury, 1932–1939*, Edinburgh, Scottish Academic Press, 1979.

Pelz, S., *Race to Pearl Harbour: The Failure of the Second London Naval Conference and the Onset of World War II*, Cambridge, Harvard University Press, 1974.

Prange, G.W., *At Dawn We Slept: The Untold Story of Pearl Harbor*, London, Penguin, 1982.

———, *Pearl Harbor: The Verdict of History*. London, Penguin, 1991.

Pratt, L., 'The Anglo-American Naval Conversations On the Far East of January 1938', *International Affairs*, 1971, vol. 47, pp. 745–63.

———, *East of Malta, West of Suez: Britain's Mediterranean Crisis, 1937–1939*, Cambridge, Cambridge University Press, 1975.

Pritchard, R.J., *Far Eastern Influences upon British Strategy Towards the Great Powers 1937–1939*, New York, Garland, 1987.

Reynolds, E.B., *Thailand and Japan's Southward Advance, 1940–1945*, London, Macmillan, 1994.

Reynolds, D., *The Creation of the Anglo-American Alliance, 1937–1941: A Study in Competitive Co-operation*, London, Europa, 1981.

Roberts, A., *The Holy Fox: A Life of Lord Halifax*, London, Macmillan, 1991.

Roskill, S., *Hankey: Man of Secrets, Vol. III 1931–1963*, London, Collins, 1974.

———, *British Naval Policy Between the Wars: The Period of Reluctant Rearmament*, London, Collins, 1976.

Rothwell, V.H., 'The Mission of Sir Frederick Leith-Ross to the Far East 1935–1936', *Historical Journal*, 1975, vol. 18, pp. 147–69.

Rusbridger, J., 'The Sinking of the "Automedon", the Capture of the Nankin, (New light On Two Intelligence Disasters in World War II)', *Encounter*, May 1985, pp. 8–14.

Rusbridger, J. and Nave, E., *Betrayal at Pearl Harbor: How Churchill Lured Roosevelt into War*, London, Michael O'Mara, 1991.

Sato, K., *Japan and Britain at the Crossroads, 1939–1941: A Study in the Dilemmas of Japanese Diplomacy*, Tokyo, Senshu University Press, 1986.

Schaller, M., *The United States Crusade in China 1938–1945*, New York, Columbia University Press, 1979.

Schroeder, P.W., *The Axis Alliance and Japanese-American Relations 1941*, Ithaca, Cornell University Press, 1958.

Shai, A., 'Was There a Far Eastern Munich?', *Journal of Contemporary History*, 1974, vol. 9 pp. 161–170.

Shai, A., *Origins of the War in the East: Britain, China and Japan, 1937–39*, London, Croom Helm, 1976.

Sheng, M.M., 'Mao, Stalin and the Formation of the Anti-Japanese United Front: 1935–37', *China Quarterly*, 1992, no. 129 pp. 149–70.

Shimada, T., 'Designs on North China, 1933–1937', in Morley, J.W. (ed.), *The China Quagmire: Japan's Expansion on the Asian Continent, 1933–1941*, New York, Columbia University Press, 1983.

Shiroyama, S., *War Criminal: The Life and Death of Hirota Koki*, Tokyo, Kodansha International, 1974.

Sims, R., *A Political History of Modern Japan 1868–1952*, New Delhi, Vikas, 1991.

Sissons, D.C.S., 'More on Pearl Harbor', *Intelligence and National Security*, 1994, vol. 9, pp. 373–9.

Smith, B., *The Ultra-Magic Deals and the Most Secret Special Relationship, 1940–1946*, Shrewsbury, Airlife, 1993.

Stafford, P., 'Political Autobiography and the Art of the Plausible: R.A. Butler at the Foreign Office 1938–39', in *Historical Journal*, 1985, vol. 28, pp. 901–72.

Stimson, H., *The Far Eastern Crisis*, New York, Harper, 1936.

Storry, G.R., *Japan and the Decline of the West in Asia 1894–1943*, London, Macmillan, 1979.

Sun, Y-L., *China and the Origins of the Pacific War, 1931–1941*, New York, St Martin's Press, 1993.

Sugihara K., 'Japan as an Engine of the Asian International Economy, c.1880–1936', *Japan Forum*, 1990, vol. 2, pp. 127–45.

Thorne, C., *The Limits of Foreign Policy: The West, The League and the Far Eastern Crisis of 1931–1933*, London, Hamish Hamilton, 1972.

———, *Allies of a Kind: The United States, Britain and the War Against Japan, 1941–1945*, Oxford, Oxford University Press, 1978.

———,*The Issue of War: The State, Society and the Far Eastern Conflict of 1941–1945*, London, Hamish Hamilton, 1985.

Toland, J., *Infamy: Pearl Harbor and its Aftermath*, London, Methuen, 1982.

Toscano, M., *The Origins of the Pact of Steel*, Baltimore, Johns Hopkins Press, 1967.

Trotter, A., *Britain and East Asia 1933–1937*, Cambridge, Cambridge University Press, 1975.

———, 'Backstage Diplomacy: Britain and Japan in the 1930s', *Journal of Oriental Studies*, 1977, vol. 15, pp. 37–45.

———, 'The Currency Weapon – Japan, Britain and the United States in China 1938–1941', *Proceedings of the British Asociation of Japanese Studies*, 1978, vol. 5, no. 1, pp. 55–77.

Tsunoda, J., 'The Navy's Role in the Southern Strategy', in Morley, J.W.

(ed.), *The Fateful Choice: Japan's Advance into Southeast Asia, 1939–1941*, New York, Columbia University Press, 1980.

Usui, K., 'A Consideration of Anglo-Japanese Relations: Japanese Views of Britain, 1937–1941', in Nish, I.H. (ed.), *Anglo-Japanese Alienation 1919–1952*, Cambridge, Cambridge University Press, 1982.

———, 'The Politics of War, 1937–1941', in Morley, J.W. (ed.), *The China Quagmire: Japan's Expansion on the Asian Continent, 1933–1941*, New York, Columbia University Press, 1983.

———, 'Japanese Approaches to China in the 1930s: Two Alternatives', in Iriye, A. and Cohen, W. (eds.), *American, Chinese and Japanese Perspectives on Wartime Asia, 1931–1949*, Wilmington, Scholarly Resources, 1990.

Utley, J.G., *Going to War With Japan, 1937–1941*, Knoxville, University of Tennessee Press, 1985.

Wark, W., 'In Search of a Suitable Japan: British Naval Intelligence in the Pacific Before the Second World War', *Intelligence and National Security*, 1986, vol. 1, pp. 189–211.

Watt, D.C., *Personalities and Policies: Studies in the Formulation of British Policy in the Twentieth Century*, London, Longman, 1965.

———, *Succeeding John Bull: America in Britain's Place 1900–1975*, Cambridge, Cambridge University Press, 1984.

———, *How War Came: The Immediate Origins of the Second World War, 1938–1939*, London, Heinemann, 1989.

Wilson, T.A., *The First Summit: Roosevelt and Churchill in Placentia Bay*, Lawrence, University of Kansas Press, 1991.

Wohlstetter, R., *Pearl Harbor: Warning and Decision*, Stanford, Stanford University Press, 1962.

Woodward, L., *British Foreign Policy in the Second World War*, London, HMSO, 1971.

Wray, H. and Conroy, H. (eds), *Japan Examined: Perspectives on Modern Japanese History*, Honolulu, University of Hawaii Press, 1983.

Xi, Wang, 'A Test of the Open Door Policy: America's Silver Policy and its Effect on East Asia', in Iriye, A. and Cohen, W. (eds.), *American, Chinese and Japanese Perspectives on Wartime Asia, 1931–1949*, Wilmington, Scholarly Resources, 1990.

Index